FAST TRACK TO A 5

Preparing for the **AP®**
English Literature and Composition Examination

To accompany
Perrine's Literature: Structure, Sound, and Sense
by Thomas R. Arp and Greg Johnson

Angelia C. Greiner
Fayetteville High School, Fayetteville, Arkansas

Skip Nicholson
University of California Riverside Extension

CENGAGE
Learning®

Australia • Brazil • Japan • Korea • Mexico • Singapore • Spain • United Kingdom • United States

National Geographic Learning/Cengage Learning is pleased to offer our college-level materials to high schools for Advanced Placement®, honors, and electives courses.
To contact your National Geographic Learning representative, please call us toll-free at **1-888-915-3276** or visit us at **http://ngl.cengage.com**.

For permission to use material from this text or product, submit all requests online at **www.cengage.com/permissions**
Further permissions questions can be emailed to **permissionrequest@cengage.com**.

ISBN-13: 978-1-285-46235-6
ISBN-10: 1-285-46235-1

Cengage Learning
200 First Stamford Place, 4th Floor
Stamford, CT 06902
USA

Cengage Learning is a leading provider of customized learning solutions with office locations around the globe, including Singapore, the United Kingdom, Australia, Mexico, Brazil, and Japan. Locate your local office at: **www.cengage.com/global**.

Cengage Learning products are represented in Canada by Nelson Education, Ltd.

To learn more about Cengage Learning Solutions, visit **www.cengage.com**.

To find online supplements and other instructional support, please visit **www.cengagebrain.com**.

Printed in the United States of America
1 2 3 4 5 6 7 18 17 16 15 14

CONTENTS

PREFACE

AP English Literature and Composition is a great course. From day one, you are immersed in so much rich poetry, fiction, and drama. Before long, you begin to spot on your own the many literary devices writers employ to make their case. And as you practice putting together essays that lay out your critical analysis, you can feel yourself finding your own distinctive voice. The course will be with you for the rest of your life.

But as spring approaches and the College Board examination begins to loom on the horizon, AP English literature can start to feel downright intimidating. The best way to deal with the AP exam is to master it, not let it master you. If you can think of the test as a way to show off how your mind works, you have a leg up; attitude *does* matter. The best way to sideline anxiety is to spend some time on focused review and practice, and this *Fast Track to a 5* is designed to help you do just that. It describes the structure of the test and suggests approaches to the various kinds of questions. Use the diagnostic test and two practice tests to make dry runs, opportunities to get a feel for the test experience and see where your strengths and weaknesses lie.

We very much appreciate the wonderful assistance we had in writing this book. We especially want to thank Carole Hamilton, Elfie Israel, and Donna Carlson Tanzer for their thoughtful comments on our writing and the presentation of ideas and Margot Mabie for her invaluable guidance and her unfailing wisdom as she helped us pull everything together into a finished book.

Angelia Greiner
Skip Nicholson
January 2014

ABOUT THE AUTHORS

ANGELIA GREINER, an English and social studies teacher for twenty-three years, has taught both AP English Literature and Composition and AP English Language and Composition for thirteen years. She now teaches high school English at Fayetteville High School in Fayetteville, Arkansas. She has been an AP reader for the past nine years.

SKIP NICHOLSON teaches courses in English, theater, and education for the University of California Riverside Extension. Head emeritus of English at South Pasadena High School in South Pasadena, California, he taught high school English for forty years. He was also a master teacher in the Folger Shakespeare Library's Teaching Shakespeare Institute. In addition to serving as a reader for the AP English Literature and Composition Examination, he is a College Board–certified consultant who conducts one-day AP workshops and week-long AP summer institutes.

Part I

Strategies for the AP Exam

PREPARING FOR THE AP® EXAM

Advanced Placement courses can be both challenging and stimulating. The rigor of an AP course, whether you are taking it at your high school or through distance education, will help you prepare for the challenges of college course work. AP English Literature and Composition focuses on two skills: critical and analytical reading and clear and coherent writing about what you have read. Unlike AP Language and Composition, which concentrates on nonfiction, AP Literature and Composition draws on imaginative literature for its texts. As you explore the expanse and variety of literature, you will develop close reading skills that enable you to see how writers of literature use structure and style, along with figurative language, imagery, symbolism, and tone, to convey meaning.

The AP English Literature and Composition exam is also a writing exam in that it tests your ability to write clearly and coherently about the details and meaning of a poetry or prose selection. It is in the essay portion of the exam that you can show off your skills as a writer. When scoring essays, readers look for variety in sentence structure, sophisticated vocabulary, logical organization of ideas, and balance between the general meaning of the selection and the specific elements by which the overall meaning is developed. Don't think of the exam as something designed to trip you up; it is an opportunity to demonstrate how well you have honed your reading and writing skills.

WHAT'S IN THIS BOOK

This *Fast Track to a 5* is keyed to *Perrine's Literature: Structure, Sound, and Sense* by Thomas R. Arp and Greg Johnson, from which many of the selections are drawn. However, it is compatible with any textbook used for an AP literature course. It is designed to familiarize you with the structure of the exam and provide you with information on how to approach the test.

At the end of this section you will find a diagnostic test. With fifty-five multiple-choice questions and three essay questions, it has all the components of the AP exam. Take the diagnostic test and then score it, paying special attention to the explanations provided for each multiple-choice question and the general scoring guidelines for each of the essay prompts. Your diagnostic test will give you an idea about your current abilities and help you identify which skills you have mastered and which you want to work on.

Part II of this book focuses on test preparation, at the heart of which is literary analysis. You will find here a close look at how to

---

analyze the different types of literature. Being able to dig deep into a selection to discern its meanings is essential. A solid understanding of literary terms is also indispensable, especially for the multiple-choice questions, so a glossary is included for you. Because annotation goes hand in hand with close analytical reading skills, a discussion on annotation and several annotated passages are included to help you prepare for reading the various selections on the exam. Knowing how to annotate is essential, but to become truly good at it you need to make a habit of annotation. Every time you read, annotation is a must for developing close reading skills.

You will also find information designed to help you prepare for specific parts of the exam. Your score on the multiple-choice section accounts for 45 percent of your exam score, so you will want a firm understanding of how to approach those questions. The second section of the AP exam is made up of three essay questions. One is based on a poetry selection; another is based on a prose selection. A third, which concerns a theme, calls on you to write an essay based on a literary work of your choice. Part II of this book begins with chapters on how to analyze literature, tone, and a list of literary terms. It ends with chapters on the three essay questions that offer you tips on how to recognize a selection's meaning, how to determine what to include—and what to leave out—when writing your essays, and how to isolate and discuss theme. There are sample prompts you can use for practice in organizing and writing the essays, as well as suggestions for creating the sophisticated writing that earns high scores.

Part III has two complete practice tests. These will give you the opportunity to practice both answering questions and managing your time on the test. The importance of practice, practice, practice cannot be stressed enough. The more familiar you are with the structure of the exam, the types of questions you will be asked, and the management of your time, the more likely you are to score well on the exam.

BEFORE THE AP EXAM

All of the books in the *Fast Track to a 5* series are designed for students to use on their own. If you have been steadily doing your homework and keeping up with the course work, you should be in good shape. The key to preparing for the AP exam is to begin early, and the first step is to set up a schedule for yourself. Take the diagnostic test to see where you are and what you want to accomplish. You may be surprised at how much material you can cover by studying thirty minutes a day for a month or so before the test. Use the practice tests to build your confidence.

The evening before the exam is not the time to cram. If you'd like, briefly review the terminology or take a quick look through class notes or your textbook, but avoid getting caught up in small details. Do get a good night's sleep. And on the day of the examination, be sure to eat breakfast—fuel for the brain. Then go get a 5.

TAKING THE AP® ENGLISH LITERATURE AND COMPOSITION EXAM

The purpose of the Advanced Placement Program hasn't changed since 1955, when it was introduced: It was designed to give students an opportunity to extend their knowledge with meaningful and engaging college-level course work. Each year hundreds of thousands of students take the AP English Literature and Composition exam! Students value the abilities to read critically, to make insightful connections between what they read and the larger world, and to write cogently about ideas. Those abilities enrich the individual. They are also the foundation for a free-thinking society.

ABOUT THE EXAM

If you are enrolled in an English Literature and Composition (or English IV AP) course, you are being given a year's instruction in the skills necessary for success on the AP exam. Most students who take the class will take the test—many took the AP English Language and Composition exam the year before. Many schools require students in AP classes to take the exam. Keep in mind that a formal year-long course is not a necessity. Any high school student may take any AP examination. Our advice to students in an AP course is always to take the test. Even if you don't get a high grade, you will have grown as a thinker and a writer. AP makes you far better prepared for college courses.

To take the test, you need to sign up with your teacher or the designated AP coordinator at your high school. There is a charge for each test. However, many states and districts offer a variety of financial incentives for taking the tests, so you may not be charged the full amount.

The AP exams are given during May at high schools worldwide. The methods of scoring and grading will be discussed in detail later, but for now just know that the exams are scored in June by AP teachers and college instructors. Students receive their grades at the beginning of July. You can have the College Board send your grades directly to the colleges of your choice. If you are not yet ready to apply to a college, you can have your scores "banked," to be sent at a later date.

AP ® and Advanced Placement Program® are trademarks registered and/or owned by the College Board, which was not involved in the production of, and does not endorse, this product.

EXAMINATION DAY

The AP English Literature and Composition exam is nearly always given in the morning and lasts approximately three and half hours. Bring a form of identification (usually your driver's license or school ID card is sufficient). In addition, you should have two well-sharpened pencils with erasers and a dark-blue or black pen. Wear comfortable clothes. We recommend layering your clothing in case the heat or air-conditioning is erratic. There is nothing worse than roasting or freezing while you are trying to concentrate on writing! It's a good idea to wear a watch so you can keep track of the time. Letting go of your cell phone can be like saying goodbye to a best friend, but they are not permitted in the testing room. In addition, no food or bottles of water are permitted in the testing room at any time.

Once you are in your seat, the proctor will take attendance, check IDs if that hasn't already been done, and give general directions. If your school has not had you provide the necessary demographic information at an earlier time, you will bubble in those sheets at this point. The proctor will then pass out a test booklet and read through the directions on filling out the answer sheet.

You will be allowed a ten-minute bathroom and water break after the multiple-choice section. If possible, get some fresh air and stretch.

Once you are back in your seat, the proctor will hand out the essay materials. The format of those materials has been changing in recent years. You will probably be given one booklet with three essay questions in it. Make your annotations in that booklet. You will get a separate booklet with lined pages for writing your essays. Each page in that booklet has a box in the upper right-hand corner where you should indicate which essay question—1, 2, or 3—you are answering. You don't have to write the essays in any particular order. If you forget to put the essay number in the box, don't worry. AP readers are trained to leave no page unturned in a student test booklet. They will read all the pages in the booklet in order to find your essay. You will not be penalized for that error.

There are three essay questions on the AP exam. One is based on poetry; another is based on a prose or drama passage; a third asks you to respond to a general statement or question, making reference to a work of literature of your own choosing. You have two hours to work on the three essay questions. All are of the same value, so it is suggested that you spend equal time—forty minutes—on each.

Writing the three essays will feel like a purging of your brain cells! It is in this section that many students begin to panic. If you feel that happening, resist it. The key to this portion of the test is managing your time. You may find yourself spending much more time on one of the essays than on the others. Rather than leaving the third essay blank and polishing the second essay to try to attain a higher score, it's better to stop where you are and focus on a response to the third essay prompt. Why? Even if you were able to raise the score on the second essay by a point, you would lose valuable time for your third essay, costing you much more than a single point. AP readers know that you don't have enough time to "polish" an essay. When you complete an essay, take a minute or two to look it over for any glaring mistakes such as omitted words or wrong names. Proctors may periodically announce how much time is left. If you have time after you've finished your final essay, go back and check all of the essays again, this time more slowly. Use any free time to check for major flaws in wording and to edit your writing where necessary.

To help stay focused on the task at hand, keep your booklet with the essay prompts in your line of sight. Seeing your notes and annotations of the essay passages can spur you on. Don't agonize over the spelling of words or capitalization rules. Some wording problems can be dismissed as well. AP readers evaluate the essays as rough drafts. Continue to write your ideas.

Quality is far more important than quantity. Many students think they must write an essay of many pages in order to earn a high score. That is not true. First, forty minutes is not enough time to write a lengthy essay. The exam is designed to evaluate your abilities to understand what the prompt is asking, and you are expected to respond with accuracy, insight, and stylistic maturity. The short time forces you to pull your thoughts together quickly and write concisely. Readers don't expect the essays to be polished, but they do expect them to present a credible thesis and demonstrate the student's control of standard written English.

At the conclusion of the two hours, you will turn in to the proctor both the booklet with your essays and the booklet with the prompts. Now you can breathe a sigh of relief. It's over! You will no doubt be exhausted, and may feel like your brain has been drained of every fact it ever possessed. Very rarely does a student think the test was easy. Take pride in the fact that you made it through a challenging exam, and give yourself a pat on the back for a job well done!

ABOUT SCORES AND GRADES

The multiple-choice section of the exam counts for 45 percent of your total score. The College Board tallies the number of correct answers—incorrect answers and questions you skip are not counted—for the multiple-choice score. That number is then multiplied by a number found by dividing the 67.5 possible points on the multiple-choice section by the number of multiple-choice questions on the test. Because the test normally has fifty-five multiple-choice questions, the multiplier is usually about 1.23. Continuing with the example above, your multiple-choice score would be about 28 x 1.23, or 34.

The three essays together count for 55 percent of your total score on the test. Each of your essays is scored on the basis of scoring guidelines that range from 1 to 9. Essays with scores of 1 to 4 are considered weak. Scores of 5 to 9 are given for essays that are acceptable to excellent. You will find detailed scoring guidelines explaining what each of these numbers means in the chapters on essay questions and in the diagnostic and practice tests. Each essay score is multiplied by 3.05. For example, if you score a 4, a 6, and a 7 on the three essays, your total score for the essay section would be approximately 52. Added to the multiple-choice score of 34, your composite score would be 86. At the end of the diagnostic and practice tests, you will find worksheets for calculating your exam scores and final AP grade.

Composite scores range from zero to a high of 150. Each year all of the composite scores are broken into five ranges, one for each final AP grade. Each final AP grade represents a level of qualification about your skills:

- a 5 means you are exceptionally well qualified;
- a 4 means you are well qualified;
- a 3 means you are qualified;
- a 2 means you are possibly qualified;
- a 1 means no recommendation.

This is very approximate, but generally, a score in the mid-70s produces a final AP grade of 3, a score in the mid-90s produces a final AP grade of 4, and a score above about 110 produces a final AP grade of 5. If you can correctly answer more than half the multiple-choice questions and earn an average of 5 on your essays, you should perform well on the exam, with a final grade of 3 or better.

When you receive notice of your final AP grade, it will be reported to you as a 1, 2, 3, 4, or 5. The notice doesn't show the scores on the two separate sections—the multiple-choice section and the essay section—of the test.

YOUR TURN

It's now time for you to get ready for the exam. A diagnostic test awaits you on the next page. You may not feel ready to take an AP exam in a timed environment, but if you feel fairly confident, by all means put the pressure on and see how well you do when faced with the mighty clock. Remember that the purpose of the diagnostic test is to help you spot both your weaknesses and your strengths. That way you will know where to focus your attention in preparation for the real deal. Be sure to check your answers carefully and read the explanation that goes with each test question. Good luck and happy testing!

A DIAGNOSTIC TEST

You can evaluate your specific strengths and the areas you need to work on by taking the diagnostic test in this chapter. You may find the test challenging. The purpose here is not to make you anxious, but to give you an experience as close as possible to the actual AP exam. Since the College Board revised the scoring of the multiple-choice questions, it is in your best interests to answer all of the questions, because there is no penalty for incorrect answers. A student who correctly answers twenty-five of the fifty-five questions—that's fewer than half—then gets the adequate, although certainly not distinguished, essay scores of 4, 5, and 6, can still get a grade of 3 on the AP exam.

OPTIONS FOR TAKING THE MULTIPLE-CHOICE TEST

You don't have to take the test under standard test conditions for it to help you—no matter what the conditions, it will still give you a feel for what to expect.

TAKING THE MULTIPLE-CHOICE TEST IN ONE SITTING

One option is to take the multiple-choice test in an hour and then check your answers. Afterward, look at the discussions of the answers and try to follow the reasoning behind them. Remember that the exam is intended to evaluate critical reading skills, so many of the questions will be interpretive and will require you to make subtle distinctions. Occasionally, two of the choices may be correct. In that case, your job is to identify the better of the two, the one best supported by the concrete details in the text. At the same time, some of the distractors will sound plausible. You want to learn to distinguish among those subtle differences. That is the nature of critical reading. We have put each question in a category. When you're done, look for patterns among the categories of questions that give you the most trouble. Those are the categories in which you'll want to pay particular attention and focus your studying.

TAKING THE MULTIPLE-CHOICE TEST IN FIVE TWELVE-MINUTE BLOCKS

Alternatively, you can take the test one block at a time. In that case, read each passage and answer the related questions. Then check your answers and read our discussion of those questions. You can finish all five blocks in one sitting or on two or more separate occasions. Twelve minutes is about the time you will have on the AP exam for each block, but for your purposes here—to get a diagnosis of your current skills—you almost certainly want to finish all the questions for that section. If a specific section takes you longer than twelve minutes, it would be a good idea to make a note of how long it takes.

WRITING THE DIAGNOSTIC TEST ESSAYS

When you get to the essays, decide how you want to approach them. Remember that on the actual AP exam, you will have two hours to complete the three essay questions. That works out to forty minutes each, although you can split the time up any way you think will help your score. With that in mind, decide if you want to write the essays in the diagnostic test in one sitting or three. After you finish, read through the detailed scoring guidelines, which give the characteristics of strong and not-so-strong essays.

Remember that to score well on the AP exam, you must practice. This part of the test is "skills-based." To hone the skills you will need, you have to practice them, just as you would do to get better at basketball or playing the saxophone. It may be hard to motivate yourself to write essays when you know no one is there to grade them. We can't send a personal trainer to your home to force you to write the practice essays. But we can tell you that writing them and then reflecting on how you did is a powerful way to prepare for this exam. There are nine essay prompts in this book, three each in the diagnostic test and two practice tests. Writing all of them will take you a long way toward scoring high on the exam.

Above all, have fun. Enjoy this challenge as you would one in a science lab, in music, in sports, or in any other activity that you find enjoyable.

A DIAGNOSTIC TEST

AP ENGLISH LITERATURE AND COMPOSITION EXAMINATION
Section I: Multiple-Choice Questions
Number of questions: 55
Total time: 1 hour

DIRECTIONS: This part consists of selections from literary works and questions on their content, form, and style. After reading each passage, choose the best answer to the accompanying questions.

QUESTIONS 1–11. Carefully read the poem "Since there's no help" by Michael Drayton before choosing your answers.

> Since there's no help, come let us kiss and part;
> Nay, I have done, you get no more of me,
> And I am glad, yea, glad with all my heart
> That thus so cleanly I myself can free;
> Shake hands forever, cancel all our vows,   5
> And when we meet at any time again,
> Be it not seen in either of our brows
> That we one jot of former love retain.
> Now, at the last gasp of Love's latest breath,
> When, his pulse failing, Passion speechless lies,   10
> When Faith is kneeling by his bed of death,
> And Innocence is closing up his eyes,
> Now, if thou wouldst, when all have given him over,
> From death to life thou mightst him yet recover.

1. The referent of the pronoun "him" in line 13 is
   (A) "death" (line 14)
   (B) "thou" (line 13)
   (C) "Love" (line 9)
   (D) "one jot" (line 8)
   (E) "help" (line 1)

2. The most obvious shift in the poem comes after
   (A) line 4
   (B) line 6
   (C) line 8
   (D) line 10
   (E) line 12

3. The words "Passion" (line 10) and "Faith" (line 11) are capitalized to
   (A) mark their use as allegories
   (B) stress their contrast
   (C) identify them as human emotions
   (D) suggest what the speaker does not want "seen in either of our brows"
   (E) reinforce the idea of clean freedom in line 4

4. The phrase "given him over" (line 13) most nearly means
   (A) ignored his "speechless lies" (line 10)
   (B) seen him recover after thinking he had died
   (C) prayed for his recovery
   (D) granted his wish to "kiss and part" (line 1)
   (E) lost hope for his recovery

5. Of the following, the most rhythmically irregular line in the poem is
   (A) line 3
   (B) line 4
   (C) line 6
   (D) line 9
   (E) line 11

GO ON TO THE NEXT PAGE

6. In lines 1–8, the tone the speaker adopts can best be described as one of
(A) vitriolic malice
(B) feigned indifference
(C) confident tenderness
(D) cynical bewilderment
(E) despairing gravity

7. The relationship of line 14 to line 1 is one of
(A) parallel structure
(B) strong reinforcement
(C) suggested reversal
(D) shared metaphor
(E) cause and effect

8. A principal purpose of the repetition of the word "Now" (lines 9 and 13) is to
(A) suggest an immediate change in the possibility of recovery
(B) underline a contrast with the previous "vows" (line 5)
(C) echo the idea in line 1 that no help will come
(D) reassure the speaker in his gladness (line 3)
(E) confirm the despair that the speaker can "former love retain" (line 8)

9. In the context of line 14, the word "yet" most nearly means
(A) motionless
(B) again
(C) up till now
(D) still
(E) even, in addition

10. The poem's closing couplet presents an example of a
(A) fervent suggestion
(B) stern ultimatum
(C) grudging agreement
(D) sharp admonition
(E) didactic instruction

11. The phrase "speechless lies" (line 10) suggests that Passion
(A) is silently presenting sham accusations
(B) is unable either to find or to utter any words
(C) asserts falsely that the "pulse" (line 10) is "failing"
(D) refuses stubbornly to answer
(E) is feigning voicelessness

QUESTIONS 12–22. Carefully read the passage from the short story "The Drunkard" by Frank O'Connor before choosing your answers.

When we did reach the pub the carriages were drawn up outside, and solemn men in black ties were cautiously bringing out consolation to mysterious females whose hands reached out modestly from behind the drawn blinds of the coaches. Inside the pub there were only the drivers and a couple of shawly women. I felt if I was to act as a brake at all, this was the time, so I pulled Father by the coattails.   5

"Dadda, can't we go home now?" I asked.

"Two minutes now," he said, beaming affectionately. "Just a bottle of lemonade and we'll go home."

This was a bribe, and I knew it, but I was always a child of weak character. Father ordered lemonade and two pints. I was thirsty and swallowed my drink at once. But that wasn't Father's way. He had long months of abstinence behind him and an eternity of pleasure before. He took out his pipe, blew through it, filled it, and then lit it with loud pops, his eyes bulging above it. After that he deliberately turned his back on the pint, leaned one elbow on the counter in the attitude of a man who did not know there was a pint behind him, and deliberately brushed the tobacco from his palms. He had settled down for the evening. He was steadily working through all the important funerals he had ever attended. The carriages departed and the minor mourners drifted in till the pub was half full.   10   15   20

"Dadda," I said, pulling his coat again, "can't we go home now?"

"Ah, your mother won't be in for a long time yet," he said
benevolently enough. "Run out in the road and play, can't you."

It struck me very cool, the way grown-ups assumed that you could   25
play all by yourself on a strange road. I began to get bored as I had so
often been bored before. I knew Father was quite capable of lingering
there till nightfall. I knew I might have to bring him home, blind drunk,
down Blarney Lane, with all the old women at their doors, saying:
"Mick Delaney is on it again." I knew that my mother would be half   30
crazy with anxiety; that next day Father wouldn't go out to work; and
before the end of the week she would be running down to the pawn
with the clock under her shawl. I could never get over the
lonesomeness of the kitchen without a clock.

I was still thirsty. I found if I stood on tiptoe I could just reach   35
Father's glass, and the idea occurred to me that it would be interesting
to know what the contents were like. He had his back to it and
wouldn't notice. I took down the glass and sipped cautiously. It was a
terrible disappointment. I was astonished that he could even drink
such stuff. It looked as if he had never tried lemonade.   40

12. It can be inferred from the passage that the boy and his father are
    (A) returning from a funeral
    (B) on their way to a wedding
    (C) shopping for the boy's ill mother
    (D) out for a father-and-son day together
    (E) trying to avoid going to work and to school

13. When the boy says, "[I]f I was to act as a brake" (line 5), he means if he were to
    (A) invent a game to play in the road
    (B) stop the carriages from leaving
    (C) keep the "shawly women" from leaving
    (D) help his father avoid going "out to work" (line 31)
    (E) prevent his father from drinking

14. The "consolation" the men brought to the "mysterious females" (lines 2–3) was most likely
    (A) notes of condolence from well-wishers
    (B) glasses of beer
    (C) soothing physical contact meant to reassure
    (D) the welcome news that their journey was almost over
    (E) shawls to keep them warm

15. The effect of limiting the boy's dialogue to the repetition of the same sentence is to
    (A) contrast with the observations of "the old women" in line 29
    (B) foreshadow the boy's tasting the pint
    (C) serve as a balance for the sadness of the "men in black ties"
    (D) emphasize the boy's discomfort
    (E) imply mild disapproval of the boy's inability to amuse himself

16. The father is characterized chiefly by
    (A) his treatment of the "mysterious females" (line 3)
    (B) what the author has him say
    (C) the old women's disapproval of him
    (D) his style of dress
    (E) the boy's account of his actions

17. In this passage, the narrator's chief purpose is best described as
    (A) giving a detailed account of his introduction to strong drink
    (B) satirizing his own youthful foolishness
    (C) revealing the reasons for his intense dislike of his father
    (D) evaluating his introduction to adulthood
    (E) meditating on the variety of reactions from different characters to a simple incident

GO ON TO THE NEXT PAGE

18. Which of the following phrases most closely describes the father's actions in lines 12–21?
    (A) "affliction's sons are brothers in distress" —Robert Burns
    (B) "sweet reluctant amorous delay" —John Milton
    (C) "Drink not the third glass, which thou canst not tame"—George Herbert
    (D) "always vulgar and often convincing" —Oscar Wilde
    (E) "divinely bent on meditation" —William Shakespeare

19. Which of the following patterns of syntax best characterizes the pervading style of the passage?
    (A) sentences with heavy subordination and complexity
    (B) a steady progression from simple to highly complex sentences
    (C) a combination of simple sentences and questions
    (D) rhetorical questions mixed with short, contrasting declarations
    (E) early sentences heavy with narrative giving way to straightforward explanation

20. The narrator's statement "I took down the glass and sipped cautiously" (line 38) is ironic when seen in relation to the phrase
    (A) "It was a terrible disappointment" (lines 38–39)
    (B) "I was still thirsty" (line 35)
    (C) "I began to get bored" (line 26)
    (D) "it would be interesting to know what the contents were like" (line 37)
    (E) "I was to act as a brake" (line 5)

21. Of the following, the scene or incident LEAST intended to have a humorous intent is
    (A) the father's sending the boy out into the road to play
    (B) the "mysterious females" reaching out of their carriages
    (C) the father preparing his pipe
    (D) the kitchen "without a clock"
    (E) the boy's reaction to his first taste of the pint

22. The narrator's overall tone in the passage is best described as one of
    (A) pedantic reproach
    (B) somber regret
    (C) amused reflection
    (D) effusive euphoria
    (E) ominous serenity

QUESTIONS 23–33. Carefully read the poem by Sylvia Plath before choosing your answers.

Mirror

I am silver and exact. I have no preconceptions.
Whatever I see I swallow immediately
Just as it is, unmisted by love or dislike.
I am not cruel, only truthful—
The eye of a little god, four-cornered.   5
Most of the time I meditate on the opposite wall.
It is pink, with speckles. I have looked at it so long
I think it is a part of my heart. But it flickers.
Faces and darkness separate us over and over.

Now I am a lake. A woman bends over me,   10
Searching my reaches for what she really is.
Then she turns to those liars, the candles or the moon.
I see her back, and reflect it faithfully.
She rewards me with tears and an agitation of hands.
I am important to her. She comes and goes.   15
Each morning it is her face that replaces the darkness.
In me she has drowned a young girl, and in me an old woman
Rises toward her day after day, like a terrible fish.

23. The poem draws its perspective primarily from the
    (A) comforting metaphor of the candles and the moon
    (B) gradual glorification of the "little god, four-cornered" (line 5)
    (C) extended personification of the mirror
    (D) illustrative allegory of the lake
    (E) ironic manipulation of light and dark images

24. The word "swallow" (line 2) is best understood to mean
    I.   absorb or envelop
    II. accept without question
    III. keep from expressing or showing
    (A) I and II
    (B) I only
    (C) II only
    (D) I and III only
    (E) I, II, and III

25. The phrase "eye of a little god" (line 5) is best interpreted to imply
    (A) the mirror's devotion to its meditation (line 6)
    (B) the mirror's close relationship to "love or dislike" (line 3)
    (C) the mirror's unassailable dominance
    (D) the value of the silver (line 1)
    (E) the woman, who brings light to "the darkness" (line 16)

26. The antecedents of the pronoun "us" in line 9 are
    (A) the woman and the "candles or the moon" (line 12)
    (B) the mirror and the pink wall
    (C) humans and their emotions
    (D) the mirror and the woman
    (E) the mirror and "love or dislike" (line 3)

27. The most notable shift that separates the two stanzas is a change in
    (A) the level of abstraction, from more concrete to more abstract images
    (B) focus, from the mirror to the woman
    (C) the rhyme scheme, from regular to random
    (D) the prevailing rhythm, from irregular to iambic pentameter
    (E) syntactic complexity, from simple to complicated

28. Which of the following best restates the meaning of line 9?
    (A) People block the mirror's view of the wall, and it cannot see it in the dark.
    (B) As humans, we repeatedly see our own futures only darkly.
    (C) Love based only on physical beauty will flicker like a candle and go out.
    (D) Only art can bridge the darkness that separates people's faces.
    (E) In the mirror's vision, the speckles on the wall become faces that peer into the darkness.

29. The speaker implies that the "candles [and] the moon" are "liars" (line 12) because
    (A) they offer a light that makes the woman appear more attractive than she is
    (B) they change through phases and are undependable
    (C) they are distorted by the mirror
    (D) they are twisted by "love or dislike" (line 3) and fail to be truthful
    (E) they are only reflections in the "lake" (line 10)

30. The poet's choice of the word "faithfully" in line 13 most directly reinforces
    (A) "meditate" (line 6)
    (B) "part of my heart" (line 8)
    (C) "unmisted" (line 3)
    (D) "cruel" (line 4)
    (E) "the candles or the moon" (line 12)

GO ON TO THE NEXT PAGE

31. Taken alone, the phrase "I see her back" (line 13) suggests that the mirror does all the following EXCEPT
(A) empathize with the woman and feel a need to reflect her "faithfully"
(B) perceive the back of the woman's body as she turns away
(C) escort the woman back to the world of reality
(D) return the woman's look
(E) understand that she has returned from "the candles or the moon"

32. "[H]er face that replaces the darkness" (line 16) refers to the
(A) woman's turning on the light
(B) biblical story of Eve in the Garden of Eden
(C) "love or dislike" (line 3)
(D) gladness the mirror feels at seeing the woman return
(E) act of creation by the "little god" (line 5)

33. Which of the following best describes the poem as a whole?
(A) a didactic, philosophical poem about humans and our relationship to our possessions
(B) a satiric anecdote exposing human vanity
(C) a lyrical demonstration of the need for love to make life significant
(D) a poignant meditation on the consolations of nature
(E) a somber reflection on our perceptions of our own aging

QUESTIONS 34–44. Carefully read the passage from William Shakespeare's *Othello*, Act I, Scene 3, before choosing your answers.

OTHELLO: Her father loved me, oft invited me,
Still questioned me the story of my life
From year to year, the battles, sieges, fortunes,
That I have passed.
I ran it through, even from my boyish days   5
To the very moment that he bade me tell it.
Wherein I spake of most disastrous chances,
Of moving accidents by flood and field,
Of hairbreadth 'scapes i' the imminent deadly breach,
Of being taken by the insolent foe   10
And sold to slavery, of my redemption thence,
And portance in my travels' history.
Wherein of antres[1] vast and deserts idle,
Rough quarries, rocks, and hills whose heads touch heaven,
It was my hint to speak—such was the process.   15
And of the cannibals that each other eat,
The anthropophagi,[2] and men whose heads
Do grow beneath their shoulders. This to hear
Would Desdemona seriously incline.
But still the house affairs would draw her thence,   20
Which ever as she could with haste dispatch,

---
[1] Caves.
[2] Cannibals.

She'd come again, and with a greedy ear
Devour up my discourse. Which I observing,
Took once a pliant hour and found good means
To draw from her a prayer of earnest heart   25
That I would all my pilgrimage dilate,
Whereof by parcels she had something heard,
But not intentively. I did consent,
And often did beguile her of her tears
When I did speak of some distressful stroke   30
That my youth suffered. My story being done,
She gave me for my pains a world of sighs.
She swore, in faith, 'twas strange, 'twas passing strange,
'Twas pitiful, 'twas wondrous pitiful.
She wished she had not heard it, yet she wished   35
That Heaven had made her such a man. She thanked me,
And bade me, if I had a friend that loved her,
I should but teach him how to tell my story
And that would woo her. Upon this hint[3] I spake.
She loved me for the dangers I had passed,   40
And I loved her that she did pity them.
This only is the witchcraft I have used.

---

[3]Opportunity.

34. From the passage it can reasonably be inferred that Othello has probably been accused of trying to win the hand of Desdemona by
(A) lying to her father about his past
(B) pretending he was wooing for a friend
(C) involving himself in the slave trade
(D) using magic
(E) fighting battles for her

35. In the passage as a whole, Othello uses a rhetorical structure that
(A) moves gradually from more general to more specific examples of his main idea
(B) anticipates counterarguments and attempts to defuse them one at a time
(C) arranges details into a narrative to support a concluding statement of his central argument
(D) begins with an indirect statement of purpose and then arranges details in order of decreasing importance
(E) presents an expository argument that works from abstract generalization to specific detail

36. The word "thence" (lines 11 and 20) is best understood to mean
(A) (away) from here
(B) (away) from there
(C) to here
(D) to there
(E) to where?

37. The lines "I would all my pilgrimage dilate, / Whereof by parcels she had something heard, / But not intentively" (lines 26–28) are best paraphrased as
(A) I would exaggerate the stories of my travels, which she had heard a little—but not much—about
(B) I would tell her of my travels, which people had told her about, but she would not listen with any attention
(C) I would tell her of my travels, which she had heard of in bits and pieces but not altogether
(D) I would tell her again of my travels, repeating what I had sent in letters that included little detail
(E) I would tell her of my travels but leaving out the parts that would offend or distress her

GO ON TO THE NEXT PAGE

38. In context, the word "passing" in line 33 has the meaning of
    (A) acceptably, moderately
    (B) extremely, surpassingly
    (C) only barely
    (D) not at all
    (E) dying

39. According to lines 33–36, Desdemona's reaction to Othello's stories is that she
    (A) felt shame and embarrassment in front of a military man who seemed so distant
    (B) wished her father could see Othello as she does
    (C) wished men like Othello could live longer lives before going to heaven so they could inspire others on Earth
    (D) hoped heaven would protect her and those she loved from creatures such as the cannibals
    (E) wished she herself could have been made such an adventurous and courageous person

40. Which two lines come closest to stating the same idea?
    (A) Lines 14 and 25
    (B) Lines 32 and 40
    (C) Lines 20 and 42
    (D) Lines 34 and 41
    (E) Lines 11 and 34

41. The first section of the passage (lines 1–18) differs from the second section (lines 18–42) in all of the following EXCEPT
    (A) sentence length
    (B) number of sentences
    (C) tone
    (D) level of abstraction
    (E) the focus of their content

42. In the context of the passage, both Desdemona and her father
    (A) repay Othello with lavish rewards
    (B) enjoy the stories Othello tells but suspect they are exaggerated
    (C) try to get away from Othello to attend to "house-affairs"
    (D) press Othello to tell the stories of his adventures
    (E) prefer the military accounts of the "battles, sieges, fortunes" to the less believable stories of cannibals and monsters

43. The line in which the poet introduces NO variety into the passage's iambic rhythm is
    (A) line 4
    (B) line 6
    (C) line 22
    (D) line 23
    (E) line 36

44. The prevailing tone of the passage taken as a whole is best characterized as
    (A) impulsively blunt and forceful
    (B) playfully pedantic and sardonic
    (C) confidently assertive and candid
    (D) aggressively supercilious and disdainful
    (E) unassumingly reticent and self-effacing

QUESTIONS 45–55. Carefully read the passage from the short story "Sonny's Blues" by James Baldwin before choosing your answers.

All I know about music is that not many people ever really hear it. And even then, on the rare occasions when something opens within, and the music enters, what we mainly hear, or hear corroborated, are personal, private, vanishing evocations. But the man who creates the music is hearing something else, is dealing   5
with the roar rising from the void and imposing order on it as it hits the air. What is evoked in him, then, is of another order, more terrible because it has no words, and triumphant, too, for that same reason. And his triumph, when he triumphs, is ours. I just

watched Sonny's face. His face was troubled, he was working hard, but he wasn't with it. And I had the feeling that, in a way, everyone on the bandstand was waiting for him, both waiting for him and pushing him along. But as I began to watch Creole, I realized that it was Creole who held them all back. He had them on a short rein. Up there, keeping the heat with his whole body, wailing on the fiddle, with his eyes half closed, he was listening to everything, but he was listening to Sonny. He was having a dialogue with Sonny. He wanted Sonny to leave the shoreline and strike out for the deep water. He was Sonny's witness that deep water and drowning were not the same thing—he had been there, and he knew. And he wanted Sonny to know. He was waiting for Sonny to do the things on the keys which would let Creole know that Sonny was in the water.

And, while Creole listened, Sonny moved, deep within, exactly like someone in torment. I had never before thought of how awful the relationship must be between the musician and his instrument. He has to fill it, this instrument, with the breath of life, his own. He has to make it do what he wants it to do. And a piano is just a piano. It's made out of so much wood and wires and little hammers and big ones, and Ivory. While there's only so much you can do with it, the only way to find this out is to try, to try and make it do everything.

And Sonny hadn't been near a piano for over a year. And he wasn't on much better terms with his life, nor the life that stretched before him now. He and the piano stammered, started one way, got scared, stopped, started another way, panicked, marked time, started again, then seemed to have found a direction, panicked again, got stuck. And the face I saw on Sonny I'd never seen before. Everything had been burned out of it, and, at the same time, things usually hidden were being burned in, by the fire and fury of the battle which was occurring in him up there.

Yet, watching Creole's face as they neared the end of the first set, I had the feeling that something had happened, something I hadn't heard. Then they finished, there was scattered applause, and then, without an instant's warning, Creole started into something else, it was almost sardonic, it was *Am I Blue.*[1] And, as though he commanded, Sonny began to play. Something began to happen. And Creole let out the reins. The dry, low, black man said something awful on the drums, Creole answered, and the drums talked back. Then the horn insisted, sweet and high, slightly detached and calm and old. Then they all came together again, and Sonny was part of the family again. I could tell this from his face. He seemed to have found, right there beneath his fingers, a damn brand-new piano. It seemed that he couldn't get over it. Then, for a while, just being happy with Sonny, they seemed to be agreeing with him that brand-new pianos certainly were a gas.

Then Creole stepped forward to remind them that what they were playing was the blues. He hit something in all of them, he hit something in me, myself, and the music tightened and deepened, apprehension began to beat the air. Creole began to tell us what the blues were all about. They were not about anything very new.

10

15

20

25

30

35

40

45

50

55

60

---

[1] A 1929 jazz standard introduced by Ethel Waters and recorded hundreds of times since then.

GO ON TO THE NEXT PAGE

He and his boys up there were keeping it new, at the risk of ruin, destruction, madness, and death, in order to find new ways to make us listen. For, while the tale of how we suffer, and how we are delighted, and how we may triumph is never new, it always must be heard. There isn't any other tale to tell, it's the only light we've got in all this darkness.

45. The clause "what we mainly hear, or hear corroborated, are personal, private, vanishing evocations" (lines 3–4) is best taken to mean that
(A) there is no "wrong way" to hear music
(B) we all have the potential to call up a power to help us create
(C) music calls up in us our own individual thoughts and memories
(D) our personal and immediate thoughts are usually contradicted by the music we hear
(E) nonmusicians actually hear music much as its creators do

46. The effect of the phrase "the man who creates the music" (lines 4–5) is most strongly reinforced by the phrase
(A) "the breath of life" (line 26)
(B) "the fire and fury" (line 38)
(C) "he couldn't get over it" (lines 51–52)
(D) "it has no words" (line 7)
(E) "Creole let out the reins" (line 46)

47. The narrator implies that Creole "held them all back" (line 13)
(A) to wait for inspiration to strike him
(B) to assert his leadership
(C) to give Sonny the chance to engage with the music
(D) to let the listeners catch up with the group
(E) to help the narrator understand the music

48. The phrase "in the water" (lines 21–22) is best read as a metaphor that implies
(A) Sonny's following Creole's direction
(B) Sonny's starting to find his way with improvisation
(C) Sonny's getting into difficulty he will not be able to get out of
(D) Creole's indifference at that point to Sonny's playing
(E) Sonny's blending into the group rather than sounding like a soloist

49. In lines 17–18 the author refers to the "the shoreline" and "the deep water"
(A) to stress the danger of the group's not pleasing the audience
(B) to heighten the contrast between Sonny's hesitation and his complete engagement with the music
(C) to contrast Sonny's mediocre talent with his intense performance
(D) as metaphors for the creation of a piano from wood, wire, and ivory
(E) as evidence of Creole's tight hold on the group's music

50. In the sentence "He and the piano stammered, started one way, got scared, stopped, started another way, panicked, marked time, started again, then seemed to have found a direction, panicked again, got stuck" (lines 33–36), the meaning is unmistakably reinforced by
   I. the consonant sounds
   II. the imagery
   III. the syntax
(A) I only
(B) I and II only
(C) II only
(D) II and III only
(E) I and III only

51. The repetition of the word "something" (lines 41–46) suggests
(A) the inadequacy of words to convey completely the experience of music
(B) the narrator's inability to understand the musicians
(C) the unimportance of the small details of the music
(D) Creole's powerlessness to lead the group without Sonny's participation
(E) the narrator's embarrassment at the weak performance

52. In the phrase "they seemed to be agreeing with him that brand-new pianos certainly were a gas" (lines 53–54), the narrator is suggesting that
(A) they became aware that Sonny did not know how well he could play when he had only old pianos to use
(B) they were happy that Sonny's gratitude for Creole's buying him a new piano began to show in his playing
(C) Sonny's suddenly inspired playing aroused and excited the whole group
(D) they recognized that the "brand-new piano" was also a curse because it came with a heavy cost
(E) the narrator disapproved of the other musicians being happy when the credit for the improved music belonged rightly to Sonny

53. In the sentence "Then Creole stepped forward to remind them that what they were playing was the blues" (lines 55–56), the narrator is doing which of the following?
(A) explaining why Creole takes on the role of a soloist and relegates the rest of the group to "playing backup"
(B) justifying Creole's stopping the music so he can talk to the group about the meaning of what they are playing
(C) disapproving of Creole's hitting out at the group and making them apprehensive about their music
(D) despairing of the group's ability to use music to overcome "ruin, destruction, madness, and death" (lines 60–61)
(E) rebuking Sonny for his unsuitable exuberance by shifting the narrative focus to Creole

54. The tone of the closing sentences of the passage is best described as one of
(A) muted but insistent affirmation
(B) frustrated but affectionate nostalgia
(C) bleak but and anguished despair
(D) amusing but mocking apprehension
(E) objective and analytical detachment

55. Taken as a whole, the passage is best characterized as
(A) a technical description of the importance of improvisation in jazz
(B) an argument developed through the use of alternating description and exposition
(C) a performance critique enlarged through both abstract and concrete comparison and contrast
(D) an expository passage chiefly concerned with establishing and extending a definition
(E) a narration that builds to an abstract statement of artistic philosophy

STOP
END OF SECTION I

Section II: Essay Questions
Number of questions: 3
Reading time: 15 minutes
Writing time: 2 hours
Suggested time for each essay: 40 minutes

Section II of this examination requires answers in essay form. Each question counts for one-third of the total essay section score. The two hours are yours to divide among the three essay questions as you think best. To help you use your time well, the proctor may announce the time at which each question should be completed. If you finish any question before time is announced, you may go on to another question. You may go back at any time and work on any essay question you want.

Each essay will be judged on its clarity and effectiveness in dealing with the assigned topic and on the quality of the writing. In response to Question 3, select a work of recognized literary merit appropriate to the question. A good general rule is to use works of the same quality as those you studied in your Advanced Placement literature course(s).

After completing each question, you should check your essay for accuracy of punctuation, spelling, and diction; you are advised, however, not to attempt many longer corrections. Remember that quality is far more important than quantity.

Write your essays clearly and legibly in dark-blue or black ink. Cross out any errors you make.

Question 1

In each of the following poems, the speaker questions God, each from a different place and time—England around 1655 in the first poem, Harlem in 1925 in the second. Carefully read each poem. Then write an essay in which you compare and contrast the two poems and analyze the relationship between them.

On His Blindness
by John Milton

When I consider how my light is spent
    Ere half my days in this dark world and wide,
    And that one talent which is death to hide
    Lodged with me useless, though my soul more bent
To serve therewith my Maker, and present   5
    My true account, lest he returning chide,
    "Doth God exact day-labor, light denied?"
    I fondly ask. But Patience, to prevent
That murmur, soon replies, "God doth not need
    Either man's work or his own gifts. Who best   10
    Bear his mild yoke, they serve him best. His state
Is kingly: thousands at his bidding speed,
    And post o'er land and ocean without rest;
    They also serve who only stand and wait."

Yet Do I Marvel
by Countee Cullen

I doubt not God is good, well-meaning, kind,
And did He stoop to quibble could tell why
The little buried mole continues blind,
Why flesh that mirrors Him must some day die,
Make plain the reason tortured Tantalus   5
Is baited by the fickle fruit, declare
If merely brute caprice dooms Sisyphus
To struggle up a never-ending stair.
Inscrutable His ways are, and immune
To catechism by a mind too strewn   10
With petty cares to slightly understand
What awful brain compels His awful hand.
Yet do I marvel at this curious thing:
To make a poet black and bid him sing!

GO ON TO THE NEXT PAGE

Question 2

Carefully read the following excerpts from "There Will Come Soft Rains" (1950), a story by Ray Bradbury, and then write an essay in which you show how the author uses literary devices to achieve his purpose. You might want to consider such literary devices as selection of detail, figurative language, allusion, and tone.

In the living room the voice-clock sang, *Tick-tock, Seven o'clock, time to get up, time to get up, seven o'clock!* as if it were afraid that nobody would. The morning house lay empty. The clock ticked on, repeating and repeating its sounds into the emptiness. *Seven-nine, breakfast time, seven-nine!*   5

In the kitchen the breakfast stove gave a hissing sigh and ejected from its warm interior eight pieces of perfectly browned toast, eight eggs sunnyside up, sixteen slices of bacon, two coffees, and two cool glasses of milk.

"Today is August 4, 2026," said a second voice from the kitchen   10 ceiling, "in the city of Allendale, California." It repeated the date three times for memory's sake. "Today is Mr. Featherstone's birthday. Today is the anniversary of Tilita's marriage. Insurance is payable, as are the water, gas, and light bills."

Somewhere in the walls, relays clicked, memory tapes glided   15 under electric eyes.

Eight-one, tick-tock, eight-one o'clock, off to school, off to work, run, run, eight-one! But no doors slammed, no carpets took the soft tread of rubber heels. It was raining outside. The weather box on the front door sang quietly: "Rain, rain, go away; rubbers, raincoats   20 for today…" And the rain tapped on the empty house, echoing.

Outside, the garage chimed and lifted its door to reveal the waiting car. After a long wait the door swung down again.

At eight-thirty the eggs were shriveled and the toast was like stone. An aluminum wedge scraped them into the sink, where hot   25 water whirled them down a metal throat which digested and flushed them away to the distant sea. The dirty dishes were dropped into a hot washer and emerged twinkling dry.

Nine-fifteen, sang the clock, *time to clean.*

Out of warrens in the wall, tiny robot mice darted. The rooms   30 were acrawl with the small cleaning animals, all rubber and metal. They thudded against chairs, whirling their mustached runner, kneading the rug nap, sucking gently at hidden dust. Then, like mysterious invaders, they popped into their burrows. Their pink electric eyes faded. The house was clean.   35

Ten o'clock. The sun came out from behind the rain. The house stood alone in a city of rubble and ashes. This was the one house left standing. At night the ruined city gave off a radioactive glow which could be seen for miles.

Ten-fifteen. The garden sprinklers whirled up in golden founts,   40 filling the soft morning air with scatterings of brightness. The water pelted windowpanes, running down the charred west side where the house had been burned evenly free of its white paint. The entire west face of the house was black, save for five places. Here the silhouette in paint of a man mowing a lawn. Here, as in a   45 photograph, a woman bent to pick flowers. Still farther over, their images burned on wood in one titanic instant, a small boy, hands flung into the air; higher up, the image of a thrown ball, and opposite him a girl, hands raised to catch a ball which never came down.

The five spots of paint—the man, the woman, the children, the ball—remained. The rest was a thin charcoaled layer.

The gentle sprinkler rain filled the garden with falling light.

Until this day, how well the house had kept its peace. How carefully it had inquired, "Who goes there? What's the password?" and, getting no answer from lonely foxes and whining cats, it had shut up its windows and drawn shades in an old-maidenly preoccupation with self-protection which bordered on a mechanical paranoia.

It quivered at each sound, the house did. If a sparrow brushed a window, the shade snapped up. The bird, startled, flew off! No, not even a bird must touch the house!

The house was an altar with ten thousand attendants, big, small, servicing, attending, in choirs. But the gods had gone away, and the ritual of the religion continued senselessly, uselessly.

Twelve noon . . .

For not a leaf fragment blew under the door but what the wall flipped open and the copper scrap rats flashed swiftly out. The offending dust, hair, or paper, seized in miniature steel jaws, was raced back to the burrows. There, down tubes which fed into the cellar, it was dropped into the sighing vent of an incinerator which sat like evil Baal in a dark corner . . .

Four-thirty. The nursery walls glowed.

Animals took shape: yellow giraffes, blue lions, pink antelopes, lilac panthers cavorting in crystal substance. The walls were glass. They looked out upon color and fantasy. Hidden films clocked though well-oiled sprockets, and the walls lived. The nursery floor was woven to resemble a crisp, cereal meadow. Over this ran aluminum roaches and iron crickets, and in the hot still air butterflies of delicate red tissue wavered among the sharp aroma of animal spoors! There was the sound like a great matted yellow hive of bees within a dark bellows, the lazy bumble of a purring lion. And there was the patter of okapi feet and the murmur of a fresh jungle rain, like other hoofs, falling upon the summer-starched grass. Now the walls dissolved into distances of parched weed, mile on mile, and warm endless sky. The animals drew away into thorn brakes and water holes.

It was the children's hour.

Five o'clock. The bath filled with clear hot water.

50

55

60

65

70

75

80

85

90

GO ON TO THE NEXT PAGE

Question 3

American clergyman Harry Emerson Fosdick wrote, "I hate war for its consequences, for the lies it lives on and propagates, for the undying hatreds it arouses, for the dictatorships it puts in the place of democracies, and for the starvation that stalks after it." War, though, has proven a rich source of material for writers, perhaps because of those consequences.

Select a novel, play, or epic poem you have studied in which a war or its aftermath plays a significant role. Then, in a well-written essay, describe the role the war plays in the work and show how that role contributes to the meaning of the work as a whole. You may choose a work from the list below or another appropriate novel, play, or epic of similar literary quality. Avoid plot summary.

A Farewell to Arms	*Mrs. Dalloway*
A Separate Peace	*Nineteen Eighty-Four*
A Tale of Two Cities	*Obasan*
A Watch on the Rhine	*Paradise Lost*
All My Sons	*Pride and Prejudice*
All Quiet on the Western Front	*Regeneration*
Antigone	*Saint Joan*
Arms and the Man	*Slaughterhouse-Five*
Beloved	*The Aeneid*
Candide	*The English Patient*
Catch-22	*The Fall*
Cold Mountain	*The Ghost Road*
Doctor Zhivago	*The Iliad*
Don Quixote	*The Kite Runner*
Going After Cacciato	*The Naked and the Dead*
Henry V	*The Painted Bird*
Johnny Got His Gun	*The Red Badge of Courage*
Julius Caesar	*The Remains of the Day*
Lysistrata	*The Sun Also Rises*
Macbeth	*The Things They Carried*
Major Barbara	*The Tin Drum*
Mother Courage and Her Children	*War and Peace*

END OF EXAMINATION

ANSWERS AND EXPLANATIONS FOR SECTION I

MULTIPLE-CHOICE ANSWER KEY

Using the table below, determine how many questions you answered correctly, how many incorrectly. Then look over the answer explanations.

1. C	2. C	3. A	4. E	5. D
6. B	7. C	8. A	9. D	10. A
11. B	12. A	13. E	14. B	15. D
16. E	17. A	18. B	19. C	20. E
21. D	22. C	23. C	24. A	25. C
26. B	27. B	28. A	29. A	30. C
31. A	32. A	33. E	34. D	35. C
36. B	37. C	38. B	39. E	40. B
41. C	42. D	43. C	44. C	45. C
46. A	47. C	48. B	49. B	50. E
51. A	52. C	53. A	54. A	55. E

EXPLANATIONS FOR THE MULTIPLE-CHOICE ANSWERS

1. ANSWER: C. *A grammar question of a kind that nearly always appears on the test.* The referent in a question is almost never close to its pronoun. Here, what "all have given over" is "Love" (line 9) that is taking its "latest breath" and has a failing pulse. "Thou" is the person to whom the poem is addressed, and the other choices do not fit that test of being "given over."

2. ANSWER: C. *A structure/shift question.* The poem shifts between lines 8 and 9. At that point it shifts into a new sentence, takes on a new tone, moves from literal to metaphorical, and reverses the suggestion about what is to be done. Each part is made up of one sentence (although the semicolon in line 1 makes the first sentence more complex than the second) and ends with a period. Lines 1–8 are literal; lines 9–14 are figurative, building the allegory of dying Love. The speaker's apparent purpose in lines 1–8 is a goodbye, whether sincere or feigned. But the farewell of the first eight lines shifts in the last six to the suggestion that the love be brought back to life.

3. ANSWER: **A.** *A punctuation question to test the range of your reading.* Wide reading brings familiarity with conventions like this one. Words used allegorically are traditionally capitalized. None of the other choices include or imply any relation between the ideas in them and why a word would begin with a capital letter.

4. ANSWER: **E.** *A vocabulary question.* The phrase has a meaning closely related to "given up." That meaning can be deduced from the context, in which Passion, Faith, and Innocence are all behaving as though they have abandoned hope.

5. ANSWER: **D.** *A prosody question.* A reader would stress the line's opening word, "Now." But because the poem's rhythm is iambic, that word sits in an unstressed position. The opposite is true of the next word, "at." A strictly iambic reading of the line would neglect the key words "last" and "love" while accentuating the minor word "of." A "regular" reading of the line would force us into "Now AT the LAST gasp OF Love's LATEst BREATH"—far from the regular iambic pentameter of the lines in the other choices.

6. ANSWER: **B.** *A tone question.* To establish the speaker's tone, the poet uses (1) diction, choosing such words as "nay" and "yea," and the informal "jot"; (2) syntax, as in the repetition of "glad" to insist on his being untroubled, as though he is trying to convince himself; (3) rhythm, though the quickness of the lines, which results from the even rhythm. Although an argument could be made for the "tenderness" in C, we're looking for the best choice, and since there's no "confidence," B is better. In D, the cynicism might be possible, but "bewilderment" is not. In A and E, both words are inaccurate.

7. ANSWER: **C.** *A relationship question.* The reversal here is from the "there's no help" in line 1 to the possibility of recovery in line 14. B is opposite the actual relationship, E makes no sense since hopelessness cannot bring about a cure. A is wrong because the lines are not parallel. D is wrong because line 14 does include the metaphor of love and illness, but line 1 has none.

8. ANSWER: **A.** *A question about repetition/diction.* By repeating the word "now," the speaker insists on the need for immediate action to bring about the recovery. The other choices are contradicted by the poem.

9. ANSWER: **D.** *A vocabulary question: words with multiple meanings.* In this line, the word has the meaning of "still." The context eliminates the other choices.

10. ANSWER: **A.** *A question of tone and purpose.* The speaker here is suggesting, almost pleading, for his lover to keep the love alive. The words "stern," "grudging," and "didactic" eliminate B, C, and E, respectively, since those choices misstate the tone. An argument could be made for the "sharp" in D, but there is no admonition in the couplet, making A the best choice.

11. **ANSWER: B.** *A vocabulary question: words with multiple meanings.* The key is in the word "lies," which here means "lie" in the sense of "to lie down." That eliminates A, C, and E. The word "stubbornly" eliminates D.

12. **ANSWER: A.** *An inference question.* The funeral in choice A is consistent with the words "consolation," "solemn," and especially "mourners." Nothing in the passage suggests a wedding or that the mother might be ill, and there is no mention of school. If the father and son were out for a day together, the father would be unlikely to send his son to play in the street.

13. **ANSWER: E.** *A question about metaphor and context.* The best choice is E, most likely echoing the boy's instructions from his mother before the story begins. Choice A has nothing to do with a brake, a tool to stop something. The boy has contact with neither the carriages nor the women in the pub, eliminating B and C. The reference to work in D comes in the boy's imagining about the future and not the immediate situation.

14. **ANSWER: B.** *An interpretation question.* Since the men are coming out of a pub, the obvious choice is B. The obvious choice isn't always the best choice, however, so we need to check the others. A and C are conceivable, but there's no reason for the men to be cautious with letters or with consoling touches. B is better because the men have to be cautious not to spill the beer. D won't work because there's no sign either that the journey is almost over or that the women react to any news. E is a common kind of distracter; it picks up a related word from another context—the "shawly women" inside the pub.

15. **ANSWER: D.** *A question about pattern.* The word "emphasize," taken with the word "repetition" in the question, makes D the best choice, and such details as the boy's pulling on his father's coat, as well as his apprehension about the trip home and his mother's reaction, reinforce the idea of discomfort.

16. **ANSWER: E.** *A characterization question.* The writer shows us a little through the father's limited dialogue but much more through the boy's narration of his father's actions at the counter and through what the boy implies about the father's actions in the past.

17. **ANSWER: A.** *A question of overall purpose and of tone.* The boy does nothing foolish here, and shows no dislike of his father, eliminating B and C. The passage presents no judgment of the boy's actions, so D is inaccurate. E won't work because we get reactions only from the boy. The details in the passage, though, from the women having drinks delivered to their carriage to the father's toying with his pint, lead up to the boy's drinking his father's beer.

18. ANSWER: B. *A question of interpretation and relationship.* Milton's line in B fits best because the "sweet" matches the father's enjoyment of the game of delaying drinking, and both "reluctant" and "amorous" fit with his actual purpose, which is to get great pleasure from drinking the pints. C can be eliminated because it is the father's first drink, not his third, as can D, because no one in the passage behaves in a vulgar way. While we might presume "affliction" and "distress" as the father's reaction to the death of a friend, other details, such as his playfulness with the pint glass, argue otherwise. In a stretch, the grown narrator might be said to be meditative, but certainly not in any divine way.

19. ANSWER: C. *A syntax question—a popular type.* C might seem a good choice since the boy's youth makes him less likely to use the more complex structures in the other choices. But it is important to remember that the actual narrator here is clearly a grown man looking back on his youth. In fact, nearly 60 percent of the sentences are simple; only nine are complex, the majority of those are "loose" sentences—those that put the main clause first and then add subordinate clauses—the easiest kind of complex sentence to read.

20. ANSWER: E. *An irony question.* The irony occurs when the boy, feeling that his job is to "act as a brake" to his father's drinking, instead takes a drink himself, the opposite of what we would expect. B also refers to his drinking, but since he is tasting something unfamiliar, it is more logical than ironic that he would "sip cautiously."

21. ANSWER: D. *An interpretation question.* Only D presents a scene without humor—the clock the mother has had to pawn because of the father's drinking, and the lasting effects of that desperation.

22. ANSWER: C. *A question of point of view and tone.* The story of a boy sneaking his first drink of beer out of his father's glass is much more humorous than reproachful, "somber," or "ominous," eliminating A, B, and E. The account is in no way "effusive" or euphoric, so D is wrong. The amusement comes from the point of view—the grown narrator looking back on an event from his childhood, one which at the time seemed so serious but which, looking back, is amusing as well.

23. ANSWER: C. *A figurative language question.* The personification of the mirror governs the poem from the first line to the last, making C the best choice. The "gradual glorification," allegory, and "ironic manipulation" included in B, D, and E do not appear in the poem. A comes closer, but the "comfort" is for the woman only, not the reader, and the image is too fleeting to be the "primary" tool the question asks for.

24. ANSWER: A. *A vocabulary question: words with multiple meanings.* The mirror "absorbs" what it sees so that it can reflect it, and it passes no judgment, so I and II are both meanings of the word in play here. It cannot, however, "keep from . . . showing," or it would fail as a mirror.

25. **ANSWER: C.** *An interpretive/implication question.* The mirror, which reflects accurately, like a god, cannot be overcome. It tells the truth, showing us as we are. This mirror is without devotion to anything, and the value of the silver is irrelevant to the poem, eliminating A and D. B is wrong because the mirror is unaffected by love or dislike, and the woman brings light simply with an electrical switch when she "replaces the darkness" (line 16).

26. **ANSWER: B.** *A grammar question.* The picture here is of the mirror staring at the wall opposite it. (Mirrors have no choice there.) It is "separated" from the wall when it's too dark to see or when people look in the mirror, putting their "faces" in the way. So B is the best answer. An "antecedent," by definition, must come before the pronoun (otherwise it's simply a "referent"), so A won't work. Sometimes it helps to slowly expand the context. That works here, because if we ask who or what is being separated over and over, it's the mirror and whatever it faces.

27. **ANSWER: B.** *A structure question.* One way to test for the type of "focus" mentioned in B is to look for the grammatical subject of each sentence. In the first stanza, all but the last two sentences have the mirror ("I") as subject. The second stanza reverses that relationship; the woman (or her face) is the subject of seven sentences, the mirror, of three. So B becomes the best choice. It can be argued that this poem shifts in its level of abstraction, but if there is such a shift, it is from abstract to concrete, eliminating A. The poet here uses no rhyme scheme at all, and although the poem has rhythmic patterns, it cannot be scanned into a namable one, eliminating C and D. E is wrong because both the length and the complexity of the sentences remain stable throughout the poem.

28. **ANSWER: A.** *An interpretation question.* Sometimes the greatest difficulty lies in accepting an answer that may appear too easy. Here, the literal meaning in A is the most accurate. Although they may sound more satisfying at first glance, the others misread the poem by forcing into the interpretation details that do not exist there.

29. **ANSWER: A.** *An implication question.* Candles and the moon, traditional symbols of romantic love, offer a dim, diffused, and more flattering light than the glare of most electric light sources.

30. **ANSWER: C.** *A diction/relationship question.* Our vision is distorted by our emotions. Mirrors can distort the world as well, as in a room full of steam where they mist up. This mirror, though, is "unmisted," both literally and figuratively, and reflects whatever is in front of it "just as it is" (line 3), "faithfully" (line 13). This "faithfully" has the meaning of "accurately," unrelated to the "faith" in religion (choice A) or love (choice B).

31. ANSWER: **A.** *A diction question: words with multiple meanings.* Only A is unrelated to a meaning of the verb "to see," and with the added problem that the mirror empathizes with the woman only in the sense that it passes on her story. Choices B, C, D, and E all play on different meanings of the word *see*—in B and D, to take in with the eyes; in C, to accompany (as in "to see someone safely home," here from the more fantastical world of the moonlight); in E, to understand (as in "to see the point").

32. ANSWER: **A.** *An interpretation question.* Again, the most literal choice is the best answer. The mirror is in a dark room until the woman comes in and turns on the light to look at herself. None of the other choices have direct support in the text of the poem.

33. ANSWER: **E.** *A question of tone and purpose.* The close of a poem—especially a short poem—often carries a key to the intended tone. That's the bit that will be ringing in readers' ears after they finish the piece, and poets take extreme care with last lines. Here, the image of the fish rising toward the woman unrelentingly ("day after day") and the fact that the fish inspires anxiety, maybe even dread ("terrible"), establish the sober feeling that the woman has as she sees the young girl she was now becoming an "old woman." So the best choice is E. The poem is without any didacticism, and its satire, if there is any, is heavily muted, eliminating A and B. The lyricism, although present, can't work toward a theme that isn't present in the poem, eliminating C. Choice D is wrong because there is almost no reference to nature anywhere in the piece.

34. ANSWER: **D.** *A question of inference.* The final line makes it clear that the speaker is trying to clear himself of the charge of witchcraft. There is no evidence that he has lied to her father, eliminating A. The reference to a friend wooing comes, indirectly, from Desdemona, not the speaker, so B is inaccurate. The events in choices C and E happened before the speaker knew her, so they can't be correct.

35. ANSWER: **C.** *An organization question.* The statement of the speaker's argument comes in the final line. The rest of the speech is an amassing of the evidence he thinks leads to that conclusion. A can't be correct since the speech remains on the same level of abstraction throughout. The entire speech constitutes one counterargument, so B is inaccurate. D is wrong because there is no statement of purpose until the end, and E strays far from the passage, because the speech is made up of anecdotes and has little, if any, exposition.

36. ANSWER: **B.** *A vocabulary question.* The context makes it clear that the speaker means "from there," so "thence" is the best choice. You want to remember this word as well as its mates "hence" (from here) and "whence" (from where?).

37. ANSWER: C. *An interpretation question.* Here the speaker says she has heard something "by parcels." Since parcels are small packets, we can guess that the meaning is little pieces. "But not" indicates an opposition or reversal, so it would be logical to assume he means not in little pieces but as a whole, making C the best choice. B and E have no root in the text. D has the attraction of "letters," a word related to "parcels," a common type of temptation to draw the unsuspecting to a wrong choice. A comes closer but deals with the overall quantity of news rather than the size of the "installments," and it introduces the erroneous idea that the speaker is intentionally exaggerating.

38. ANSWER: B. *A vocabulary question.* The context makes it clear that the word means "surpassingly" or "exceedingly," although we don't often use it that way now. The parallel with "wondrous" in the next line helps make it clearer. Substituting the words in A and C into the context shows that they don't make sense there. D makes the sentence contradict itself, and E simply plays on the modern euphemism without making sense in that context.

39. ANSWER: E. *An interpretation question.* It might be necessary to read the line twice to see that "her" is the object of the verb "made," that it does not mean "for her," as it first might appear. In any case, none of the other choices offers the option of the meaning that she wanted such a man made for her, so E becomes the best choice. The others don't fit the context, or, as in the case of A, contradict it.

40. ANSWER: B. *A relationship/interpretation question.* Both lines 32 and 40 say that as a result of hearing the speaker's stories, Desdemona loved/sighed for him. Choice A is inviting because of the relationship between the words "heaven" and "prayer," another instance of a surface relationship unrelated to the actual meaning in context. Choice D does almost the same.

41. ANSWER: C. *A section contrast question.* "Except" questions can eat up time. Check first to see if there's an obvious answer. Since this passage has a consistent tone, C quickly becomes a good choice. Having a probable answer in hand often makes it easier to eliminate the others. A quick check for periods can eliminate A and B since the first part has two and the second, five. Since the parts are of nearly equal length, the one with more than twice the number of sentences will average sentences of about half the length. E can be eliminated because in the first part, the speaker talks of his adventures; in the second part, he addresses Desdemona and his relationship with her. D is inaccurate because the first section is built on the specific details of places, events, and sights, while the second leans more heavily on abstract statements of emotion. So C remains the best choice.

42. ANSWER: D. *An inference question.* Both the father (lines 1–2) and Desdemona (lines 19, 32, 38–39) say and show that they want to hear the stories. B and E can be eliminated quickly because we don't hear the reactions of the listeners. We know only what the speaker tells us, and he doesn't mention what his listeners might suspect is exaggerated or which stories they prefer. He mentions no rewards beyond the "sighs" (line 32). C is wrong because Desdemona tries to "dispatch" the "house affairs" with "haste" so that she can get back to the speaker's stories.

43. ANSWER: C. *A prosody question.* Only line 22 scans perfectly: "she'd COME a-GAIN and WITH a GREE-dy EAR." Line 4 is a half line only, eliminating A. Lines 6 and 23 will end up with an extra syllable, even with the opening "To the" condensed into one syllable, as must be done, so B is wrong. D and E won't fit either because of an extra syllable in each.

44. ANSWER: C. *A tone question.* All three of the words in C fit the speaker's attitude toward his speech, making it the best choice. The careful ordering of the details argues against the "impulsively" in A. None of the three words in B and in E describe the passage. One could argue for the aggression in D, but not the other two terms there.

45. ANSWER: C. *An interpretation question.* The passage implies that those of us who are not musicians hear music in terms of what it makes us think of and what it reminds us of, so C is the best choice because C speaks of "our own individual thoughts and memories." Choice A may be true, but the passage doesn't say so. B and E can be eliminated because they present ideas that the passage does not. D is close to the opposite of what the phrase actually says.

46. ANSWER: A. *A question of reference or allusion.* The "breath of life" is imparted by the creator of human beings in nearly all accounts of the creation, including the one in the Bible. Only choice A links that breath to a creator—here, one who makes the music "come alive." None of the other choices have anything to do with the process of creating or making something come alive.

47. ANSWER: C. *A "motivation" question.* The writer gives Creole's reason only at the end of the following sentence, ". . . he was listening to Sonny." The other choices have no basis in the passage.

48. ANSWER: B. *A figurative language question.* The water is a metaphor for the simultaneous creating and playing of the music; that leads to B as the best choice. This question demands a look at the context of the phrase quoted. The writer begins the extended metaphor four lines earlier: "He wanted Sonny to leave the shoreline and strike out for the deep water." So Creole does care what Sonny does, eliminating D, and that the "deep water" is something good, not bad, eliminating C. Creole needs to tell him that "deep water and drowning were not the same thing," implying that Sonny sees a risk. There's no risk, though, to blending in, only in striking out alone, so E is incorrect. And since Creole is not telling Sonny what to do, but waiting to see what he does, A doesn't fit.

49. **ANSWER: B.** *A figurative language question.* This question asks much more directly about the metaphor than question 48, which requires more analysis. Here, only B speaks to the parallel contrasts between the shoreline and the water on the one hand and Sonny's not being "with it" and his later finding the "brand-new piano." A can be dismissed because the audience is not mentioned or even hinted at here. C is wrong because the word "mediocre" is clearly inaccurate. D doesn't work because it speaks of combining things to make a piano. The metaphor, though, has nothing to do with combination. It builds instead on the contrast between the safe "shoreline" and the risky "water." E comes closer because Creole at this point is exerting his control, but the metaphor applies only to Sonny, not to the other musicians.

50. **ANSWER: E.** *A diction/syntax question.* To reinforce the hesitation and the faltering in Sonny's playing, the syntax falls into short, chopped phrases. Of the thirty words, eleven are verbs. The diction supports the syntax by lining up words full of stops forced by the consonant sounds—t's, d's, p's, k's, and hard c's and g's—that keep the sentence from finding a rhythm, just as Sonny can't find a rhythm on the piano. Twice it seems to pick up: "another way" has no stops but is followed immediately by "panicked," which has two. "Then seemed to have found a direction" stops only three times but ends in another "panicked." So I and III figure prominently in the construction of this long sentence. The sentence, though, has no imagery beyond the arguable auditory results of the diction and cannot be said to provide any "unmistakable" reinforcement.

51. **ANSWER: A.** *A diction question.* A is the best choice because in spite of his understanding, the narrator is forced to express one art—music—using the tools of another—literature—and those tools prove inadequate in places, as the writer stresses with the very meaning of the word "something" as the narrator searches for the right word but can't find it and repeats the vague "something." Nothing in the text supports D or E. C looks tempting at first, but words and phrases such as "something awful" and "insisted" argue that the discussion here does not involve small details but the whole tone of the performance. B can't be accurate because the narrator leads the reader to a profound understanding of the musicians.

52. **ANSWER: C.** *An interpretation question.* Choice C accounts for all the details of Sonny's becoming "part of the family again." A and B (and possibly D) fail to see that the piano is "brand-new" only in a metaphoric sense. Sonny is playing the same old piano; it is his changed relationship to it that makes it new. The word "damn" in the description of the piano is a slang expression, which makes D a weaker choice than C. Further, although the passage says the musicians were "risking ruin," the leap from that potentiality to the flat statement that the piano "came with a heavy cost" is too great.

53. **ANSWER: A.** *An interpretation question.* Creole hears and understands the exhilaration in the group's music but knows he must subdue that joy somewhat to fit the music. So he does what choice A outlines: He moves out in front with his bass so the others can follow his lead and restore the mood of the blues. B fails to understand that Creole is communicating with music, not words. C misinterprets Creole's motivation, which is to inspire not apprehension but confidence. The passage is guarded in any optimism it has, but there is no despair, so D is wrong. E is incorrect because there is no rebuke from the characters, the narrator, or the writer.

54. **ANSWER: A.** *A tone question.* Choice A accounts for all the details, from the "triumphant" (line 7) in the first paragraph to "keeping it new" (line 49) in the last. The piece ends with the insistence on that reaffirmation of "how we are delighted, and how we may triumph." C and D are inaccurate because the passage has no apprehension, and since it offers hope, the sentence cannot be said to be despairing. It may border on objectivity at times since the narrator is something of an outsider to the scene, but he is far too involved to be considered "detached," eliminating E. A case could be made for B, although there's little evidence of frustration on the part of the narrator, making this response too narrow.

55. **ANSWER: E.** *A purpose and type question.* The passage has almost no description or exposition, eliminating A, B, and D. It does not critique the performance beyond implying that it improves when Sonny finds his "brand-new piano," eliminating C. Only E has all the details right. The passage tells a specific and detailed story that leads to the two final sentences, which provide a philosophy on the purpose of not only music but all art.

SCORING GUIDELINES FOR SECTION II

The score reported for each essay reflects the reader's judgment of the quality of the essay as a whole. Readers are instructed to reward the writers for what they do well. The score for an exceptionally well-written essay may be raised by one point. A poorly written essay can be scored no higher than a 3.

SCORING GUIDELINES FOR QUESTION 1

9–8 These essays compellingly treat both poems in some depth and are specific about how the two are different and how they are similar. They also discuss, explicitly, the relationship between the two and comment on the specific circumstances of the speakers. The scrutiny of the poems may or may not include technical comment on the form and prosody; if it does, the essay offers comment on the purpose or effectiveness of those aspects. Frequent references to the text are specific and fit the analytical context in which they appear. Although they may have flaws, these essays show a sensitive grasp of both poems and express it with dependable precision and maturity.

7–6 These essays present a rational and credible comparison and contrast between the two poems. Although in their interpretations they do not show the precision or the thoroughness of the top papers, they are thoughtful and attend to the tasks of the prompt. They enumerate and discuss both similarities and differences, although with less depth than the top essays. They may show less stylistic maturity or occasional wanderings. Nevertheless, they support their commentary clearly with specific and appropriate detail from the text, although possibly without the fine balance of the 8–9 papers. The writing style may be more workmanlike and have more hesitations but is still competent and generally comfortable.

5 These acceptable essays may be superficial in their understanding of explanations but they present plausible interpretations of both poems. They may slight the analysis of the relationship between the two poems or either the comparison or the contrast of the two. They may depend on generality instead of specificity in their comparisons and contrasts or marshal support that is too thin or only marginally appropriate to the student's commentary. They may fall into paraphrase, but that paraphrase, however overextended, will be in the attempted service of analysis. They may show a minor misreading of the poems. Although the writing may be unsophisticated and inexact or include distracting surface errors, it is still adequate to the expression of the writer's ideas.

4–3 These "lower-half" essays are incomplete in their understanding of either the prompt or the poems, or both. They may indulge in a more serious misreading of the poems or slight one of them completely. They often paraphrase more than they comment or comment without rooting their commentary in the text. The writing may fail to show organization and control over the content and the form. This is the highest score for an essay that discusses only one of the poems or whose organizational or mechanical weakness forces continuous backtracking and rereading.

2–1 These essays compound the weaknesses of the 3–4 papers. They may completely misconstrue the poems or pay little heed to the instructions. Typically they are unacceptable in form, in content, or both. While they address the prompt, they do so in a cursory, fleeting, or ineffective way. Essays scored 2 will include some analysis, however rudimentary. Essays scored 1 include no worthwhile comment on the poems.

0 These essays may refer to the prompt but make no attempt to respond to it.

— These essays are blank or do not mention the prompt or the poems.

SCORING GUIDELINES FOR QUESTION 2

9–8 These essays offer a persuasive analysis of how Bradbury uses literary devices to achieve his purpose. They select apt devices and choose appropriate, specific examples for analysis. They relate that analysis to a sound interpretation of Bradbury's purpose, whether they state that purpose directly or imply it clearly. These essays move well beyond the simple idea of the personification of the house to analyze such elements as the passage's tone, the religious allusions, the ironic details, and the sustained use of metaphor. These drafts may not be error free, but they demonstrate a perceptive reading of the passage and clear, well-organized, and well-detailed writing. Their analysis is sophisticated, and the writing shows an adept control of language

7–6 These essays offer a reasonable analysis of Bradbury's use of literary devices to achieve his purpose. They choose appropriate devices to analyze and provide suitable textual support balance with explanation and analysis. They show an accurate reading of the passage and an awareness of how the literary devices contribute to the achievement of Bradbury's purpose. They may offer a less clear identification of that purpose and a less detailed clarification of the contribution of the techniques to its achievement. They may not be free of errors, but their presentation of the major ideas is clear and shows control over the elements of effective composition.

5 These essays offer a plausible reading of the passage. Their analysis, though, may tend toward superficiality and predictability. They may lack a convincing development of how Bradbury uses literary devices, or they may fail to either state or imply a clear understanding of his purpose. They identify devices to analyze but may devote a large part of that analysis simply to listing examples of the most obvious techniques—typically the personification of the house. They may lapse into partial summary or paraphrase. They show an acceptable control of language and composition, although they may not maintain a strong organization, and the meaning may suffer from surface errors of mechanics and usage.

4–3 These essays offer an unsatisfactory understanding of the passage or of how Bradbury uses literary devices to make his point. They may identify techniques but offer little analysis beyond naming those techniques and indicating their use. Their support from the text tends to be thin or inappropriate. They may move away from the task to offer extended summary or paraphrase. They often fall into repetition of one or two simplistic ideas. Some may reduce the story's purpose to a moralistic platitude, or they may omit it altogether. They may misread the passage or—particularly in the case of essays scoring 3—they may read in details not found in the text. They tend to force the rereading of passages because of confusing sentence structure or wording. Errors in mechanics and usage demonstrate a lack of control over the elements of effective composition.

2–1 These essays show a lack of understanding of the passage and the techniques it uses. They may fail to identify its speculative nature or may assume the people will return to the house or left it of their own volition. Most—not all—will be unacceptably brief, although in the case of essays scoring 2, there will be some attempt at analysis, however insufficient. Ideas in these essays may be difficult to locate or to follow because of a lack of focus and organization. Mechanical and usage faults are often joined by deeper structural errors that impede reading and understanding. Essays scored 1 are marked by evident incoherence or incompetence.

0 These essays may refer to the text or the prompt but do not attempt a response.

— These essays either are written on topics unrelated to the assigned task or are left blank.

SCORING GUIDELINES FOR QUESTION 3

9–8 These persuasive essays identify a war, battle, or other military action in an appropriate novel, play, or epic. They explain with precision and rich concrete detail from the text the role the war plays in it. They articulate clearly a meaning of the work as a whole and show compellingly how the role they have defined of the war relates to it. While it's possible the war itself is not central to the literary work, it is to these essays. They are not without flaw, but they are focused and organized, and alternate with skill between the details of the text and the writer's comment on that detail. They show that the writer reads with perception and has a practiced and sophisticated control over the techniques of expressing that perception. A paper scored 9 will show particular polish and grace.

7–6 These essays present a rational and credible explanation of the war's impact on a clearly stated meaning of the work. The account of that relationship may be more mechanical or less smoothly articulated, and the essays less thorough or specific than the top papers, but they demonstrate both an accurate reading of the work and sufficient control over the elements of writing about literature. Essays scored 7 will have stronger textual support for their claims and, generally, more expertise of expression than those scored 6.

5 These acceptable essays may be superficial in their expression of the relationship of the war to a meaning of the work. They may overexplain the obvious or belabor predictable ideas rather than offer insight. Plot summary may play too large a role, but plot summary is still linked to an attempt at analysis. While the writing may be inexact in diction and lack grace in syntax, it is still adequate to the expression of the writer's ideas.

4–3 These "lower-half" essays are incomplete, either in their understanding of the prompt or of the works they purport to analyze, or both. They may choose a conflict they cannot successfully relate to a meaning of the work or they may be unable to articulate such a meaning clearly. Often they will relate a battle or campaign at great, unnecessary length and fail to comment meaningfully on its role in the work. They may fail to go beyond restating what is evident in a plot line or be carried away by plot summary. The writing may fail to show organization and control over the content and the form. This is the highest score for an essay that avoids identifying a meaning of the work as a whole or whose organizational or mechanical weakness forces continuous rereading and backtracking.

2–1 These essays compound the weaknesses of the 4–3 papers. They may completely misconstrue the actual purpose of an author's using the events of a war or pay little heed to the instructions. Typically they are unacceptable in form, in content, or both. While they address to the prompt, they do so in a cursory, fleeting, or ineffective way. Essays scored 2 will include some analysis, however rudimentary. Essays scored 1 offer no worthwhile comment on the poems.

0 These essays may refer to the prompt but make no attempt to respond to it.

— These essays are blank or do not mention the prompt or the poems.

CALCULATING YOUR AP EXAM GRADE FOR THE DIAGNOSTIC TEST

Please keep in mind that these numbers are approximate. Two variables affect the computation every year: the number of multiple-choice questions and the difficulty levels of the essays. There is a slight adjustment every year in terms of the numbers. However, remember that earning 15 points on the three essays combined and getting 55 percent right on the multiple-choice questions will generally produce a grade of 3.

SCORING THE MULTIPLE-CHOICE SECTION

$$\underline{\hspace{3cm}}_{\text{number correct}} = \underline{\hspace{3cm}}_{\text{multiple-choice score}}$$

SCORING THE FREE-RESPONSE SECTION

$$\underline{\hspace{2cm}}_{\substack{\text{Question 1}\\(0–9 \text{ score})}} + \underline{\hspace{2cm}}_{\substack{\text{Question 2}\\(0–9 \text{ score})}} + \underline{\hspace{2cm}}_{\substack{\text{Question 3}\\(0–9 \text{ score})}} = \underline{\hspace{2cm}}_{\text{total essay score}}$$

CALCULATING THE COMPOSITE SCORE

$$1.23 \times \underline{\hspace{3cm}}_{\text{multiple-choice score}} = \underline{\hspace{3cm}}_{\text{weighted section I score}}$$

$$3.05 \times \underline{\hspace{3cm}}_{\text{free-response score}} = \underline{\hspace{3cm}}_{\text{weighted section II score}}$$

$$\underline{\hspace{3cm}}_{\text{weighted section I}} + \underline{\hspace{3cm}}_{\text{weighted section II}} = \underline{\hspace{3cm}}_{\text{composite score}}$$

DETERMINING YOUR AP EXAM GRADE

You now have a number between 0 and 150. The composite scores are divided into five ranges, one for each AP grade. Each year that scale is adjusted. Generally, it goes like this:

Composite Score Range	AP Grade
112–150	5
95–111	4
76–94	3
50–75	2
0–49	1

Part II

Reviewing for the AP English Literature and Composition Exam

HOW TO ANALYZE LITERATURE

You have taken on an exciting adventure in developing skills of literary analysis. Literature offers answers to life's great questions about who we are, our place in the universe, and how we live with one another and ourselves. It gives us, as Tennessee Williams said, "truth in the pleasant disguise of illusion." That truth is what the AP exam in English Literature and Composition calls "the meaning of the work as a whole." The analysis that helps us get to that truth is the careful and deliberate study of what writers have created through the use of fictional characters, settings, plots, and language.

The skill of literary analysis is not easy to learn. It isn't a list of things to do, but a new way of thinking. Like other worthwhile skills, it takes time, patience, and dedication. Yet that heavy lifting will repay you in new ways to read on a more rewarding level.

Good basketball players focus on one element at a time: they practice shooting free throws until they feel comfortable at the line; then they move on to practicing passing or perimeter defense. Good players know they are never done improving, but they put in the time necessary to get to a zone of comfort. Similarly, good cello players work on their skill with a bow until they feel competent before moving on to focus on fingering or phrasing. Those principles apply just as clearly to literary analysis. Readers with less experience with serious literature improve their skills by focusing on one element at a time. They may work on recognizing the patterns in complex writing, or the ambiguities, or the structure, and then move on to another skill. Good readers know they are never done, that it's never perfect, but they put in the time necessary to get to a zone of comfort.

The question here is, *How do I analyze literature?*, and the course in Advanced Placement English Literature and Composition is the answer. Here we offer an overview of the basic skills you'll need to best find meaning in a variety of written work.

When we talk about *analysis,* we mean breaking something down to its elements to see what they are and how they work together to produce the whole. In literature we can divide those elements into two categories: the actual parts of a work and the tools writers use to convey meaning.

The "parts" include books, sections, chapters, and paragraphs in fiction; acts, scenes, and lines in drama; and stanzas, lines, and cantos in poetry. We'll look at some of those in relation to each of the three types of literature. The elements of literature up for analysis fall into two groups: those common to all imaginative literature and those particular to one or two types. We'll look at both, because you'll want to draw on both kinds in your analysis. First let's consider some points to help you read more deeply and then use that reading to both speed up and strengthen your analysis.

READING ANALYTICALLY

Most of the works in an AP English course call for a different and more active style of reading than does the commercial literature we read simply for plot. With literary fiction you want to take careful notice not only of the plot but also of how the writer uses literary tools to guide your reactions and thinking. These works are open to multiple interpretations, and practice in analysis will extend your grasp on the writer's aims and in the process make the reading richer and more enjoyable. Active reading here includes being alert to any devices, similarities, contrasts, or shifts.

To maintain control of the process, you will need to make annotations within the text. Annotating is a way to keep your mind engaged with the work because it asks you to respond to it, anticipate what is coming, and ask questions as you read. You will probably develop your own system, but here are some ideas for getting started:

- This reminds me of _____.
- I wonder why _____.
- I didn't see _____ coming.
- I like that _____.
- I don't think I'm pleased that _____.
- I'm really interested that _____.

If you own the book, write in it. If you don't, use sticky notes or pieces of paper with the page numbers written on them.

Individual elements of literature will deserve more attention in some works than in others. Start with story components:

- the setting and setting changes
- characters' first appearances
- the point of view and the identity of the narrator
- symbols
- ambiguity
- foreshadowings and warnings
- unusual or effective uses of language
- patterns—recurrences and echoes

Stay attentive to what the writer is doing. Remember that the AP exam in English Literature and Composition is built on the idea that the structure and meaning of a work are closely connected. For purposes of analysis, your personal response to a work is less important. You won't be asked to describe your personal reactions to a work; instead, you will be asked to explain how the writer conveys meaning as a whole. There is no credit for identifying those tools or pointing out where a writer uses them unless you explain how they function to bring out meaning. The mantra here is "no *what* without *why*."

FOUR COMPONENTS OF LITERATURE

STRUCTURE

Narrative fiction offers writers near-complete freedom in how to structure a work. Some writers divide their novels—even their short stories—into parts, books, or chapters. Pay attention to any titles authors give those units. For example, "Flight to the Ford" in *Lord of the Rings* telegraphs to the reader that Frodo and his allies will reach the place to cross a river but, because it says only "to" and not "across," leaves open the question of whether they will succeed. Another approach is to use summaries or quotations to introduce units of a work, as with "How a Little Sound Produced a Great Dream" in Thomas Hardy's *The Return of the Native*, which sends a clue that Eustacia's exotic dream in the chapter results from—and is linked to— two words she overheard earlier.

The most traditional structure for a story is in five parts: (1) a beginning, where things are in order; (2) an inciting incident, which threatens the order and begins the conflict; (3) rising action, during which the conflict continues; (4) the climax, the highest point of the story, where the conflict is traditionally resolved, for better or worse; and (5) falling action, when loose ends are tied up and the original order is restored or a new one is established. Some works vary that pattern slightly.

A few writers invent their own structures. Vladimir Nabakov's *Pale Fire* is a 999-line poem followed by a line-by-line commentary written by a scholar who, we come to learn, is telling us the story of the novel in a most roundabout way. The epistolary novel normally combines a series of letters or other documents into a collection from which a story emerges. Saul Bellow used letters in *Herzog*; in *Dracula*, Bram Stoker included diary entries and news accounts. Nick Bantock's *Griffin & Sabine* epistolary trilogy includes pages with actual envelopes containing letters and cards.

PACE

Writers use tools to manipulate the tempo of the reader's progress through the work. They can make use of syntax, slowing us down with complex or long sentences or speeding us up with short, simple ones. They can use diction to speed up the reading with simple words and literal language or slow it down with less familiar vocabulary and abstract or figurative expressions. Quick dialogue or long descriptive passages will affect our reading speed as well. Accomplished writers will use these and other techniques with intention. Because the shifts in pace don't happen accidentally, we have to ask why they occur and what the writer wants us to think about. (In some infrequent cases when writers are paid by the word—think Dickens and Dostoevsky— the pace may at times be dictated by publication necessities, but those are rare circumstances.)

Some works use time in an unusual way, presenting events out of chronological order, as Tim O'Brien's *Going After Cacciato* does. Some use flashbacks to show action from before the work's opening, as *Death of a Salesman* does when Arthur Miller inserts the scene with the woman in Boston. When that happens, it's important to think about why the author made such a choice.

NARRATION

At the start of every work, one of your first questions is to find out who is telling the story. Because we can know only what narrators show or tell us, we must find out quickly as much as we can about them. Are they inside the story, like Nick Carraway, who narrates *The Great Gatsby,* or outside, like E.M. Forster's anonymous narrator in *A Room with a View*? If they're inside, what opinions and biases might they have that will influence what they let us see?

Guard against the temptation to assume that the narrator is the author. An author must create a narrator who believes the characters are real people, even though the author knows they are not; there is always some distance between the author and the narrator. That distance may be quite small, or it may be enormous. Jane Austen's and Nathaniel Hawthorne's narrators stay very near their authors; we come to rely on those narrators because what they tell us continues to turn out to be accurate. We know, though, that Huckleberry Finn is not Mark Twain because Twain constantly gives us evidence that Huck is incapable of understanding what is happening around him.

Narrators rarely knowingly lie to us, but the so-called "unreliable narrator" has become a favorite of modern writers. These narrators often think they are telling the truth, but sometimes they can't distinguish reality from their own delusions. Huckleberry Finn and Holden Caulfield are too unsophisticated or gullible and naïve (or kind and trusting, depending on your reading of the novels) to notice that what they are telling us is frequently contradicted by the action around them. Kurt Vonnegut's Billy Pilgrim in *Slaughterhouse-Five* and some of Tim O'Brien's narrators find their ability to think so ravaged by war that they have created a reality separate from that in which they live, and from which they tell us their stories. Some narrators, even though they are not part of the plot, stay closer to some characters by giving readers more detail about what those characters see or hear than they do with others.

DETAIL

All imaginative literature exaggerates some details and downplays or omits others. The writer's choices about which details to stress or to describe in depth direct attention in some way to a theme of the work. The use of detail is related to the pace of a work because description slows the tempo of the narrative. When that happens, you must again consider why.

THREE LANGUAGE TOOLS

DICTION

Diction is the writer's choice of words. In analysis, we talk about diction in two related ways. The first is the *level* of diction. High or elevated diction usually depends on a Latinate vocabulary of multisyllabic words, and the writer will avoid the colloquial language of normal conversation. Nathaniel Hawthorne often exploits high diction to achieve a tone of solemn meditation. Neutral or middle diction sounds more like the normal conversation of educated people, as in many of the works of F. Scott Fitzgerald or Gabriel García-Márquez. Low diction covers a range, from informal conversation to substandard usage. It appears in fiction most often in the dialogue of characters, some of whom may be intelligent or even wise, but who are likely untrained or uneducated. We hear such voices, for instance, in the novels of Toni Morrison and Tim O'Brien.

The second way we think about diction is through the use of adjectives that communicate more about the attitudes of the speakers and narrators than about their station. Here's a partial list of words commonly used to describe diction.

HIGH

academic	esoteric	pompous
archaic	flowery	preachy
bookish	formal	pretentious
cultivated	intellectual	refined
cultured	learned	scholarly
didactic	ornate	stuffy
educated	ostentatious	superior
elegant	pedantic	teachy

NEUTRAL

everyday	ordinary	unadorned
casual	plain	uncomplicated
conversational	relaxed	
informal	simple	

LOW

abrupt	laconic	slangy
colloquial	provincial	terse
homespun	rural	unpolished
jargon	rustic	vulgar

Notice that the levels here are not "good" or "bad." All three levels include words with positive, neutral, and negative connotations. The adjectives in the following group are not tied to the levels and could describe diction in any of the three.

ᴀᴘᴘʟɪᴄᴀʙʟᴇ ᴛᴏ ᴀʟʟ ʟᴇᴠᴇʟs

banal	euphemistic	precise
bland	exact	proud
bombastic	flat	self-righteous
ceremonial	grotesque	sensual
coarse	insipid	sensuous
connotative	lyric	simple
conventional	melodious	specific
decisive	moralistic	trite
detached	obscure	unemotional
emotional	poetic	

FIGURATIVE LANGUAGE

Figurative language is a way of saying something and meaning something else. It's the coin of the realm in poetry, but nearly all imaginative literature will use and even depend on it. In analysis we direct attention to how figures of speech bring out theme. Analysis never includes simple identification of a device a writer is using without showing how the device enhances the meaning of the work as a whole.

Some sources list more than two hundred different figures of speech. (You'll find definitions of the most important figures of speech in "A Glossary of Literary Terms," pp. 67–73.) Still, just four pairs make up a writer's basic equipment: personification and apostrophe, irony and paradox, metaphor and simile, and synecdoche and metonymy. A good understanding of each of these will serve you well.

One caution about figurative language: avoid using figures of speech in literary analysis. Write literally, especially on tests—including the AP exam—and save figures of speech for your own fiction writing.

SYNTAX

Syntax is based on a Greek word that means "arrangement." When we analyze syntax as a literary device, we look at sentence structure, complexity, and length. In poetry, in particular, word order becomes significant. Longer, more complex sentences tend to slow the reader; shorter sentences pick up the tempo. The arrangement of sentence patterns helps reinforce the meaning of a passage and, finally, of the work as a whole. Be especially aware of patterns of repetition of phrases or of kinds of phrases within and among sentences. Notice where the writer uses specific constructions. Loose sentences begin with the main clause and then add modifying clauses, creating a more relaxed, conversational tone, as Willa Cather does in *The Song of the Lark*: "She sank back into the hansom and held her muff before her face, lowering it occasionally to utter laconic remarks about the people in the carriages they passed, interrupting Fred's narrative in a disconcerting manner." Periodic sentences begin with subordinate ideas and delay the main clause to the end, creating a more formal tone because the structure isn't standard everyday speech. Margaret Atwood uses it to strong effect in *Oryx and Crake*: "Stick in hand, rehearsing the story he'll tell them, he goes along the path to their encampment." Parallel constructions signal parallel ideas, as in the opening of Alan Paton's *Cry, the Beloved Country*: "The ground is holy . . . . Keep it, guard it, care for it, for it keeps men, guards men, cares for men. Destroy it and man is destroyed." Be alert, as well, to heavy subordination, and to strings of prepositional or infinitive phrases. And always ask yourself why each author makes the syntactical choices he or she does.

ANALYZING NARRATIVE FICTION

Seven elements play major roles in both novels and short stories. Because of their length and complexity, novels paint with a broader brush; a writer's closer attention to these elements can be easier to see in a short story because the genre is more concentrated, so an especially attentive reading of short stories pays great dividends in both understanding and enjoyment. Always keep in mind that these elements are not separate—they work together to communicate a work's themes.

PLOT

In conversation, we often use the word *plot* as a synonym for *story*. In analysis, however, plot is the way the writer arranges the story. Any analysis of plot needs to include consideration not only of *what* (the story), but also of *when* and *why*. The events in many stories will appear in chronological order. In others, however, the writer will move back and forth in time, as Faulkner does in "A Rose for Emily," keeping the earliest events of the story as a surprise ending. The *why* involves causality—the idea that each event in a story is caused by a preceding event. Careful writers who break those links of causality are giving us a signal to meaning. When an event can't be explained by whatever has preceded it, ask why the author withheld that information. Was it to develop empathy for a character the readers might dislike if they knew his background? What is the author leading the reader to conclude?

Plot implies conflict. Normally the main characters face conflicts with other characters, with natural or supernatural forces, or within themselves. A strong analysis should cite any conflict and explain how the writer resolves it, while also demonstrating its connection to an overall theme.

SETTING

Setting includes the entire context of a story. An analysis of setting will include the time (era, century, year, season, weather, time of day, and the like) and the place (urban or rural, indoors or out, and so forth). But setting also takes in the historical and social background. Knowing that Nadine Gordimer set her story "Once upon a Time" in South Africa in the 1980s demands that any analysis must mention the country's policy of apartheid at the time. In some stories the geography is key; a good part of the meaning of Faulkner's "A Rose for Emily" depends on its setting in a declining South. In other stories the time provides keys to meaning, as in F. Scott Fitzgerald's "Babylon Revisited," which is set in Paris between the two world wars. Some depend on their social setting, as John Cheever's "The Swimmer" does on its upper-class milieu. In some stories the immediate setting becomes key—as in, for example, Herman Melville's "Bartleby, the Scrivener," which is about a lowly clerk in the claustrophobic confines of an office, or in Charlotte Perkins Gilman's "The Yellow Wallpaper," whose main character is imprisoned in a bedroom. Setting not only supplies hints about why the characters act as they do; it contributes to the mood and atmosphere of the text.

CHARACTER

Writers use three principal devices to reveal character: characters' actions, characters' words, and what others—including the narrator—say about them. Keep in mind that there are times when characters might say inaccurate or misleading things about themselves; others may too—even when it's the narrator speaking. Physical descriptions will sometimes provide clues to characters, as will objects, places, or situations that surround them. Likewise, a name may suggest something about a character, as in the case of the wretched Sowerberrys in Charles Dickens's *Oliver Twist*. It may also be ironic, as in the case of the unexpectedly emotionally burdened Holly Golightly in Truman Capote's novella *Breakfast at Tiffany's*.

Occasionally an object or a setting can be considered a character; when that happens, any analysis must link that character to a theme about humanity. In Ray Bradbury's "There Will Come Soft Rains" the main character is the house, but the meaning of the story concerns the people, who are absent.

We describe some characters as "round," or complex and deep, more like real people, and others as "flat," or one-dimensional and unchanging. Nearly all characters fall somewhere on a continuum between these two extremes. Flat characters are often stock characters. Like shoe salesmen who keep a range of sizes and colors in a back stockroom, writers have a set of characters for quick use as a plot device. Writers depend on our knowing them from other reading or movies and television. We can quickly recognize the typical hardened criminal, the harlot with a heart of gold, the pair of naïve lovers, and countless others. These characters are generally not of central importance to the plot, but they help move the story along. In a ten-page story or a thirty-minute TV program, we can't possibly get to know and understand every bus driver, sales clerk, or doctor the main characters will meet. These stock characters are an economical tool for keeping a story moving forward.

The purpose of a foil character is to reveal by contrast the characteristics or traits of a main character. Foils can be fully developed characters in their own right, or minor characters whose purpose is simply to help us understand someone else. In Shakespeare's *Romeo and Juliet,* for instance, Benvolio serves as a foil to Romeo, for while Romeo is passionate, Benvolio is even-tempered, a contrast that serves to enhance Romeo's volatile actions.

POINT OF VIEW

Point of view pertains to the identity of the narrator and how much that narrator knows. Think of point of view as the eyes through which we see the story. It is common practice to distinguish four types of narrational point of view, three "third person" and one "first."

The first-person point of view presents a story told by a major or minor character who says "I" and "me." Such narrators can tell us everything they feel and think, as well as what they see and hear, but they can't get into the minds of other characters. In addition, sometimes first-person narrators are unreliable because they are involved in the story.

Third-person narrators stand outside the story rather than being part of it. The three most common types are the omniscient, the limited, and the objective narrator. Omniscient narrators know all of the details from the past, present, and future, as well as what every character is thinking and feeling. They can tell us anything they like. But even an omniscient narrator must choose what to tell us and what to leave out, or the story would never end. The omniscient narrator frequently stays close to one character, or at least to one character at a time. In J. K. Rowling's *Harry Potter* series, for instance, the narrator remains outside the story but manages to stay closer to Harry than to the other characters.

In a limited third-person point of view the narrator can see inside one character but not the others. This will sometimes include the technique called *stream of consciousness*, in which the narration imitates the way we think: in incomplete sentences, combining thoughts related to the present with thoughts of the future, and without logical transitions among ideas or impressions. In a novel, the writer can sometimes shift from one character's point of view to another's, as William Faulkner does from chapter to chapter in *As I Lay Dying* and from section to section in *The Sound and the Fury*. This type of narrator is different from the omniscient narrator in being limited to one character at a time.

The objective narrator relates the action and, in some cases, the characters' thoughts, but without judgment or comment. In the short story "Hills Like White Elephants," Ernest Hemingway's narrator remains objective by presenting only factual narration and direct quotations. Of course, the author can't be completely objective, because the choice of details inescapably influences any interpretation.

Keep in mind that while the writer of a memoir is also the narrator, in novels and short stories that is never the case. The narrator must believe that the story being told is true, that its world exists, and that these characters are real.

Occasionally, novelists and other writers use their own names for a narrator—as Proust does with a narrator named Marcel in *In Search of Lost Time*—but bear in mind that in doing so, they are projecting a persona. Such writers project some of themselves into the character, but there is not a direct one-to-one relationship.

SYMBOL

A symbol is an element in a story that suggests more than what it is. Symbols do not *mean*, they *suggest* or *remind* or *reflect*. Stories will clue us in to symbols, but you must have your antennae up and receiving to get the signals. Even experienced readers don't notice everything symbolic on a first reading. The "one ring" in Tolkien's *The Lord of the Ring,* for example, is first and foremost a ring, but it's a ring that suggests power—especially dangerous power that can be easily abused.

Symbols are not hidden secrets; writers use them to enhance and enrich meaning, not to hide it. Hunting for symbols most often leads to finding some that are not there. Seeing those that are there takes some experience in careful reading and, in short stories, often a repeated reading. At the same time, you don't want to assume that everything is symbolic. A writer may use an owl in a story to suggest thoughts of wisdom or of patience or death, but sometimes an owl is just an owl. To confirm that something is a symbol, look elsewhere in the story for proof of your analysis of it.

HUMOR

Inexperienced readers lose some of the enjoyment of reading (and some of the points on the AP English Literature exam) by missing the clues that a writer intended a work or a passage to be humorous. For purposes of analysis, however, you must recognize where humor was intended, even when the humor doesn't appeal to you. Here are four common sources of humor:

- VERBAL HUMOR, notably the pun—for example, Mark Twain's comment that "Denial ain't just a river in Egypt"—and the malapropism—for example, Shakespeare's police constable Dogberry saying, "Our watch, sir, have indeed *comprehended* two *auspicious* persons"

- INCONGRUITY IN TONE, primarily when a writer uses
  - a serious tone to describe a comic or absurd subject or a comic tone for a serious subject
  - overstatement / exaggeration / hyperbole, or speaking of small or unimportant things as though they were significant
  - understatement, or speaking of big or valuable things as though they were small or of minimal value

- COMEDY FROM NONSENSICAL STATEMENTS
  - sheer nonsense, as in Wilde's *The Importance of Being Earnest,* when Cecily is talking to Algernon after knowing him for only about five minutes, and mentions his letters. When Algernon says he could not have written her any because he didn't know her, she answers, "You need hardly remind me of that. . . . I remember only too well that I was forced to write your letters for you. . . . The three you wrote me after I had broken off the engagement are so beautiful, and so badly spelled, that even now I can hardly read them without crying a little."
  - *non sequitur* (Latin for "does not follow"), when one thing follows another to which it is completely unrelated. An example is when Algernon says he has an appointment he must miss in London and Cecily responds, "Well, I know, of course, how important it is not to keep a business engagement, if one wants to retain any sense of the beauty of life."

- the reversal of what a reader or audience expects, as in Algernon's comment about a widow: "I hear her hair has turned quite gold from grief." Or it can reverse a well-known phrase, as when he declares that "Divorces are made in Heaven."

- SATIRE, which holds foolishness, weakness, or vice up for ridicule. It can surface in a short passage, as when Shakespeare uses the workmen's play in *A Midsummer Night's Dream* to mock popular melodrama. Often satire pervades an entire long work, as in Molière's satirical comedies, Voltaire's *Candide,* or modern works such as Joseph Heller's *Catch-22.*

THEME

The issue of theme deserves special consideration. The word has two different meanings, and it's essential that you understand the differences. Often theme is simply the name of an abstract idea that a work of literatures addresses: "injustice," "family and belonging," "war-induced madness," and the like.

What the AP exam generally refers to as "the meaning of the work as a whole" is commonly called the theme. When it has this meaning, a "theme" is expressed in a full sentence that states what the work says about the topic. It also relates the work to the human experience: (1) our relationship to universal and divine forces, (2) our relationships with one another, or (3) our personal conceptions of ourselves and our place in our world. Themes in literature are not hidden messages we must hunt for. Rather, they require us to think and talk about the characters, events and details, and symbols and patterns in the work, and then construct a statement of theme based on what we uncover. The statement of theme you as an individual generate will differ slightly from statements of theme made by other readers. But each interpretation is accurate if it passes two tests: nothing in the work contradicts it, and it accounts for all of the work's details. There is, therefore, never one "right" reading of a complex work, although there could be many "wrong" readings. Note that even though the AP exam uses the phrase "the meaning," complex works, especially novels and plays, have multiple meanings, so we often do well to speak or write of "a theme" or "a major theme" rather than "*the* theme." The following, for example, are among the myriad accurate but arguable themes of *Hamlet:*

- In a society marked by political and moral corruption, it becomes difficult or impossible to establish truth.

- As humans, we must learn to trust that the supernatural force that governs the universe keeps it in order, even if that order is not always apparent to us.

- We can never be certain in our knowledge of others. The search for that certainty, however, may bring a more significant understanding of ourselves and of the world.

Themes are truths—as the writer sees them—about life, so a statement of theme will never mention characters or details from a work, because those elements are fictional. One more caution: avoid reducing the theme to a moral about how to live ("Telling lies is wrong and leads to trouble") or into a cliché ("Slow and steady wins the race").

We'll return to themes again, in "The Open Essay Question."

ANALYZING DRAMA

As a reader, you approach plays differently than you approach novels or short stories. Playwrights compose their works as scripts to be staged and acted rather than as books to be read, and we rarely have a narrator to guide us. You'll find that if you shift your role from reader to director, you'll start asking the questions necessary to any analysis of a play. Some are bigger questions: "Who should play this role?" or "What should the stage look like?" Others might be more detailed: "What colors should he wear?" or "Should she pause and look around before she says that line?" As the "director," you need to be constantly thinking about how actors should speak their lines, where they should pause, what facial expressions they might make, and so forth.

Many modern playwrights do a lot of the directing through their introductions and stage directions. Arthur Miller, Tennessee Williams, and Lorraine Hansberry, for instance, provide detailed descriptions of the stage setting and directions for speaking many of the lines: "[turning away]" or "[with rising resentment]." Those directions can guide a reader to visualize what happens on stage and, finally, what a play means.

In the texts of older plays, though, we do not have those guides. For Shakespeare and Molière, for example, we have only the characters' lines. Often those lines will direct the actor. For example, in Shakespeare's *Richard III,* Gloucester's line asking Anne "Why dost thou spit at me?" makes it clear what she has to do before he can say it. In most editions of those plays, editors have added stage directions, but because those are editorial and not authorial, you are free to change them. So "reading" such a play becomes more of an adventure because we're free to make many more decisions. In *A Raisin in the Sun* we are told "Ruth is about thirty," and we know Walter yells the line "they get to a point where they can't insult you man to man" in anger because the stage direction says "[in fury]." But in *Othello*, we know no one's age, and even a line as simple as "My name is Roderigo" can send at least four different messages to an audience, depending on which of the four words the actor stresses. Part of your job as the "director" is to decide which way you think the lines should be read.

When possible, seeing actual stage productions and videos of plays is ideal, for drama is most powerful when viewed. Keep in mind that there will probably be considerable similarities among productions of modern plays because modern playwrights are also often their own first directors. For older plays, each director starts almost from scratch with his or her own production. Avoid thinking that there's one right way a play is supposed to be produced.

The following are questions to consider in analyzing a play. Keep in mind that after the answer to each, you must then ask "Why?" A successful analysis requires you to show how the playwright used various dramatic tools to build or reinforce a meaning of the work as a whole. When you encounter a selection from an unfamiliar play on the

AP exam, you won't have time to attend to all these questions. Experience with considering them, however, will help you spot the primary dramatic tools and will pay in a clearer, richer analysis.

- **SET:** Is it indoors or out? open? claustrophobia inducing? If it's a room, how is it furnished? Which colors dominate? Why?

- **COSTUMES:** Are the costumes described? If not, what should the characters be wearing and when and why do they change? Is the makeup neutral, used only to compensate for lighting and distance, or does it exaggerate something about the character? Why?

- **SOUND:** How and where does the playwright use sound effects or music? As a director, where do you want to add sound or music? Why?

- **LIGHTING:** Is the lighting realistic, so spectators don't notice it? Is it warm? cold? colored? Is part of the stage darker or lighter than the rest at times? Is one character or object lit differently from the rest of the stage? Why?

- **PROPERTIES:** Do some objects take on special meaning through their size or placement or because they reappear? Why?

- **BLOCKING:** Are some characters still, or do they all move around a lot? Does anyone fidget? Do some pairs or combinations of characters stay close to each other? Do they keep a noticeable distance? Do some stay in the background? Why?

- **GESTURES AND STAGE BUSINESS:** Do any of the characters have distinct physical characteristics, disabilities, or idiosyncratic mannerisms? Do any have specific "stage business,"—that is, do they make movements or actions intended especially to establish character or atmosphere? Why?

Such annotations will go a long way in helping you visualize what the play looks like, and, through that visualization, understand the meanings it conveys.

ANALYZING POETRY

READING POETRY

Because poems are the richest, most intense form of literature, their analysis requires special treatment. A good analogy for analyzing poetry is getting to know a person. You make some judgments quickly based on appearance and the first things you hear people say. As you see them in different surroundings, at times when you are in different moods, you rework what you think about them. You listen to what they say, watch what they do, and come to know them better. So it is with poems: you need to read them repeatedly, in different times, places, and moods. No one reads a good poem once or twice and "gets it all." The AP exam doesn't give you time for much rereading, but if you develop the habit of returning to poems, you will develop a sense of how poems slowly disclose their meaning. That can help when you encounter an unfamiliar one on a test.

Read poems repeatedly and aloud. Ears pick up a great deal that eyes can miss. Let punctuation guide you. Although there is always a pause, even if very brief, at the end of each line, read sentences rather than lines. Read a variety of poets; to do well on the AP exam, you want to become comfortable with works from the Renaissance through modern times.

On a timed exam, when you're faced with a poem you've never seen before, you'll need a system for getting to know it fast. Many find a mnemonic, a memory aid, useful in helping to recall a set of questions that can make a good introduction to any poem. It's almost essential to have one for high-stakes exams. This one is "TP-COASTT." Think of it as a way to "COASTT through a poem." (How you remember the "TP" part is up to you!)

- TITLE: How many meanings can the title have?

- PARAPHRASE: What do you discover when you put the poem into your own words? What do you learn about the meaning? What about the poet's choice of words?

- CONNOTATION: What meanings has the poet given the poem beyond its literal meanings? Use a dictionary to look up words that are used in a new or unusual way, and a dictionary of synonyms for help with the words' connotations.

- ORGANIZATION: What does the poem look like on the page? Does it have identifiable parts? What kind of progression has the poet given the piece? Are ideas arranged in order of time? place? importance? something else?

- ATTITUDE: What is the speaker's tone? Is the poet's the same, or has the poet created some distance between the two?

- SHIFTS: Where are the major shifts in the poem: in setting? in tone? in syntax? in diction? In rhythm or rhyme?

- TITLE: Look back at the title after analyzing the poem. Does it suggest new interpretations?

- THEME: What is the theme of the poem—the meaning of the work as a whole? You might begin with the topic—loneliness, joy, loss, family—and then phrase the theme, which is what the poem says about the topic. Remember to phrase your statement of the theme in a complete sentence, and not simply with a label.

SOUND PATTERNS

The primary characteristic of poetry—what separates it from prose—is the poet's attention to sounds and their patterns. Some poetry, especially contemporary poetry, is unrestricted by any regularized rhythm and follows no standard pattern. The term "free verse" reflects that open form. But most poetry follows a predictable pattern. The "fixed forms" have a prescribed rhythm and number of lines and the poet chooses or establishes a pattern.

Of the standard rhythms, you'll need to know the four most common "feet," or sets of syllables:

- the iamb: two syllables, one unstressed followed by one stressed (to-**day**)

*I **do** not **like** them, **Sam-I-am**.*

■ the trochee: two syllables, one stressed followed by one un stressed (**fa**-ther)

when we *look* around and *won*der

■ the anapest: three syllables, two unstressed followed by one stressed (in-ter-**cept**)

and the *sheen* of their *spears* was like *stars* on the *sea*

■ the dactyl: three syllables, one stressed followed by two unstressed (**light**-ning rod)

Romeo **Mon**tague, *living* in *It*aly

Each rhythmic style creates a different mood and tempo. Iambic feet sound most like natural English speech. An anapestic line moves fast—it's perfect for a poem about a horse race, for example.

Poets frequently choose words that echo each other so as to link elements and stress moods or ideas. Alliteration is the use of different words beginning with the same sound—usually consecutive words. For instance the sounds of /g/, /b/, /p/, and /d/ slow the pace because they all stop the air coming from the lungs. So when *Romeo and Juliet's* Mercutio doesn't talk of "Cupid's arrow," which would keep the line moving quickly, but of the "blind bow-boy's butt-shaft," the pace must slow four times. (Cupid was believed to be blind, and the reference is to his bow and arrow.) Assonance is the repetition of vowel sounds to link ideas; in "if a cheerfulest Elephantangelchild should sit," e. e. cummings uses assonance twice in the line about "a proud round cloud in white high night."

Rhyme adds to our enjoyment with pleasing sound, but more importantly, it becomes an organizational tool, linking rhyming lines. Pay particular attention to any variation in a rhyme pattern. When the poem doesn't offer the rhyme we might have expected, the poet is doubtless calling our attention to the word or line for a purpose. Likewise, the caesura is a full pause or rhythmic break in a line of poetry, normally as a way to indicate a break in thought or continuity or rhythm.

Once again, remember that in analysis, naming the rhythm or rhyme scheme is of no value without commentary on how the sound pattern enhances the poem's meaning.

FIXED FORMS

Poems are said to be in a fixed form if they are written to fit a pre-established pattern. Of the three patterns most commonly used in English, the sonnet is overwhelmingly the most popular, but be sure to familiarize yourself as well with the villanelle and the sestina, two somewhat complex forms.

IMAGERY

All imaginative literature involves imagery—words or phrases that appeal to the senses—but poetry depends on it most heavily. Visual images, those that call up pictures, are the most common, but take note of those that address the other senses as well. Sounds, textures, smells, and tastes can reinforce and enhance meaning in a work. Be particularly attentive to patterns of imagery; watch for repetition of appeals to the same or multiple senses. Remember that the purpose of analysis is always to bring out and explain meaning. You want to mention elements such as imagery when you are showing how the poet uses them to help communicate the meaning of the poem as a whole.

ALLUSION

Because of the compact nature of poems, poets often depend highly on brief references to other literature or history, alluding most often to the Bible, classical mythology, Shakespeare, history, fables, fairy tales, and current cultural phenomena, and they count on readers to recognize those allusions. As you build up the store of works you've read and remember, you will become more attuned to the allusions in newer works. In analyzing a poem, the key question is why the writer chose a given allusion, how it enhances the work or a part of it, and, finally, how it relates to a meaning of the work as a whole.

Working on the skills outlined here will help you reach a comfort zone in understanding literature. Like the ever-practicing basketball player and cellist at the beginning of this chapter, even the most proficient readers need to keep at it. But you will develop habits of reading that will greatly increase your understanding and enjoyment of literature and prove valuable long after the one-day exam is over.

A WORD ABOUT TONE

An understanding of tone and the abilities to recognize and speak or write about it are essential to any analysis of literature. Tone plays such a key role in all forms of art that even in informal criticism, people talk about books, movies, music, and art in terms of tone. Movies are routinely described as "creepy" or "feel-good" or "suspenseful," for example. In conversation, we can show attitude toward what we are saying with vocal inflection, pauses, facial expressions, and gestures. Except in drama, those are not available to written literature, so novelists and poets use diction, figurative language, choice of details, imagery, and sentence type and length. The overall purpose of analysis is to understand how an author develops meaning and suggests tone through diction and literary techniques.

Tone is key to literary analysis, and it figures prominently on all AP English Literature and Composition exams. Your exam will include questions—both multiple-choice and essay—that will require you to explore tone with precision. On a recent AP "released exam," fully 20 percent of the multiple-choice questions asked directly or indirectly about tone. Tone can be a difficult literary concept to grasp, but understanding what it is—and is not—will help you understand what an author is saying.

Many students confuse tone with mood. Although different, both tone and mood can have the same emotional impact. The author's *attitude* toward a subject, whether stated or implied, is referred to as tone. Some possible attitudes are optimism, earnestness, bitterness, humor, and exuberance. An author's tone can be revealed through choice of words and details and through figurative language and syntax. If the subject is an abstract concept such as death, discerning the tone of such a passage requires figuring out the narrator's or speaker's attitude or feelings about death. (The word "narrator" generally refers to the person telling a story, while the word "speaker" refers to the person from whose perspective a poem is told. Keep in mind that the narrator or speaker is not the same as the author.) Does the narrator seem afraid of death? Does the narrator see death as a natural part of life? To find out, you must look for clues to how the narrator feels about death. Is the narrator reliable? Look at the opening lines from Edgar Allan Poe's "The Tell-Tale Heart":

> True!—nervous—very, very dreadfully nervous I had been and am; but why *will* you say that I am mad? The disease had sharpened my senses—not destroyed—not dulled them. Above all was the sense of hearing acute. I heard all things in the heaven and in the earth. I heard many things in hell. How, then, am I mad? Hearken! and observe how healthily—how calmly I can tell you the whole story.

From the beginning the reader understands that the narrator is mentally ill. The description of the exaggeration of the senses is a detail that the author includes to let the reader know that, despite the narrator's claims, he is indeed insane. The deranged tone is reinforced by the syntax—sentences broken by exclamation points, a rhetorical question, the hyperbole of the narrator's hearing "all things in the heaven and in the earth." Determining whether the narrator is reliable is not often this easy. Still, when you begin reading a passage, you should always separate the narrator's thoughts from the author's. In essence, you are deconstructing the passage, looking at its parts in order to determine its overall meaning.

Tone is often created through words. All words have a denotative meaning—that is, every word has a literal definition. Many words also have a connotative meaning—a positive or negative feeling associated with them. For example, the word "lady" has a denotative meaning much the same as the word "woman." Both are defined as a female person. However, do the two words call up the same feelings? Let's add another word that means *female* to the group—the word "broad," a slang term used as a slur. The connotation, or feeling, is negative. If an author uses the word "lady" in reference to a character, the attitude toward the character would be much more positive than the attitude toward a character referred to as a "broad." Pay particular attention to the connotative powers of words. In general, authors who feel strongly about a subject want you to feel the same way.

Edgar Allan Poe is often a favorite of those who like a good horror story. Many of Poe's stories center around the subject of death, and the tone he creates is one of apprehensive melancholy. Continuing with "The Tell-Tale Heart":

> It is impossible to say how first the idea entered my brain; but once conceived, it haunted me day and night. Object there was none. Passion there was none. I loved the old man. He had never wronged me. He had never given me insult. For his gold I had no desire. I think it was his eye! yes, it was this! One of his eyes resembled that of a vulture—a pale eye, with a film over it. Whenever it fell upon me, my blood ran cold; and so by degrees—very gradually—I made up my mind to take the life of the old man, and thus rid myself of the eye forever.

As the story proceeds, it becomes clear that it is not enough to kill the old man because of his deformity, or "evil eye," as the narrator describes it. Instead, the old man must be hacked to pieces and hidden under the floorboards of his own home. We know through the narrator's actions that he is indeed insane, though he professes that he is not. The narrator views his actions as inevitable and tries to justify the old man's brutal murder. But this is the attitude toward death that we get from the narrator, not from the author. What is the author's attitude?

> No doubt I now grew *very* pale; —but I talked more fluently, and with a heightened voice. Yet the sound increased—and what could I do? It was a *low, dull, quick sound—much such a sound as a watch makes*

when enveloped in cotton. I gasped for breath—and yet the officers heard it not. I talked more quickly—more vehemently; but the noise steadily increased. I arose and argued about trifles, in a high key and with violent gesticulations; but the noise steadily increased. Why *would* they not be gone? I paced the floor to and fro with heavy strides, as if excited to fury by the observations of the men—but the noise steadily increased. Oh God! what *could* I do? I foamed—I raved—I swore!

We know from the actions of the narrator that the author wants us to understand that the motives for the murder are not justified and that murder is an insane act. Death is not something deserved or something that always comes upon us naturally or peacefully. The tone of the story is then disturbingly melancholic.

Because the reader and the author often have the same feelings about a character or a situation, it's easy to confuse tone with mood. "Mood" refers to the climate of feeling or atmosphere in a literary work. It is the overall sense a reader gets from a particular passage or poem. The choices of setting, objects, details, images, and diction all help to create a specific mood. Keep in mind that how you, the reader, feel about a subject is not necessarily the same as how the author feels about it, but the two may overlap. When we read horror stories, often we are filled with dread. We may even feel suspense and fear. That's what the author wants us to feel. And that's why mood and tone are often described with the same words.

Determining the tone of a literary work can be difficult, especially in poetry. A T-chart can be helpful in understanding tone. Draw a *T* on a piece of paper and label the left side *positive,* the right side *negative.* As you read, list words with a positive or a negative connotation (emotion) on the appropriate side of your T-chart. Before long, you will begin to see that one side of your T-Chart has grown a lot longer than the other. You can then begin to find the right words to convey tone. When you write about tone, refer to your T-chart for specific words to support your conclusions.

Tone isn't divisible only between positive and negative, happy and sad. Rather, the tone of a work or passage lies somewhere along a continuum; some writing lies near the middle of the continuum and is said to be neutral. You commonly encounter this type of writing in learning materials such as handbooks, textbooks, and manuals, which are labeled *didactic.* Even these, though, take on a variety of tones. Some can be accurately described by such increasingly negative labels as *staid, terse, pedantic, pompous,* and *pretentious.* Others would be better described with more neutral words such as *straightforward, dispassionate, formal,* or *impartial.* We hope most of your school reading has a more positive tone—one that is provocative, informative, incisive, and vibrant.

Tone shifts in most works of literature, especially in poetry. A poem may start out, say, cynically doubtful, and then shift to a scene or statement of hopeful serenity. There may be more than one shift in tone.

When we discuss poetry in more depth, we will look at the importance of identifying shifts in tone.

The literary fiction and poetry that we read not only for enjoyment, but to help us understand the universe, the divine, others, and ourselves—the kind of literature common in AP courses—is marked by two separate tones, each producing its own effect while combining to create a deeper meaning and feel. Work at combining two words in order to describe tone with more precision and richness. Since you'll use adjectives to describe tone, find the best two and turn the secondary one into an adverb. You'll finish with something like "audaciously irreverent" or "playfully mocking." Below is a list of words for describing tone, divided into four general categories: positive, negative, neutral, and contextually determined. Those in the last group can be positive or negative, depending on the context. A provocative tone, for example, might be a positive attribute, indicating something that prompts a reader to pause and reflect, but it could also be negative, conveying the idea of hostile aggression. Be sure you know the meanings of these tone words. You need a sophisticated vocabulary for literary analysis. Simply saying the tone is positive or negative or neutral doesn't provide any clarity. Likewise, labeling tone as "happy" or "sad" is of little or no value and can even hurt your analysis. Nuanced vocabulary that describes tone, on the other hand, will give your writing a boost. The multiple-choice section of the AP exam will include many questions testing your ability to discern tone and understand words in context—there is one question of this type for nearly every passage.

Tone Vocabulary

Positive Attitude Words

affectionate	delightful	humorous	persuasive
amused	ebullient	incisive	playful
authoritative	elated	instructive	reverent
bantering	elegiac	jocund	rousing
benevolent	empathetic	joyful	sanguine
caring	encouraging	lighthearted	serene
ceremonial	enthusiastic	loving	stirring
cheerful	euphoric	meditative	sympathetic
cheery	excited	mirthful	tender
compassionate	expectant	ominous	thoughtful
complimentary	exuberant	optimistic	vibrant
conciliatory	gleeful	passionate	whimsical
confident	hilarious	pensive	wistful
	hopeful		wry

NEGATIVE ATTITUDE WORDS

accusing	despairing	indignant	resigned
ambivalent	desperate	inflammatory	sarcastic
angry	diabolic	insipid	sardonic
annoyed	disappointed	insolent	satiric
anxious	disdainful	irreverent	scared
apprehensive	disgusted	irritated	scornful
audacious	distressed	lethargic	selfish
bewildered	disturbed	lugubrious	silly
bitter	enraged	melodramatic	simpering
blunt	facetious	miserable	sinister
bossy	fatalistic	moralistic	sneering
brusque	fearful	mournful	somber
candid	flippant	nervous	staid
choleric	foreboding	outraged	strident
cold	frantic	paranoid	suspicious
conceited	frightened	pathetic	taunting
condemnatory	frustrated	patronizing	terse
condescending	furious	pedantic	threatening
contemptuous	gloomy	pessimistic	timorous
contentious	grave	petty	turgid
critical	greedy	pompous	uncaring
cynical	grim	pretentious	unconcerned
depraved	gushy	proud	uneasy
depressed	haughty	psychotic	unsympathetic
derisive	holier-than-thou	regretful	vitriolic
derogatory	hopeless	remorseful	worried
desolate	horrific		wrathful

NEUTRAL ATTITUDE WORDS

clinical	factual	lyrical	questioning
cool-headed	impartial	matter-of-fact	reflective
cultured	indifferent	objective	reminiscent
detached	informative	official	restrained
didactic	instructive	pithy	scholarly
disinterested	learned	placid	straightforward
dispassionate		plain-speaking	

CONTEXTUALLY DETERMINED ATTITUDE WORDS

admonitory	effusive	mock-heroic	romantic
allusive	fanciful	mock-serious	sentimental
baffled	fervent	mysterious	serious
burlesque	formal	nostalgic	skeptical
casual	impatient	outspoken	sober
colloquial	intimate	provocative	solemn
concerned	introspective	questioning	stoic
confused	ironic	reflective	suspenseful
diffident	laid-back	relaxed	tense
doubtful	measured	reminiscent	urgent
dramatic	melancholic	reticent	zealous

Adding these words and the fine shades of meaning they can express to your critical and analytical vocabulary will greatly increase your pleasure in reading. It will also pay dividends in your ability to read perceptively on exams, and to talk with others about literature and other forms of art, because you will no longer be dependent on "happy" and "sad" as the only words you can find to describe a writer's or filmmaker's attitude toward the action of a novel or movie.

A GLOSSARY OF LITERARY TERMS

Literary terms make the job of analysis easier by providing a common vocabulary for discussing literature. That vocabulary is a tool for analysis, not the purpose of analysis. The following is a list of some of the terms that are used in analyzing works of literature. You will no doubt encounter some of these words in the multiple-choice questions.

ACTIVE VOICE: Active voice pertains to any sentence with an *active* verb. Active voice expresses more energy than does passive voice. For example: "Robert crushed the tomato with his fist" is in the active voice. "The tomato was crushed by Robert" is in the passive voice.

ALLEGORY: An extended narrative (in poetry or prose) in which the characters and actions—and sometimes the setting as well—are contrived to make sense on the literal level and at the same time to signify a second, correlated order of characters, concepts, and events. In other words, an allegory carries a second, deeper meaning, as well as its surface story.

ALLITERATION: The repetition of a consonant sound at the beginning of several words in a sentence or a line of poetry. For example: "Black reapers with the sound of steel on stones / Are sharpening scythes" — Jean Toomer.

ALLUSION: A reference to another person, another historical event, another work, and the like. To make allusions, you should be familiar at the very least with Greek and Roman mythology, Judeo-Christian literature, and Shakespeare. Identify the impact of an allusion the same way you would a metaphor. For example, the title "By the Waters of Babylon" by Stephen Vincent Benét is a reference to Psalm 137.

ANALOGY: A term that signifies a comparison of or similarity between two objects or ideas. For example, "Nature's first green is gold" — Robert Frost.

ANAPHORA: The deliberate repetition of a word or phrase at the beginning of several successive poetic lines, prose sentences, clauses or paragraphs. It is used to emphasize an idea. For example: "**This** royal throne of kings, **this** sceptred isle, / **This** earth of majesty, **this** seat of Mars, / **This** other Eden, demi-paradise, / **This** fortress built by Nature for herself" —William Shakespeare.

APHORISM: A brief statement of an opinion or elemental truth. "Vision is the art of seeing what is invisible to others" —Jonathan Swift.

APOSTROPHE: This is a direct address to someone who is not present, to a deity or muse, or to some other power. "O eloquent, just, and mighty Death!" —Sir Walter Raleigh.

ASSONANCE: Repetition of a vowel sound within a group of words or lines. Notice the recurrent long "I" in the following lines: "Thou still unravish'd bride of quietness, / Thou foster-child of silence and slow time" —John Keats.

BLANK VERSE: Blank verse consists of lines of *iambic pentameter,* which of all verse forms is closest to the natural rhythms of English speech. Most of Shakespeare's plays are in blank verse.

CAESURA: A pause within a line of poetry in order to make the meaning clear or to follow the natural rhythm of speech. "To err is human, / to forgive, divine" —Alexander Pope.

CARPE DIEM: Latin for "Seize the day."

CONNOTATION: The associations or moods attached to a word. Words generally are negative, positive, or neutral. An author's choice of words, especially words with a particularly strong connotation, is usually the key to determining the author's tone and intention.

CONSONANCE: The repetition of a sequence of two or more consonants but with a change in the intervening vowel. For example: "live-love," "lean-alone," "pitter-patter."

COUPLET: A pair of rhymed lines. For example, "Into my empty head there come / a cotton beach, a dock wherefrom" —Maxine Kumin.

DENOTATION: The dictionary definition of a word.

DIALECT: A regional speech pattern. When using a dialect, a writer is relying on language to make a passage feel personal and authentic. For example: "You mean, you mad 'cause she didn't stop and tell us all her business. . . .The worst thing Ah ever knowed her to do was taking a few years offa her age and dat ain't never harmed nobody" —Zora Neale Hurston.

DICTION: Word choice; the specific words an author uses in his or her writing.

ELEGY: A formal meditative poem or lament for the dead. An example is "To an Athlete Dying Young" by A. E. Housman.

ELLIPSES: Three dots that indicate words have been left out of a quotation. Ellipses are also often used to create suspense. For example: "The dark car appeared at the end of the alley and Herman, the handsome hero, was trapped against the wall at the opposite end. The engine revved . . ."

EPISTROPHE: The ending of a series of lines, phrases, clauses, or sentences with the same word or words, used to emphasize the word or group of words for emotional impact. "[This] government of the people, by the people, and for the people shall not perish from the earth" —Abraham Lincoln.

EUPHEMISM: To use an inoffensive or more socially acceptable word for something that could be inappropriate or offensive to some. For example, "she passed away" instead of "she died."

FOIL: A minor character whose situation or actions parallel those of a major character and thus by contrast set off or illuminate the major character. Most often the contrast is complimentary to the main character. For example, Unferth is the foil to Beowulf.

FOOT: The combination of stressed and unstressed syllables that make up the metric unit of a line. The most commonly used feet are the iambic foot and the trochaic foot. The iambic foot consists of an unstressed syllable followed by a stressed syllable. For example: "When **I** / con-**sid** / er **how** / my **light** / is **spent**" —John Milton. The trochaic foot is the reverse—a stressed syllable followed by an unstressed syllable. For example: "**There** they / **are,** my / **fif**-ty / **men** and / **wo**-men" —Robert Browning.

FREE VERSE: Poetry that doesn't follow a prescribed form but is characterized by irregularity in the length of the lines and a lack of a regular metrical pattern and rhyme. Free verse may use other repetitive patterns including words, phrases, or structures.

HYPERBOLE: Exaggeration of an event or feeling—"I nearly died laughing!"

IMAGERY: Language that appeals to one or another of the five senses (sight, sound, touch, taste, or smell). Imagery can be created by using particularly vivid adjectives, similes, and metaphors.

IRONY: The use of words to express something other than—and often the opposite of—the literal meaning. There are three types of irony. Verbal irony contrasts what is said and what is meant. For example, in Shakespeare's *Julius Caesar,* Antony calls Brutus "an honorable man" when, in fact, he wants the people to think just the opposite. Situational irony contrasts what happens and what was expected to happen. In "The Monkey's Paw" by W. W. Jacobs, the Whites expect the paw (a talisman) to bring them happiness, but instead it brings them only grief. Dramatic irony contrasts what the character thinks to be true and what the reader knows to be true. In Shakespeare's *Romeo and Juliet,* Friar Lawrence arrives too late to inform Romeo of Juliet's deception in faking her own death. Romeo takes his own life thinking Juliet is dead, while the audience knows that she is not. You should be familiar with all three types of irony.

JARGON: A pattern of speech and vocabulary associated with a particular group of people. Medical doctors, computer analysts, teachers—all have a unique vocabulary, or jargon, that is used by members of that profession.

JUXTAPOSITION: The placement of one idea next to its opposite to make it more dramatic—for example, playing the song "What a Wonderful World" while showing scenes of war and violence.

LYRIC: Any poem in which a speaker expresses intensely personal emotion or thoughts. The term was originally applied to poems meant to be sung; now the term is sometimes used to refer to any poem that has a musical quality.

MALAPROPISM: A wonderful form of comic wordplay in which one word is mistakenly substituted for another that sounds similar. The name comes from the character of Mrs. Malaprop in Richard Sheridan's play *The Rivals*. She said things like "He is the very pineapple of politeness" rather than "He is the very pinnacle of politeness."

METAPHOR: A figure of speech in which an implicit comparison is made between two things that are essentially dissimilar. Metaphors, unlike similes, do not use the words "like" or "as." "Once I seen a **human ruin** / In a elevator-well. / And his members was bestrewin' / All the place where he had fell" —Ambrose Bierce. ("Human ruin" is a metaphor referring to a man's body.)

METER: The pattern of stressed and unstressed syllables or the units of stress patterns.

METONYMY: A figure of speech in which the name of one thing is substituted for another with which it is closely associated. For example: The crown spoke with authority about the growing crisis within the country. "Crown" is not literal, but is meant to represent a king or queen.

METRIC LINE: A line named according to the number of feet composing it, starting with *monometer,* a line of one foot, followed by *dimeter, trimeter, tetrameter, pentameter, hexameter, heptameter,* and *octameter,* a line of eight feet.

ODE: A lyric poem that is serious in subject and treatment, elevated in style, and elaborate in its stanzaic structure. An example is "Ode on a Grecian Urn" by John Keats.

ONOMATOPOEIA: A figure of speech in which a word when spoken imitates the sound associated with the word. For example, "buzz" echoes the sound of bees.

PARADOX: A figure of speech that seeks to create mental ambiguity, which then forces the reader to pause and seek clarity. For example: "My **silent** love **grows loude**r with each passing moment."

PARALLELISM: A pattern of language that creates a rhythm of repetition often combined with some other language of repetition. Parallel sets of sentences or parallel clauses can exist within a sentence. One type of parallelism is balance—"This is the place where girls become women, boys become men, dreams become reality." A second is antithesis—for example, "It was the best of times, it was the worst of times" —Charles Dickens.

PANEGYRIC: A literary expression of praise—for example, "O Captain! My Captain!" by Walt Whitman.

PASSIVE VOICE: The opposite of active voice. The passive voice is used when something happens to someone. For example, "Samantha was choked by the assailant" rather than "The assailant choked Samantha," which is in the active form. Use of the passive voice indicates that Samantha is the important character here.

PASTORAL: A reference to or a description of simple country life. Older pastoral poems usually include shepherds who live in an idyllic setting. Generally, the word "pastoral" suggests being carefree or a return to a time of innocence. An example of a pastoral is Christopher Marlowe's "The Passionate Shepherd to His Love."

PERSONIFICATION: Giving human characteristics to nonhuman things. For example, "Because I could not stop for Death— / He kindly stopped for me—" —Emily Dickinson.

PLOCE: One of the most commonly used figures of stress, it means repeating a word within the same line or clause. For example: "Make war upon themselves; blood against blood / Self against self" — William Shakespeare.

POINT OF VIEW: The perspective from which the writer chooses to tell his or her story. Point of view can be in the first or third person, and limited, omniscient, or objective. Additionally, the reader must determine the state of mind of the narrator or speaker. Remember that the narrator of a story is not the author and the speaker of a poem is not the poet. How is the narrator connected to the story itself? Is the narrator part of the action or an objective bystander? If the narrator is part of the events of the story, his or her retelling of events may be biased. Is the narrator reliable? In other words, are we sure that what we are being told is what really happened?

PUN: A play on words used to create humor or comic relief. "I've always regarded archery as an aimless sport," he said with a quiver.

REFRAIN: A line, part of a line, or group of lines repeated in the course of a poem, sometimes with slight changes—for example, the word "nevermore" in Edgar Allan Poe's "The Raven."

REPETITION: The repeating of a word or phrase for emphasis. Repetition is often used in poetry. Sometimes repetition reinforces or even substitutes for meter (the beat), the other chief controlling factor in poetry.

RHYME: The echo or imitation of a sound. A rhyme scheme is a regular pattern of rhyming words in a poem. Rhyme can and often does contribute to the rhythm of a poem. There may be internal rhyme (rhyme within the line), end rhyme (last word of each line rhymes), slant or half rhyme (two words that sound close but not exactly alike, such as "alight/white," "grace/haste"), and perfect rhyme ("time/lime," "shot/hot").

RHYTHM: The sense of movement attributable to the pattern of stressed and unstressed syllables. Although rhythm is sometimes used to signify meter, it includes tempo (pacing) and the natural fluctuations of movement.

SATIRE: A form of writing in which a subject (usually a human vice) is made fun of or scorned, eliciting amusement, contempt, or indignation. The purpose of satire is to provoke change or reform. Examples of satire are Jonathan Swift's *Gulliver's Travels* and George Orwell's *Animal Farm.*

SHIFT: A change in setting (place or time), tone, or speakers. Identifying shifts in poetry is especially important for determining the overall purpose and tone of a poem.

SIMILE: A figure of speech in which an explicit comparison is made using "like," "as," or "than" between two very different things in order to express an idea that is more familiar or understandable. "Oh, my love is like a red, red rose." —Robert Burns.

SOLILOQUY: A speech in which a character in a play, alone on stage, expresses his or her thoughts. A soliloquy may reveal the private emotions, motives, and state of mind of the speaker. Hamlet's "To be or not to be" speech is a well-known soliloquy. Soliloquy is also known as *dramatic monologue.*

SONNET: A fixed form of fourteen lines, normally in iambic pentameter, with a rhyme scheme conforming to or approximating one of two main types. Shakespearean sonnets are divided into three quatrains and a concluding couplet and have the rhyme scheme *abab cdcd efef gg.* Italian or Petrarchan sonnets begin with an octave (eight lines) with the rhyme scheme *abbaabba.* The octave generally includes the "problem" that the sonnet will develop. It is followed by a sestet (six lines), which has as its rhyme scheme *cdcdcd* (or some variation thereof). The "problem" is resolved in the sestet.

STANZA: A group of lines that forms one division of a poem.

SYMBOL: An object that signifies something greater than itself. For example, the bald eagle is often used as a symbol of the United States.

SYNECDOCHE: A figure of speech in which a part is used for the whole—for example, "All hands on deck." (We assume the sailors' bodies will follow.)

THEME: An insight into life conveyed by a poem or story. The theme is the main point the author wants to make with the reader, and is often a basic truth, an acknowledgment of our humanity, or a reminder of human beings' shortcomings. This general insight is usually about life, society, or human nature. Themes often explore timeless and universal ideas. Most themes are implied rather than stated explicitly. Short works of fiction may have only one or two themes; however, a novel may include many themes because of the number and depth of the characters and the numerous events within the plot.

VERSE: Lines of poetry or metrical language in general, in contrast to prose.

A Closer Look at Multiple-Choice Questions

You are allotted sixty minutes for Section I of the AP exam, which consists of approximately fifty-five multiple-choice questions based on four or five selections. The selections are drawn from poetry, prose, and drama by American, British, and world writers from the sixteenth century to the present. You are not allowed to bring a dictionary or thesaurus, so it is in your best interest to be familiar with how language has been used over that span of time. A good anthology, such as *Perrine's Literature: Structure, Sound, and Sense* by Thomas R. Arp and Greg Johnson, is invaluable. There you will find gathered in one place literature that represents a variety of genres, time periods, writers, and styles.

The multiple-choice questions are designed to test your ability to read analytically, to recognize literary devices and their role in the work in question, and to understand the techniques writers use to express their ideas. For success with the multiple-choice questions, practice close reading under timed conditions. Answering fifty-five questions in sixty minutes gives you little time to think about each question.

Your score on this section of the exam will be 45 percent of your total score.

The Importance of Annotation

Make it a habit to annotate while you read. Annotation—highlighting, circling, or underlining words or phrases and writing your thoughts in the margins—is key to developing close reading skills. Many teachers begin each school year with several weeks of highlighting diction (to find the tone), circling or underlining metaphors and similes (imagery), and making brief notes in the margins (connecting with the text for meaning). These marks and scribbled notes are annotations.

Have you ever found yourself reading and suddenly a character or event reminds you of an experience you have had? Have you ever read a line of poetry and said, "Huh?" These are perfect places to annotate. If a word in the text sounds like gibberish, underline it and place a question mark in the margin. As you read on, you may be able to understand the line. If not, the question mark is a reminder to bring the word up during a class discussion. Either way, you are learning to pay *close attention* to what you are reading. When you come across a line of prose that is particularly descriptive or comical or that prompts you to say, "Aha!" make a brief note—"vivid colors," "slapstick action," "he confesses his love"—in the margin.

When you annotate, you are interacting with what you are reading. You begin to pay more attention to diction, imagery, similes and metaphors, and a host of other literary devices. When you slow down just long enough to highlight or jot down a note or a question in the margin, you will notice more and more details. Connecting to the text helps you remember details and recognize ideas within the text.

There is such a thing as too much annotation. When you are learning to annotate, it often happens that you look back over a passage you have read and see nothing but an ocean of highlighter fluid and a zillion scribbled notes. Don't worry! Eventually you'll learn to recognize what is and is not important.

AN EXAMPLE OF ANNOTATION

The following is a passage from "The Story of an Hour" by Kate Chopin. Pencil in hand, annotate it as you read. When you are finished, look at the sample annotated version of the passage. (No peeking!) The idea is to compare your annotations with ours.

Knowing that Mrs. Mallard was afflicted with a heart trouble, great care was taken to break to her as gently as possible the news of her husband's death.

It was her sister Josephine who told her, in broken sentences, veiled hints that revealed in half concealing. Her husband's friend Richards was there, too, near her. It was he who had been in the newspaper office when intelligence of the railroad disaster was received, with Brently Mallard's name leading the list of "killed." He had only taken the time to assure himself of its truth by a second telegram, and had hastened to forestall any less careful, less tender friend in bearing the sad message. 5 ... 10

She did not hear the story as many women have heard the same, with a paralyzed inability to accept its significance. She wept at once, with sudden, wild abandonment, in her sister's arms. When the storm of grief had spent itself she went away to her room alone. She would have no one follow her. 15

There stood, facing the open window, a comfortable, roomy armchair. Into this she sank, pressed down by a physical exhaustion that haunted her body and seemed to reach into her soul. 20

She could see in the open square before her house the tops of trees that were all aquiver with the new spring life. The delicious breath of rain was in the air. In the street below a peddler was crying his wares. The notes of a distant song which some one was singing reached her faintly, and countless sparrows were twittering in the eaves. 25

There were patches of blue sky showing here and there through the clouds that had met and piled one above the other in the west facing her window.

She sat with her head thrown back upon the cushion of the chair, quite motionless, except when a sob came up into her 30 throat and shook her, as a child who has cried itself to sleep continues to sob in its dreams.

She was young, with a fair, calm face, whose lines bespoke repression and even a certain strength. But now there was a dull stare in her eyes, whose gaze was fixed away off yonder on one of those patches of blue sky. It was not a glance of reflection, but rather indicated a suspension of intelligent thought. 35

There was something coming to her and she was waiting for it, fearfully. What was it? She did not know; it was too subtle and elusive to name. But she felt it, creeping out of the sky, reaching toward her through the sounds, the scents, the color that filled the air. 40

Now her bosom rose and fell tumultuously. She was beginning to recognize this thing that was approaching to possess her, and she was striving to beat it back with her will—as powerless as her two white slender hands would have been. 45

When she abandoned herself a little whispered word escaped her slightly parted lips. She said it over and over under her breath: "Free, free, free!" The vacant stare and the look of terror that had followed it went from her eyes. They stayed keen and bright. Her pulses beat fast, and the coursing blood warmed and relaxed every inch of her body. 50

She did not stop to ask if it were not a monstrous joy that held her. A clear and exalted perception enabled her to dismiss the suggestion as trivial. 55

She knew that she would weep again when she saw the kind, tender hands folded in death; the face that had never looked save with love upon her, fixed and gray and dead. But she saw beyond that bitter moment a long procession of years to come that would belong to her absolutely. And she opened and spread her arms out to them in welcome. 60

Now that you have read the passage and annotated your connections to it, let's look at a sample of what an annotated version of the passage might look like.

weak

Knowing that Mrs. Mallard was afflicted with a heart trouble, great care was taken to break to her as gently as possible the news of her husband's death.

It was her sister Josephine who told her, in broken sentences, veiled hints that revealed in half concealing. Her husband's friend Richards was there, too, near her. It was he who had been in the newspaper office when intelligence of the railroad disaster was received, with Brently Mallard's name leading the list of "killed." He had only taken the time to assure himself of its truth by a **in the past?** second telegram, and had hastened to forestall any less careful, less tender friend in bearing the sad message. **husband dead**

She did not hear the story as many women have heard the same, with a paralyzed inability to accept its significance. She wept at once, with sudden, wild abandonment, in her sister's arms. When the storm of grief had spent itself she went away to her room alone. She would have no one follow her. **not like other women?**

There stood, facing the open window, a comfortable, roomy armchair. Into this she sank, pressed down by a physical exhaustion that haunted her body and seemed to reach into her soul. **Personification**

She could see in the open square before her house the tops of trees that were all aquiver with the new spring life. The delicious breath of rain was in the air. In the street below a peddler was **?** crying his wares. The notes of a distant song which some one was singing reached her faintly, and countless sparrows were twittering in the eaves. **Spring life v. Death of husband**

There were patches of blue sky showing here and there **personified** through the clouds that had met and piled one above the other in the west facing her window.

She sat with her head thrown back upon the cushion of the chair, quite motionless, except when a sob came up into her throat and shook her, as a child who has cried itself to sleep continues to sob in its dreams. **simile** — **so, not weak?**

Young/spring — She was young, with a fair, calm face, whose lines bespoke **??** — repression and even a certain strength. But now there was a dull stare in her eyes, whose gaze was fixed away off yonder on one of **diction (south or west)** those patches of blue sky. It was not a glance of reflection, but rather indicated a suspension of intelligent thought. **more nature**

There was something coming to her and she was waiting for it, fearfully. What was it? She did not know; it was too subtle and elusive to name. But she felt it, creeping out of the sky, reaching toward her through the sounds, the scents, the color that filled **suspense!** the air.

Now her bosom rose and fell tumultuously. She was beginning to recognize this thing that was approaching to possess her, and she was striving to beat it back with her will—as **Diction—Is she in danger?** powerless as her two white slender hands would have been.

When she abandoned herself a little whispered word escaped her slightly parted lips. She said it over and over under her breath: "Free, free, free!" The vacant stare and the look of terror that had followed it went from her eyes. They stayed keen and bright. Her pulses beat fast, and the coursing blood warmed and **free v. repression** relaxed every inch of her body.

5

10

15

20

25

30

35

40

45

50

She did not stop to ask if it were not a (monstrous joy) that held
her. A clear and exalted perception enabled her to dismiss the   55
suggestion as trivial.

She knew that she would weep again when she saw the kind,
tender hands folded in death; the face that had never looked save
with love upon her, fixed and gray and dead. But she saw beyond
that bitter moment a long procession of years to come that would   60
belong to her absolutely. And she opened and spread her arms
out to them in (welcome)

Ends positive
Started negative.

Husband dies and now she is
free—free from marriage?

ANSWERING MULTIPLE-CHOICE QUESTIONS

Depending on how many selections are used in the multiple-choice
section, you will have approximately 12 to 15 minutes to read and
annotate each selection and answer the corresponding multiple-choice
questions. Most students find that the selections and their questions
are challenging but manageable when there is no clock ticking. When
you begin preparing for the AP exam, don't worry too much about the
clock. However, it is important to include the occasional timed session.
You need to be up to speed—literally—by the day of the test.

HOW TO APPROACH A SELECTION AND ITS QUESTIONS

Multiple-choice questions consider every aspect of a selection, from
the smallest detail to the broadest concepts. They might ask about the
meaning of a word or phrase, information that is directly stated and
information that is implied in a selection, literary devices and
techniques, style, tone, theme. In short, they cover a lot of ground.
Here are some suggestions:

■ Some students like to skim the questions before reading the
selection—it helps them focus their reading to find the information
they are going to need. Other students find it slows them down or
gives them too much information to deal with. Try both approaches
and see which works best for you.

■ Annotating the selection as you read will save you a lot of time. It
allows you to quickly locate the literary devices, clues to tone, and
transitions you spotted in your reading.

■ The AP exam, unlike some standardized tests, does not start with
the easiest questions and progress to the most challenging. The
questions are generally arranged to move in sequence from the
beginning to the end of the selection. When you encounter a
difficult question, don't assume that the next question will be even
more difficult. It may be easier. In other words, read every
question.

■ Answers are always based on information that is given or
implied. Don't go out on a limb to answer a question. The
answer should be based on the passage, not on your personal
experience or another, similar passage.

- Eliminate obvious wrong answers. If you know an answer choice is incorrect, cross it out as an option.
- Watch out for the tricky distractor. This is the answer choice that is really, really close to the right answer but is not right. If you've narrowed your answer choices down to two, one is probably the tricky distractor. Reading the question again often will help you see the best choice between the two.
- You can work on the selections in any order. If a reading bogs you down from the very beginning, you may want to skip it and move on to the next selection. Sometimes finding a more familiar or engaging selection can jump-start you. But be careful! Make sure to mark your answers to the selection you are working on in the proper place on your answer sheet.
- Pace yourself. It's best not to spend too much time on any one question. If a question is really stumping you, skip it and come back to it later. If you really have no idea what the answer is, leave it blank and move on. However, it's best to make a decision on a question before you move to the next passage on the test.
- Predict the answer. After you read the question, make an educated guess before you look at the answer choices. If you see an answer that is similar to your own, it may well be the correct answer. However, be sure to read through all the answer choices before selecting your final answer.

Now let's try some multiple-choice questions. Make annotations as you go through them, then compare your annotations with ours.

MULTIPLE-CHOICE QUESTIONS FOR AN EXCERPT FROM "THE STORY OF AN HOUR" BY KATE CHOPIN

THE QUESTIONS

1. In lines 39-43, the narrator does which of the following?
   (A) creates a shift in tone
   (B) introduces a foreshadowing of death
   (C) describes Mrs. Mallard's sorrow
   (D) emphasizes Mrs. Mallard's physical weakness
   (E) creates a sense of excitement

2. The term "monstrous joy" (line 54) is an example of
   (A) a paradox
   (B) an oxymoron
   (C) a colloquialism
   (D) a chiasmus
   (E) antithesis

3. Lines 12–16 ("She did not hear . . . have no one follow her") suggest that Mrs. Mallard
   (A) is stronger than others believe her to be
   (B) is mentally unstable
   (C) reacted to the news of her husband's death as any woman would
   (D) feels hopelessly lost without her husband
   (E) is in shock over the death of her husband

4. In line 24, the word "crying" means
   (A) lamenting
   (B) weeping
   (C) shouting
   (D) howling
   (E) singing

5. When saying, "whose lines bespoke repression" (lines 34–35), the narrator does which of the following?
   (A) makes a general reference to the overall condition of women
   (B) introduces the idea of slavery
   (C) emphasizes the theme of death
   (D) suggests the need for change
   (E) connects a youthful appearance with nature

6. The news of Mr. Mallard's death is in contrast to the narrator's description of
   (A) a storm
   (B) Mrs. Mallard's emotional state
   (C) Mrs. Mallard's sister
   (D) Mrs. Mallard's physical health
   (E) nature

7. In lines 57–62, the narrator conveys a sense of
   (A) sanguinity
   (B) nostalgia
   (C) contentment
   (D) skepticism
   (E) arrogance

8. All of the following are personified in the passage EXCEPT
   (A) "rain" (line 23)
   (B) "hands" (line 58)
   (C) freedom (lines 41–42)
   (D) "heart trouble" (line 1)
   (E) "physical exhaustion" (lines 18–19)

9. What does the pronoun "it" in lines 39–41 refer to?
   (A) freedom
   (B) death
   (C) hope
   (D) misfortune
   (E) fear

THE QUESTIONS WITH ANNOTATIONS

1. In lines 39-43, the narrator does which of the following?
   ✓ (A) creates a shift in tone *Beginning was sad then suspenseful*
   ? (B) introduces a foreshadowing of death *?Maybe*
   ✗ (C) describes Mrs. Mallard's sorrow
   ✗ (D) emphasizes Mrs. Mallard's physical weakness
   ✗ (E) creates a sense of excitement *wrong word*

2. The term "monstrous joy" (line 54) is an example of   *opposites*
   ? (A) a paradox *usually a situation*
   ✓ (B) an oxymoron *phrase*
   ✗ (C) a colloquialism
   ✗ (D) a chiasmus
   ✗ (E) antithesis

3. Lines 12–16 ("She did not hear . . . have no one follow her") suggest that Mrs. Mallard
   ✓ (A) is stronger than others believe her to be *thought she was weak*
   ✗ (B) is mentally unstable
   ✗ (C) reacted to the news of her husband's death as any woman would *said she didn't!*
   ✗ (D) feels hopelessly lost without her husband *No*
   ? (E) is in shock over the death of her husband *Maybe. Would she want to be alone?*

4. In line 24, the word "crying" means *peddler sells goods*
   ✗ (A) lamenting —*why would he be crying?*
   ✗ (B) weeping —*same*
   ? (C) shouting —*shout*
   ✓ (D) howling —*long wail —close to cry*
   ✗ (E) singing *happy*

5. When saying, "whose lines bespoke repression" (lines 34–35), the narrator does which of the following? *setting is in the past*
   ✓ (A) makes a general reference to the overall condition of women *DEATH FREE*
   ? (B) introduces the idea of slavery *Maybe but she's married & no mention of slavery*
   ✗ (C) emphasizes the theme of death *No. She's not dead*
   ✗ (D) suggests the need for change *What change?*
   ✗ (E) connects a youthful appearance with nature *opposite Death/Life ——▶Spring*

6. The news of Mr. Mallard's death is in (contrast) to the narrator's description of
   ✗ (A) a storm
   ✗ (B) Mrs. Mallard's emotional state
   ✗ (C) Mrs. Mallard's sister
   ✗ (D) Mrs. Mallard's physical health
   ✓ (E) nature

7. In lines 57–62, the narrator conveys a sense of
   ✓ (A) sanguinity
   ✗ (B) nostalgia *No.*
   ? (C) contentment *Maybe but more emotion than that*
   ✗ (D) skepticism
   ✗ (E) arrogance

8. All of the following are personified in the passage EXCEPT
   ✗(A) "rain" (line 23)
   ✗(B) "hands" (line 58)
   (C) freedom (lines 41–42) **freedom implied**
   ✓(D) "heart trouble" (line 1)
   ✗(E) "physical exhaustion" (lines 18–19)

9. What does the pronoun "it" in lines 39–41 refer to?
   ✓(A) freedom
   ✗(B) death
   ✗(C) hope
   ✗(D) misfortune
   ✗(E) fear

ANSWERS AND EXPLANATIONS FOR THE MULTIPLE-CHOICE QUESTIONS

1. In lines 39-43, the narrator does which of the following?
   (A) creates a shift in tone
   (B) introduces a foreshadowing of death
   (C) describes Mrs. Mallard's sorrow
   (D) emphasizes Mrs. Mallard's physical weakness
   (E) creates a sense of excitement

ANSWER: A. The passage begins on a sad note as the reader and Mrs. Mallard are made aware of the death of Mr. Mallard. In lines 40–41, there is a shift in tone as the reader begins to feel some suspense evoked by the words "fearfully," "elusive," and "creeping." Answer B is a good distractor, but the passage gives no indication of death as Mrs. Mallard welcomes a new sense of freedom. Answer C indicates that Mrs. Mallard feels only sorrow, which is not the correct emotion in lines 39–43. Answer D suggests that the passage focuses on Mrs. Mallard's physical weakness, something that's not even mentioned. Answer E suggests there's a feeling of excitement, which has a more positive connation than the diction of the passage suggests.

2. The term "monstrous joy" (line 54) is an example of
   (A) a paradox
   (B) an oxymoron
   (C) a colloquialism
   (D) a chiasmus
   (E) antithesis

ANSWER: B. The paired words "monstrous" and "joy" have opposite connotations. Monstrous suggests something horrible or terrible and joy implies a feeling of extreme happiness. It is an unusual combination and fits the definition of an oxymoron. Although the pair of words is odd, it is not a colloquialism, so answer C is wrong. Answer D implies that there is a repetition of paired phrases, but there is no repetition within the sentence. Answer A does point toward a contrast in meanings; however, a paradox is a statement or situation including apparently contradictory or incompatible elements. Answer

E also points toward a contrast in meanings; however, antithesis is the juxtaposition of opposing ideas in balanced phrases or clauses.

3. Lines 12-16 ("She did not hear . . . have no one follow her") suggest that Mrs. Mallard
   (A) is stronger than others believe her to be
   (B) is mentally unstable
   (C) reacted to the news of her husband's death as any woman would
   (D) feels hopelessly lost without her husband
   (E) is in shock over the death of her husband

ANSWER: **A.** The statement that she "would have no one follow her" seems rather commanding in tone and suggests that Mrs. Mallard is not as fragile as previously supposed. There is no mention or suggestion of mental instability (B). Answer C is incorrect because the passage notes that Mrs. Mallard doesn't react as another women might to the death of her husband. Answer D is simply not supported by the passage. Answer E says that Mrs. Mallard is in shock, but she doesn't show physical signs of shock, and wanting to be alone doesn't indicate that she is in shock.

4. In line 24, the word "crying" means
   (A) lamenting
   (B) weeping
   (C) shouting
   (D) howling
   (E) singing

ANSWER: **C.** This is a question that requires you to consider other definitions of a commonly used word. Answers A and B are too similar in meaning to "crying" and suggests the peddler is sad, but the passage doesn't give the reader information about the peddler's emotional state. Answer E is an action one would take if he or she was happy, but again we know nothing about the peddler's emotional state. Answer D is a loud sound similar to a shout; however, the word is associated with pain or distress. The only word in the list that suggests a loud sound but is the least emotional is the word "shout," answer C.

5. When saying, "whose lines bespoke repression" (lines 34–35), the narrator does which of the following?
   (A) makes a general reference to the overall condition of women
   (B) introduces the idea of slavery
   (C) emphasizes the theme of death
   (D) suggests the need for change
   (E) connects a youthful appearance with nature

ANSWER: **A.** Line 35 begins to hint at the overall theme of the story. As readers we are, at first, perhaps shocked by the word "repression." The word has a negative connotation, and the line suggests that Mrs. Mallard has been controlled or dominated by something or someone. In this case, as the passage continues, it is clear that her husband and the institution of marriage have controlled her. There are little hints within the story that point toward an earlier time in history when the use of the telegraph and the railroad were common. Answer E has nothing to do with repression, but rather, with a new beginning. Answer D is too vague in meaning. The phrase doesn't emphasize death (C), which is a different state than repression. Answer B would be the best distractor because slavery is, in fact, a state of repression. But the best answer is A because the repression seems to center on a restraint that is not physical but social, one common during a period when women had few rights during marriage. Mrs. Mallard is "free" only after the death of her husband.

6. The news of Mr. Mallard's death is in contrast to the narrator's description of
    (A) a storm
    (B) Mrs. Mallard's emotional state
    (C) Mrs. Mallard's sister
    (D) Mrs. Mallard's physical health
    (E) nature

ANSWER: E. Lines 1–20 focus on the news of Mr. Mallard's death and Mrs. Mallard's emotional response to the news. Lines 21–29 repeatedly mention nature with its "delicious breath," "new spring life," "distant song," and "patches of blue sky." All are in direct contrast to the idea of death. Answer A suggests there is a storm; however, the only storm is that of grief (line 15). Answer B suggests that Mrs. Mallard's emotional state at hearing the news of her husband's death would be the opposite of grief, which is not the case in the beginning of the passage. There is not enough information on Mrs. Mallard's sister (C), and answer D suggests that Mrs. Mallard's physical health is deteriorating, which it is not.

7. In lines 59–62, the narrator conveys a sense of
    (A) sanguinity
    (B) nostalgia
    (C) contentment
    (D) skepticism
    (E) arrogance

ANSWER: A. Mrs. Mallard's emotional state at the end of the passage suggests that she is welcoming what lies ahead of her now that her husband is dead. She doesn't look back to the past with longing, as answer B would suggest. She is not skeptical (answer D) about what awaits her. There is no doubt that she feels she is in control of her own life now, but Mrs. Mallard doesn't show any sense of arrogance, as answer E would suggest. Answer C is a good distractor in that she indeed seems content, but she is in a heightened emotional state that goes beyond contentment. The word "sanguinity" means cheerfully optimistic, and Mrs. Mallard is indeed optimistic about her future.

8. All of the following are personified in the passage EXCEPT
    (A) "rain" (line 23)
    (B) "hands" (line 58)
    (C) freedom (lines 41–42)
    (D) "heart-trouble" (line 1)
    (E) "physical exhaustion" (lines 18–19)

ANSWER: D. The only answer can be heart trouble. "The delicious breath of rain" (A), "the kind, tender hands folded in death" (B), freedom "creeping out of the sky, reaching toward her through the sounds, the scents, the color that filled the air" (C), and "a physical exhaustion that haunted her body and seemed to reach into her soul" (E) are examples of personification.

9. What does the pronoun "it" in lines 39–41 refer to?
    (A) freedom
    (B) death
    (C) hope
    (D) misfortune
    (E) fear

ANSWER: A. Chopin here offers an unusual description of the feeling of freedom. It is intentional because the narrator wants the reader to understand that "being free" as a woman is both liberating and frightening. In a close reading of the text, one would notice the use of the telegraph to receive information about Mr. Mallard's death. Even if one didn't notice this detail, the lines after 39–43 make clear that the emotion Mrs. Mallard was fearful of was being "free." During the late 1800s and early 1900s, women were expected to marry; all property that belonged to a woman before marriage became the property of her husband. A married woman had legal power only when she became a widow. It was indeed a "monstrous joy" because Mrs. Mallard's new sense of freedom was a direct consequence of her husband's death.

THE POETRY ESSAY QUESTION

Your preparation for Section II of the AP exam should include a heavy emphasis on honing your writing skills. Over the course of the school year, you will have many opportunities to write about literary works. The type of writing you do depends on its purpose, but may include one or more of the following:

- ■ WRITING TO UNDERSTAND: writing that responds to literature through reading journals, annotative reading, or free writing
- ■ WRITING TO EXPLAIN: essays that focus on a particular aspect of language or structure in literature and on the analysis of a written passage
- ■ WRITING TO EVALUATE: essays that demonstrate an ability to develop and explain a position and to assess the connections between literature and social and cultural values

As you practice your ability to understand, explain, and evaluate both poetry and prose passages, remember that the work of analysis is only part of the exam scoring criteria—it also takes into account the clarity of your writing and your stylistic maturity. AP readers look for the following:

- ■ Do you balance the general with the specific in your analysis—do you write general statements and then provide specific examples to support those statements?
- ■ Do you use transitions effectively so that the reader is able to understand the logical connections between general statements and specific details and among related ideas?
- ■ Is your vocabulary strong, or do you use words that are vague, such as *things, like, good,* and *bad*? Is your vocabulary rich and varied? If you wait until the AP exam time to use new words, you may still be unfamiliar with them—and therefore run the risk of sounding unsure of their meanings or of using them only to impress your reader. Instead, build them into your vocabulary as you go. When you encounter a new word, try to use it in your next writing assignment or class discussion. The more familiar you are with a variety of words, the more likely you will be to use them in your writing on the test.
- ■ Do you use multiple sentence structures in your writing? Don't be afraid to include, say, an appositive or an infinitive or a variety of short and long sentences. Your writing will be more interesting and will demonstrate your control of language.
- ■ Does your paper sound like *you*? That is, does your writing have a voice? If you have developed a sense of voice, it will show in your choice of vocabulary, sentence arrangement, and organization.

When someone can recognize your writing without seeing your name on the paper, you are well on your way to developing both a voice and stylistic maturity.

GETTING A HANDLE ON A POEM

One essay question is based on poetry. Poetry can be difficult to understand, especially if it uses unfamiliar vocabulary or allusions. It's always a good idea to have a dictionary handy when reading poetry, though you won't have that luxury when taking the AP exam.

Thomas Arp and Greg Johnson, the authors of *Perrine's Literature: Structure, Sound, and Sense,* say that "poetry might be defined as a kind of language that says *more* and says it *more intensely* than does ordinary language." Indeed, poets choose their words carefully, in order to convey a specific meaning and evoke specific emotions. As a consequence, poetry needs to be read slowly and thoughtfully. Although poems generally call for far fewer words than the average short story, they often are able to convey greater emotion and reflect more profound themes.

To get the most out of a poem, use TP-COASTT (see p. 58). Follow these steps as you read:

- Read the title of the poem and consider possible meanings.
- Read the poem through once, and then paraphrase it in your own words. What is the poem saying?
- Note the diction. Is the connotation of the words generally positive or negative? Look—and listen—for poetic devices such as rhyme, similes, metaphors, personification, symbolism, allusions, alliteration, assonance, and onomatopoeia.
- Determine the poem's subject—for example, love, death, a town, a time of day. Look at the poem's organization and the sequence of ideas and images.
- To determine the point of view, first figure out who is speaking. Is it a child, an invalid, a grandmother, a dog? Use your tone vocabulary to determine the speaker's attitude toward the subject.
- Locate shifts—for example, changes in time, place, speaker, tone—in the poem.
- Return to the title. Has the meaning or significance of the title changed since the first time you read it?
- Put it all together—what is the poet saying about the subject, the theme of the poem?

All of these aspects of a poem are essential to determining its overall meaning. Although it is important to identify poetic devices such as similes, personification, and onomatopoeia, your essay should not be a mere laundry list of devices. It's more important that you understand how a given particular device contributes to the overall meaning of the poem. If the poem includes alliteration, why did the poet use it? If there is imagery in the poem, what connotation does the imagery have? How does the imagery add to the reader's experience of the poem? Analysis is not simply identifying various literary and poetic devices; it is determining how those devices add to the overall meaning of the prose or poem.

AN EXERCISE IN ANALYZING POETRY

As an exercise in analyzing poetry, read the following poem, "There is no Frigate like a Book," by Emily Dickinson. After you've read it, make your annotations: write any comments or thoughts you had in response in the margins, circle words that stand out to you or that are unfamiliar to you. Take time to paraphrase the poem in your mind. Determine the poem's overall tone and its theme.

> There is no Frigate like a Book
> To take us Lands away
> Nor any Coursers like a Page
> Of prancing Poetry—
> This Traverse may the poorest take   5
> Without oppress of Toll—
> How frugal is the Chariot
> That bears the Human soul.

There are several poetic devices in this poem, but the major one is diction—word choice. (For more about word choice, see the chapter "Denotation and Connotation" in *Perrine's Literature: Structure, Sound, and Sense*.) Yes, there are similes, alliteration, and the like, but the play of words is what gives the reader insight into the poem's meaning. The following are some questions you might ask yourself about diction in this poem:

- What is the significance of the title?
- Who is "us" (line 2)?
- What is a frigate? a courser? a chariot?
- Why does the speaker use the word "prancing" (line 4)? What images does that word evoke?
- What is a traverse (line 5)?
- What is meant by line 5: "This Traverse may the poorest take"?
- What is a toll (line 6)? How could a toll "oppress" someone?
- What does the word "frugal" mean?
- Why is "Human" (line 8) capitalized?

Remember that the goal is not just to understand the devices, but to understand the meaning of the poem and how the devices contribute to that meaning. Here, then, are more questions to ask yourself:

- What is the poem's subject?
- How does the speaker feel about the subject—what is the tone?
- What is the speaker saying about the subject?

Now look at one annotation of the poem, bearing in mind that each reader's annotation will be unique.

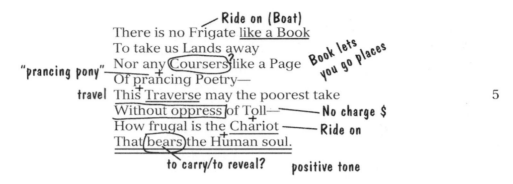

- *What is the subject of the poem?* The subject is books—we know this because the speaker specifically uses the word "book."
- *How does the speaker feel about the subject—what is the tone?* The speaker is admiring, exuberant. We know this because the speaker says books *take us Lands away* and *the poorest take / Without oppress of Toll.* (They can take us to faraway, perhaps exotic places, and because it costs little or nothing at all to read a book, even the poor can take part in the adventure.) Other words in the poem have a positive connotation: *prancing, chariot, human.*
- *What is the speaker saying about the subject?* At this point, we know the speaker is enthusiastic about books—serious and adventurous books (Frigate), as well as books of poems (prancing Poetry). The speaker's message is that books are more than *frigates, coursers,* and *chariots*—note that these words denote various means of transportation (*traverse*). Books are greater than these modes of transportation because they are economical. Books allow us to experience so much for so little (*frugal*) and take us to places of adventure (*lands away*), beauty (*prancing poetry*), and romance (*chariot*) in our own minds.

With the subject, tone, and theme of the poem, you have what you need to write a solid essay.

A SAMPLE POETRY ESSAY QUESTION

When you take the AP exam, you may be asked to analyze not one but two poems—in recent years, the poetry question has occasionally called on students to compare and contrast two poems. The poems may have been written in two very different historical eras but share the same theme; they may explore a similar subject but through different viewpoints and tone; they may consider a similar topic but differ in their imagery, structure, and point of view. The following is an AP exam-type question contrasting two poems. As you read the poems, make annotations to help you answer the question.

Question 1

Carefully read the following two poems. Then, in a well-written essay, examine the speakers' differing views of war. In your essay, consider such elements as point of view, imagery, and structure.

Dulce et Decorum Est
by Wilfred Owen

Bent double, like old beggars under sacks,
Knock-kneed, coughing like hags, we cursed through
    sludge,
Till on the haunting flares we turned our backs
And towards our distant rest began to trudge.
Men marched asleep. Many had lost their boots   5
But limped on, blood-shod. All went lame; all blind;
Drunk with fatigue; deaf even to the hoots
Of tired, outstripped Five-Nines[1] that dropped behind.

Gas! GAS! Quick, boys!—An ecstasy of fumbling,
Fitting the clumsy helmets just in time;   10
But someone still was yelling out and stumbling
And flound'ring like a man in fire or lime . . .
Dim, through the misty panes and thick green light,
As under a green sea, I saw him drowning.
In all my dreams, before my helpless sight,   15
He plunges at me, guttering, choking, drowning.

If in some smothering dreams you too could pace
Behind the wagon that we flung him in,
And watch the white eyes writhing in his face,
His hanging face, like a devil's sick of sin;   20
If you could hear, at every jolt, the blood
Come gargling from the froth-corrupted lungs,
Obscene as cancer, bitter as the cud
Of vile, incurable sores on innocent tongues,—
My friend, you would not tell with such high zest   25
To children ardent for some desperate glory,
The old lie: Dulce et decorum est
Pro patria mori.[2]

[1] Shells that explode on impact and release poison gas.
[2] Latin: "It is sweet and becoming to die for one's country."

King Henry V, Act 4, Scene 3
by William Shakespeare

King Henry V is about to lead his outnumbered army into a battle against the French. His cousin, the Earl of Westmoreland, has just expressed a wish that some of the men back in England were there to fight with them. Henry V responds to Westmoreland here, in what is referred to as the St. Crispin's Day speech. The king's army won the Battle of Agincourt the next day, October 25, 1415, the feast day of the twins Crispin and Crispinian, third-century martyrs who became the patron saints of shoemakers.

    What's he that wishes so?
My cousin Westmoreland? No, my fair cousin:
If we are mark'd to die, we are enough
To do our country loss. And if to live,
The fewer men, the greater share of honour.   5
God's will! I pray thee, wish not one man more.
By Jove, I am not covetous for gold,
Nor care I who doth feed upon my cost.
It yearns[1] me not if men my garments wear;
Such outward things dwell not in my desires.   10
But if it be a sin to covet honour,
I am the most offending soul alive.
No, faith, my coz, wish not a man from England.
God's peace! I would not lose so great an honour
As one man more, methinks, would share from me   15
For the best hope I have. O, do not wish one more!
Rather proclaim it, Westmoreland, through my host,
That he which hath no stomach to this fight,
Let him depart; his passport shall be made
And crowns for convoy[2] put into his purse.   20
We would not die in that man's company
That fears his fellowship to die with us.
This day is called the feast of Crispian.
He that outlives this day, and comes safe home
Will stand a tip-toe when the day is named,   25
And rouse him at the name of Crispian.
He that shall live this day and see old age
Will yearly on the vigil feast[3] his neighbours,
And say 'To-morrow is Saint Crispian:'
Then will he strip his sleeve and show his scars.   30
And say 'These wounds I had on Crispin's day.'
Old men forget: yet all shall be forgot,
But he'll remember with advantages[4]
What feats he did that day. Then shall our names,
Familiar in his mouth as household words,   35
Harry the king, Bedford and Exeter,
Warwick and Talbot, Salisbury and Gloucester,

[1] saddens
[2] money for travel
[3] host a feast for
[4] a little exaggeration

Be in their flowing cups freshly remember'd.
This story shall the good man teach his son;
And Crispin Crispian shall ne'er go by,   40
From this day to the ending of the world,
But we in it shall be remember'd.
We few, we happy few, we band of brothers—
For he today that sheds his blood with me
Shall be my brother; be he ne'er so vile,[5]   45
This day shall gentle his condition[6]—
And gentlemen in England now a-bed
Shall think themselves accursed they were not here,
And hold their manhoods cheap whiles any speaks
That fought with us upon Saint Crispin's Day.   50

After reading and annotating the two poems, compare your annotations with those below.

[5] humble, low born
[6] make him a gentleman

WAR

He feels just the opposite

Dulce et Decorum Est
by Wilfred Owen

Bent double, like old beggars under sacks,
Knock-kneed, coughing like hags, we cursed through
    sludge,
Till on the haunting flares we turned our backs
And towards our distant rest began to trudge.
Men marched asleep. Many had lost their boots   5
But limped on, blood-shod. All went lame; all blind;
Drunk with fatigue; deaf even to the hoots
Of tired, outstripped Five-Nines[1] that dropped behind.   *soldiers at war*

Gas! GAS! Quick, boys!—An ecstasy of fumbling,   —*gas attack WWI?*
Fitting the clumsy helmets just in time;   10
But someone still was yelling out and stumbling
And flound'ring like a man in fire or lime . . .
Dim, through the misty panes and thick green light,
As under a green sea, I saw him drowning.   ← *awful!*
In all my dreams, before my helpless sight,   15
He plunges at me, guttering, choking, drowning. *action verbs*

If in some smothering dreams you too could pace   —*talking to reader*
Behind the wagon that we flung him in,
And watch the white eyes writhing in his face,
His hanging face, like a devil's sick of sin;   20
If you could hear, at every jolt, the blood   *jolt of wagon*
Come gargling from the froth-corrupted lungs,
Obscene as cancer, bitter as the cud   *horrible way to die*
Of vile, incurable sores on innocent tongues—   —*young soldiers?*
My friend, you would not tell with such high zest   25
To children ardent for some desperate glory,
The old lie: Dulce et decorum est
Pro patria mori.[2]   *Title too*

Negative tone

*He says it is a lie
that it is sweet to
die for your country*

_____

[1]Shells that explode on impact and release poison gas.   **Why Latin?**
[2]Latin: "It is sweet and becoming to die for one's country."

King Henry V, Act 4, Scene 3
by William Shakespeare

King Henry V is about to lead his outnumbered army into a battle against the French. His cousin, the Earl of Westmoreland, has just expressed a wish that some of the men back in England were there to fight with them. Henry V responds to Westmoreland here, in what is referred to as the St. Crispin's Day speech. The king's army won the Battle of Agincourt the next day, October 25, 1415, the feast day of the twins Crispin and Crispinian, third-century martyrs who became the patron saints of shoemakers.

POV—king commanding an army

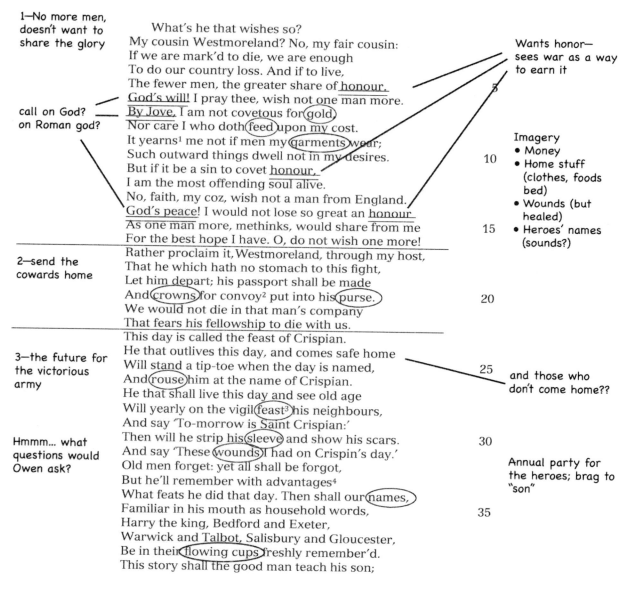

1—No more men, doesn't want to share the glory

    What's he that wishes so?
My cousin Westmoreland? No, my fair cousin:
If we are mark'd to die, we are enough
To do our country loss. And if to live,
The fewer men, the greater share of honour.
God's will! I pray thee, wish not one man more.

call on God? on Roman god?

By Jove, I am not covetous for gold,
Nor care I who doth feed upon my cost.
It yearns[1] me not if men my garments wear;
Such outward things dwell not in my desires.
But if it be a sin to covet honour,
I am the most offending soul alive.
No, faith, my coz, wish not a man from England.
God's peace! I would not lose so great an honour
As one man more, methinks, would share from me
For the best hope I have. O, do not wish one more!

Wants honor—sees war as a way to earn it

Imagery
• Money
• Home stuff (clothes, foods bed)
• Wounds (but healed)
• Heroes' names (sounds?)

2—send the cowards home

Rather proclaim it, Westmoreland, through my host,
That he which hath no stomach to this fight,
Let him depart; his passport shall be made
And crowns for convoy[2] put into his purse.
We would not die in that man's company
That fears his fellowship to die with us.

3—the future for the victorious army

This day is called the feast of Crispian.
He that outlives this day, and comes safe home
Will stand a tip-toe when the day is named,
And rouse him at the name of Crispian.
He that shall live this day and see old age
Will yearly on the vigil feast[3] his neighbours,
And say 'To-morrow is Saint Crispian:'

and those who don't come home??

Hmmm... what questions would Owen ask?

Then will he strip his sleeve and show his scars.
And say 'These wounds I had on Crispin's day.'
Old men forget: yet all shall be forgot,
But he'll remember with advantages[4]
What feats he did that day. Then shall our names,
Familiar in his mouth as household words,
Harry the king, Bedford and Exeter,
Warwick and Talbot, Salisbury and Gloucester,
Be in their flowing cups freshly remember'd.
This story shall the good man teach his son;

Annual party for the heroes; brag to "son"

5

10

15

20

25

30

35

[1] saddens
[2] money for travel
[3] host a feast for
[4] a little exaggeration

                And Crispin Crispian shall ne'er go by,   40
                From this day to the ending of the world,
                But we in it shall be remember'd.
                                                                           brothers to the
4—invitation   We few, we happy few, we band of brothers—   king?? big P.R.
to the   For he today that sheds his (blood) with me   push?
brotherhood   Shall be my brother; be he ne'er so vile,[5]   45
                This day shall gentle his condition[6]—
                And gentlemen in England now (a-bed)   neg. tone for
                Shall think themselves accursed they were not here,   those not there
                And hold their manhoods cheap whiles any speaks
                That fought with us upon Saint Crispin's Day.   50

PLANNING YOUR ESSAY

In preparing to write the essay, you will need to read and analyze each poem fairly quickly, identifying major differences in the poems and determining which poetic devices are most important in developing each speaker's point of view. Avoid summarizing the poems as you begin your essay. The AP reader already knows the poems well, and your simply summarizing them does not show any insight.

Sometimes the prompt will be worded to offer suggestions on what to look for or where to start in your analysis, as is the case here. The wording of this question encourages you to pay close attention to such elements as point of view, imagery, and structure. Remember that those are suggestions only. That key phrase "such elements as" means that you may choose the elements you think will make the best essay. You will not identify every poetic device used in a poem, and you must avoid simply listing devices. Along with summarizing, listing devices without explaining their purpose or effect is a trap students often fall into in their responses. Instead, your task is to demonstrate how you used the poem's devices to interpret its meaning. Remember to *always* support your ideas. Always.

Refer to the voice in the poem as the *speaker*, not the *narrator* (that term is reserved for prose), and definitely not as the author or poet. Writing "The poet says . . ." is inaccurate. You should say "The speaker says . . ." or "The speaker feels . . ." because the speaker and the poet are not one and the same. The speaker may be anyone from a child to a lonely old man. In fact, there may be a shift in speakers as viewpoints change within a poem.

Don't forget to discuss all shifts—a change in the time of day, a change in the speaker from child to adult, a change in tone as seen through a shift in the speaker's attitude. If you are reading a poem and determine that the tone is somber and depressing, for instance, be sure there are no shifts near the end to indicate hope, vindication, or salvation. A poet may use gloomy imagery throughout the poem (suggesting a negative tone), only to show the power of sacrifice or patriotism in the last lines of the poem. Such shifts are powerful and contribute greatly to the overall theme of a poem.

THE SCORING GUIDELINES

The scoring guidelines, below, follow the concepts and language of the scoring guidelines used by the College Board. To receive a score of 6 or higher, you must respond successfully to the prompt. AP readers score each essay knowing it was composed as a rough draft. Your essay may have mistakes—they're found even in papers scoring a 9. However, an essay with many distracting errors in mechanics or usage will not be scored higher than a 3.

9–8 Essays in this scoring range illustrate a persuasive comparison of both poems and an effective and insightful analysis of how such devices as point of view, imagery, and structure function in both poems. These essays show consistent and effective control of language. Writing is clear, cohesive, and stylistically mature. An essay scoring a 9 is particularly insightful in its interpretation of both poems and uses a sophisticated style appropriate to the analysis of poetry.

7–6 Essays in the upper-half range offer a reasonable comparison of both poems, as well as effective analysis of poetic devices used in both poems. There may be a range of interpretations for each poem. Writers use textual evidence to suggest how devices such as point of view, imagery, and structure function within each poem. Writers show more consistency in their analysis than in an essay scored a 5. Essays scoring a 7 exhibit more sophistication in both the effectiveness of their analysis and their overall style.

5 These essays demonstrate an ability to respond to the prompt with an acceptable overall reading of both poems, but they offer only a superficial analysis of the poems. Often these essays show some analysis, but also some paraphrasing. There is very little or no consistency in the development of ideas. Essays scored a 5 may begin to discuss a particular poetic device or technique (such as point of view, imagery, or structure) used in a poem, but then fail to show how the device or technique adds to the overall meaning of the poem. These essays demonstrate adequate writing skills but are often marred by many errors in mechanics and spelling. Many times an essay scored a 5 seems superficial and predictable.

4–3 These essays attempt to respond to the prompt but may misinterpret one of the poems or fail to develop a cohesive compare-and-contrast analysis of the two. Many essays in this scoring range lack a proper development of ideas and resort to paraphrase rather than analysis and interpretation. They may simply state that one poem opposes war and the other does not and then restate that simplistic idea rather than drawing on the text for specific detail. Errors in usage and punctuation are pervasive, especially in those essays scoring a 3. The essay may be repetitive in its commentary, and have few textual examples to support ideas in the essay, or even none at all. An essay in which the writing is particularly simplistic will be scored 3.

2–1 Essays in this range may attempt to answer the prompt but include a serious misreading of one or both poems. They may respond to the prompt in a general way, with no specific reference to either poem. These essays lack development in responding to the prompt. Many essays scored 2 or 1 are very short—often less than a page. These essays lack a control of language and show repeated errors in sentence structure, and may depend on simple diction insufficient to express ideas clearly. They fail to show any attempt at analysis and often ramble. Papers with no development of ideas are scored 1.

0 An essay that merely repeats the prompt is scored 0.

— This mark indicates a blank response or one that is completely off topic.

SAMPLE STUDENT POETRY ESSAYS WITH COMMENTS

A STUDENT ESSAY SCORED 8

"Dulce et Decorum Est" and "Henry V" offer differing views regarding war. Both speakers use imagery to describe their view of war; however, the speaker in "Dulce et Decorum Est" is a soldier who has experienced the horror of war in a very real way by marching "knock-kneed, coughing like hags, we cursed through sludge." Henry sees battle as providing a potential for heroism and even a little immortality. Both poems focus their attention on war, but Owen's speaker warns the reader not to tell "the old Lie" that war is glorious and to die for one's country is "sweet and becoming" to children. Ironically, King Henry views war as glorious and turns his focus to the results for the victors who live through the battle, ignoring those who are maimed or die.

"Dulce et Decorum Est" vividly portrays the horrors of war and in particular the gassing of soldiers and the violent death of soldiers that succumbed to the poisonous gas. As the speaker explains, "In all my dreams, before my helpless sight, / He plunges at me, guttering, choking, drowning." He invites the reader to join him in his nightmare and see the dead with agony etched in their faces. The tone is one of revulsion toward the act of war. The overall structure of the poem begins with a rather unexpected image of soldiers exhausted and "bent double" like old men with uniforms hanging on their emaciated bodies like "sacks." The image of these soldiers is not the image we expect, which echoes the point the poem makes—war is never what we "expect." A shift to present tense signals the reader that a decisive moment for the soldiers is occurring—live with a mask or die from gas. There is no glorious confrontation with the enemy in human form, just a poisonous gas. The speaker then shifts to his nightmares of dying soldiers and ends with a plea to the reader to tell war as it is—abominable. The use of the words "devil" and "sick of sin" suggests that war is a sin and that to encourage the idea that to die in war is glorious is a sin as well.

In Henry's speech, a king with a talent for motivating his men presents war as an adventure, a way to achieve "honour" and to make their name "household words." He begins by refusing to want a larger army because the honor would have to be divided among more men and each share would be smaller. He moves in line 17 to criticism of any of his men who might not have the "stomach to this fight." In line 23 he turns to his main argument, the honor and fame his men will share after the war. Englishmen not in the battle, he says, will hold only "cheap" manhood.

Instead of the imagery of sickness and agony in Owen's poem, Shakespeare focuses on images of home and normal life. Henry does mention the man "that sheds his blood with me," but he never allows a thought of dying. Instead, the man who "sheds his blood" (but evidently not a lot of it because he lives) will become a brother to the king. The only other signs of the violence of war are in the healed "scars" and "wounds" that the veterans show their sons. The other images focus on money, on "gold," "crowns," and "purse," and on celebration, using festive words like "fed," "rouse," "feast," and "flowing cups." So the point of view here is the one of a general leading his men and needing to inspire them to fight bravely—a sharp contrast to the miserable foot soldier in Owen's poem.

The tone of Henry's speech is rousing, heroic, courageous and conveys the confidence the king feels his men must have in their leaders. He draws his details to establish that tone from peaceful life and celebrations, not from the trenches of the battlefield. The syntax reinforces that tone. Henry's language is emotional but careful and formal. He has none of the exclamations or broken sentences that Owen uses to show the chaos. Henry's is obviously a much different war—or a different outlook on war—from Owen's. Owen must have known the speech from Shakespeare, and he puts it in the same category as the "old lie" on the statue. It is impossible for Owen's speaker to think that any sane men would "think themselves accursed they were not here."

COMMENT

This essay effectively compares and contrasts the passages. The writer understands that the subject of both poems is war, but that they are told from opposing points of view and, therefore, create different tones (passionately condemnatory in one, rousingly heroic in the other). The essay gives apt and specific examples from both passages of imagery and the effect it has in creating tone. The quotations are appropriately brief—usually only a word or two—and are worked smoothly into the student's own writing. The essay effectively analyzes how point of view, diction, syntax, structure, and imagery affect the overall themes of the passages, and it demonstrates the maturity of the writer's style. The exceptionally smooth ending that ties the two pieces together moves the essay close to a 9.

A STUDENT ESSAY SCORED 6

"Dulce et Decorum Est" by Wilfred Owen and "Henry V" by Shakespeare have many similarities and differences. Both poems are about war, but one poem tells about war in a very vivid way and the other is told by a king who wants his men to fight bravely in a war. The two poems are written from two different point of views which has an effect on the tone in both poems as well.

Wilfred Owen explores the violence of war through the point of view of a soldier who is facing the realities of war, in particular deadly gas that can drown you "under a green sea" (line 14). The soldier describes the terrible condition he and his fellow soldiers are in. "Men marched asleep" (line 5) are further described as "Bent double, like old beggars under sacks" (line 1). The soldier describes the horror of seeing one of the soldiers die from gas and the reader can't help but grimace in horror. He makes war sound so terrible that to think about war as being something glorious doesn't seem right. The soldier even says that if you had really experienced war as he had, you wouldn't tell children "the old Lie" (line 27) that "Dulce et decorum est / Pro patria mori"—"It is sweet and becoming to die for one's country." The tone is depressing and horrific.

In Shakespeare's "Henry V" war is seen through the eyes of a king. He seems to talk only about the positive aspects of fighting and war, about the rewards the men will have after the war as honored veterans. He seems to ignore all the realities of war or at least to keep his men from thinking about them. Instead he talks about the glory. He promises that his men's names shall be "familiar in his mouth as household words" and that they will "Be in their flowing cups freshly remember'd." He adds that the men who are not there will regret it. They "shall think themselves accursed they were not here, / And hold their manoods cheap whiles any speaks / That fought with us upon Saint Crispin's Day." This is the view of war Owen's soldier warns the reader about.

There is not a lot of vivid imagery in "Henry V"; however, the speaker mentions "the vigil feast" (line 28) and the "flowing cups" (line 38) calling up a picture of the celebrations after the men return home. He uses formal diction because he is a king and wants to inspire his men. He uses other rhetorical techniques. He calls the men by name, drawing them in as part of an audience. He moves from talking about not needing more men to what to do with the cowards, then to the celebrations. But what he leaves out is the battle. So he focuses only on the positive and leaves out the reality of war.

Owen wants to warn the reader about the true horror of war and Shakespeare seems to want to have King Henry focus on the celebration of a happy outcome.

COMMENT
This essay does compare and contrast the two poems and explains the general differences between the two poems based on the different points of view. The reading of both pieces is accurate and shows some insight. However, the analysis is thin, and the essay bogs down under the weight of excessively long quotations. Some repetition may be a sign that the student began writing without setting out a clear plan. It stays on task, though, and avoids falling into paraphrase or summary. The style is not as mature as an essay that is given a higher score, but it is generally free of any major writing problems.

A STUDENT ESSAY SCORED 4

In the two poems, "Dulce et Decorum Est" and "Henry V" a description of war is given but they are quite different. There are many differences between the two poems that can be seen in their point of view, imagery, alliteration, diction, and similes.

First, the poem "Dulce et Decorum Est" describes war from the point of view of a soldier who is actually fighting in the war. The imagery is very vivid and paints a picture in your mind as to what war is really like. The soldiers are "bent double, like old beggars under sacks." He uses many similes as well like "as under a green sea" (line 14) and "bitter as the cud" in (line 23). He also uses alliteration when he says "Knock-kneed, coughing like hags, we cursed through sludge" which repeats the sound of a K. This poem really lets the reader know how horrible war is.

The second poem "Henry V" is told from the view of a king leading his men into battle. He promises his men that they will live to tell their sons about the battle. The diction of this poem is very positive. He talks about money and "flowing cups" (line 38). To him war is a place to prove if your brave or a coward hasn't realized how horrible war can be because he's the king and doesn't fight in the battles. He does not use similes but speaks directly and literally. His tone is enthusiastic. The structure is in iambic pentameter and fits the speech of a king. He doesn't use alliteration as Owen does. He pays a lot of attention to the future of his men, even if some of them may not survive the battle, but he does not describe the battle itself as Owen does. So for him, war is more about honor.

These are some of the more important similarities and differences between the two poems.

COMMENT

This essay attempts to analyze the two poems but falls short in both depth of analysis and maturity of writing. The writer lists poetic devices rather than explain why they are used and how they affect the meaning in the two poems.

THE PROSE ESSAY QUESTION

Another of the three essay questions in Section II of the AP exam is based on a prose passage. As with poetry, you begin by analyzing the prose passage to figure out what the author is trying to say and the tools he or she uses to say it. To deepen your understanding—and enjoyment—of fiction, refer to "The Elements of Fiction," the first part of *Perrine's Literature: Structure, Sound, and Sense*. You'll find a lot of valuable information about how prose fiction is organized and constructed. Again, keep in mind that annotation is an essential tool. It helps you zero in on the important details and will save you valuable time when you are writing your essay.

Analyzing a Prose Passage

Analyzing and evaluating a prose passage is a task much like that for poetry. You are looking for answers to three questions:

- What is the passage about?
- How does the author view the subject—what is the tone of the passage? How does the author use language and literary devices to create tone and meaning?
- What is the importance of this passage? What does the author want us to understand about the subject?

Try annotating the following excerpt from "The Most Dangerous Game," a short story by Richard Connell.

> "Off there to the right—somewhere—is a large island," said Whitney. "It's rather a mystery—"
> "What island is it?" Rainsford asked.
> "The old charts call it 'Ship-Trap Island,'" Whitney replied. "A suggestive name, isn't it? Sailors have a curious dread of the place. I don't know why. Some superstition—"   5
> "Can't see it," remarked Rainsford, trying to peer through the dank tropical night that was palpable as it pressed its thick warm blackness in upon the yacht.   10
> "You've good eyes," said Whitney, with a laugh, "and I've seen you pick off a moose moving in the brown fall bush at four hundred yards, but even you can't see four miles or so through a moonless Caribbean night."
> "Nor four yards," admitted Rainsford. "Ugh! It's like moist black velvet."   15
> "It will be light in Rio," promised Whitney. "We should make it in a few days. I hope the jaguar guns have come from Purdey's. We should have some good hunting up the Amazon. Great sport, hunting."   20

"The best sport in the world," agreed Rainsford.

"For the hunter," amended Whitney. "Not for the jaguar."

"Don't talk rot, Whitney," said Rainsford. "You're a big-game hunter, not a philosopher. Who cares how a jaguar feels?"   25

"Perhaps the jaguar does," observed Whitney.

"Bah! They've no understanding."

"Even so, I rather think they understand one thing— fear. The fear of pain and the fear of death."   30

"Nonsense," laughed Rainsford. "This hot weather is making you soft, Whitney. Be a realist. The world is made up of two classes—the hunters and the huntees. Luckily, you and I are the hunters. Do you think we've passed that island yet?"   35

After a close reading and annotation of the passage, go back to the three questions:

- What is the passage about?
- How does the author view the subject—what is the tone of the passage? How does the author use language and literary devices to create tone and meaning?
- What is the importance of this passage? What does the author want us to understand about the subject?

Now let's put it all together. First, compare your annotation with ours:

"Off there to the right—somewhere—is a large island," said Whitney. "It's rather a <u>mystery</u>—" **A lot of dashes**

"What island is it?" Rainsford asked.

"The old charts call it 'Ship-<u>Trap</u> Island,'" Whitney replied. "A suggestive name, isn't it? Sailors have a   5
curious <u>dread</u> of the place. I don't know why. Some <u>superstition</u>—" **suspenseful**

"Can't see it," remarked Rainsford, trying to peer through the dank tropical night that was palpable as it
smothering <u>pressed</u> its thick warm <u>blackness</u> in upon the yacht.   10

"You've good eyes," said Whitney, with a laugh, "and I've seen you pick off a moose moving in the brown fall bush at four hundred yards, but even you can't see four miles or so through a <u>moonless</u> Caribbean night." **place**

"Nor <u>four yards</u>," admitted Rainsford. "Ugh! It's like   15
(<u>moist black velvet.</u>")   **Simile—nice**

"It will be light in Rio," promised Whitney. "We should make it in a few days. I hope the jaguar guns have come from Purdey's. We should have some <u>good hunting up the Amazon</u>. <u>Great sport, hunting</u>." **Hunting**   20

"The <u>best sport</u> in the world," agreed Rainsford. **really must like hunting to**

"For the hunter," amended Whitney. "Not for the **travel so far**
jaguar."

"Don't talk rot, Whitney," said Rainsford. "You're a big-game hunter, not a philosopher. Who cares how a jaguar feels?" **Wow! Harsh!**   25

"Perhaps the jaguar does," observed Whitney.

"Bah! They've no understanding." **Cold! How does he know?**

"Even so, I rather think they understand one thing—fear. The fear of pain and the fear of death."   30

"Nonsense," laughed Rainsford. "This hot weather is making you soft, Whitney. Be a realist. The world is made up of two classes—the hunters and the huntees. **Survival of the fittest** Luckily, you and I are the hunters. Do you think we've passed that island yet?" **Why does he ask this?**   35
Worried? Curious?

Now compare your answers with those provided below:

WHAT IS THE PASSAGE ABOUT? The subject is hunting. We know this because the dialogue is about hunting jaguars. It is interesting to note that the topic of hunting comes up when Whitney refers to Ship-Trap Island.

HOW DOES THE AUTHOR VIEW THE SUBJECT—WHAT IS THE TONE OF THE PASSAGE? We know how Whitney and Rainsford feel about it—it's the "best sport in the world." Whitney says he thinks that animals understand one thing, "fear." Rainsford believes that the animal doesn't understand anything—in fact, he suggests that there are only two classes, "the hunters and the huntees." Rainsford has no sympathy for the animals being hunted and suggests that Whitney is getting "soft." The author seems to be questioning the idea of whether hunted animals have feelings. Rainsford comes across as being not only a realist but an insensitive one at that. *How does the author use language and literary devices to create tone and meaning?* The images and diction—for example, *mystery, curious dread, Ship-Trap Island, dank tropical night that was palpable as it pressed its thick warm blackness in upon the yacht*—suggest a tone that is both suspenseful and menacing. Note as well the author's use of dashes to suggest pauses in the conversation that emphasize what's being said and also build suspense: *"I rather think they understand one thing—fear."*

WHAT IS THE IMPORTANCE OF THIS PASSAGE? WHAT DOES THE AUTHOR WANT US TO UNDERSTAND ABOUT THE SUBJECT? The passage suggests suspense and a sense of dread in its opening lines. The author wants us to feel both of these emotions as the topic switches quickly from the mysterious Ship-Trap Island to the act of hunting. We know the men have traveled a great distance to hunt and consider it a great sport. It is unexpected that the two hunters would discuss the idea that animals have feelings. Is the author's point of view spoken through Whitney? Perhaps. The reader characterizes Rainsford as callous and therefore undeserving of our sympathy or support. Given the dialogue between the two men, the question is whether hunting is humane. The author wants us to think about the act of hunting and not simply pass it off as "rot" or foolishness. Note that Whitney believes that animals (the jaguar, at least) feel fear, but that he is willing to hunt and kill them anyway.

We now see several important aspects of the passage. Taken all together, they give us the basis for not one but several good essays. Consider the following two prompts, both of which could be used as the basis for an essay on the passage from "The Most Dangerous Game."

- Carefully read the following passage. In a well-written essay, analyze the characters and the relationships among them.
- Carefully read the following passage. In a well-written essay, explain how the author uses point of view and imagery to provide social commentary.

Now it's your turn.

A SAMPLE PROSE ESSAY QUESTION

Question 2

The following passage is an excerpt from Tim O'Brien's *The Things They Carried*, a novel about life as a soldier during the Vietnam War. Carefully read the passage. Then, in a well-written essay, discuss the complex attitude of the narrator toward the Vietnam War through the author's use of such literary devices as imagery, detail, and syntax.

They carried plastic water containers, each with a two-gallon capacity. Mitchell Sanders carried a set of starched tiger fatigues for special occasions. Henry Dobbins carried Black Flag insecticide. Dave Jensen carried empty sandbags that would be filled at night 5 for added protection. Lee Strunk carried tanning lotion. Some things they carried in common. Taking turns, they carried the big PRC-77 scrambler radio, which weighed thirty pounds with its battery. They shared the weight of memory. They took up what 10 others could no longer bear. Often, they carried each other, the wounded or weak. They carried infections. They carried chess sets, basketballs, Vietnamese-English dictionaries, insignia of rank, Bronze Stars and Purple Hearts, plastic cards imprinted with the 15 Code of Conduct. They carried diseases, among them malaria and dysentery. They carried lice and ringworm and leeches and paddy algae and various rots and molds. They carried the land itself—Vietnam, the place, the soil—a powdery orange-red dust that 20 covered their boots and fatigues and faces. They carried the sky. The whole atmosphere, they carried it, the humidity, the monsoons, the stink of fungus and decay, all of it, they carried gravity. They moved like mules. By daylight they took sniper fire, at night they 25 were mortared, but it was not battle, it was just the endless march, village to village, without purpose, nothing won or lost. They marched for the sake of the march. They plodded along slowly, dumbly, leaning forward against the heat, unthinking, all blood and [30] bone, simple grunts, soldiering with their legs, toiling up the hills and down into the paddies and across the rivers and up again and down, just humping, one step and then the next and then another, but no volition, no will, because it was automatic, it was anatomy, and the [35] war was entirely a matter of posture and carriage, the hump was everything, a kind of inertia, a kind of emptiness, a dullness of desire and intellect and conscience and hope and human sensibility. Their principles were in their feet. Their calculations were [40] biological. They had no sense of strategy or mission. They searched the villages without knowing what to look for, not caring, kicking over jars of rice, frisking children and old men, blowing tunnels, sometimes setting fires and sometimes not, then forming up and [45] moving on to the next village, then other villages, where it would always be the same. They carried their own lives. The pressures were enormous. In the heat of early afternoon, they would remove their helmets and flak jackets, walking bare, which was dangerous [50] but which helped ease the strain. They would often discard things along the route of march. Purely for comfort, they would throw away rations, blow their Claymores and grenades, no matter, because by nightfall the resupply choppers would arrive with [55] more of the same, then a day or two later still more, fresh watermelons and crates of ammunition and sunglasses and woolen sweaters—the resources were stunning—sparklers for the Fourth of July, colored eggs for Easter. It was the great American war chest— [60] the fruits of science, the smokestacks, the canneries, the arsenals at Hartford, the Minnesota forests, the machine shops, the vast fields of corn and wheat— they carried like freight trains; they carried it on their backs and shoulders—and for all the ambiguities of [65] Vietnam, all the mysteries and unknowns, there was at least the single abiding certainty that they would never be at a loss for things to carry.

After reading and annotating the passage, compare your annotations with those below.

The following passage is an excerpt from Tim O'Brien's *The Things They Carried*, a novel about life as a soldier during the Vietnam War. Carefully read the passage. Then, in a well-written essay, discuss the (complex) attitude of the narrator toward the Vietnam War through the author's use of such literary devices as imagery, detail, and syntax.

Soldiers

They carried plastic water containers, each with a two-gallon capacity. Mitchell Sanders carried a set of *odd* starched tiger fatigues for special occasions. Henry Dobbins carried Black Flag insecticide. Dave Jensen carried empty sandbags that would be filled at night   5
for added protection. Lee Strunk carried (tanning lotion.) Some things they carried in (common.) Taking *Share* turns, they carried the big PRC-77 scrambler radio, which weighed thirty pounds with its battery. They shared the weight of memory. They took up what   10
others could no longer bear. Often, they carried each other, the wounded or weak. They carried infections. They carried chess sets, basketballs, Vietnamese-English dictionaries, insignia of rank, Bronze Stars and Purple Hearts, plastic cards imprinted with the   15
Code of Conduct. They carried diseases, among them malaria and dysentery. They carried lice and ringworm and leeches and paddy algae and various rots and molds. They carried the land itself—Vietnam, the place, the soil—a powdery orange-red dust that   20
covered their boots and fatigues and faces. They carried the sky. The whole atmosphere, they carried it, *Place is part of them* the humidity, the monsoons, the stink of fungus and decay, all of it, they carried (gravity.) They moved like *heavy burden* mules. By daylight they took sniper fire, at night they   25
were mortared, but it was not battle, it was just the endless march, village to village, without purpose, —*no glory* nothing won or lost. They marched for the sake of the *sounds lost or* march. They plodded along slowly, dumbly, leaning *frustrated* forward against the heat, unthinking, all blood and   30
bone, simple grunts, soldiering with their legs, toiling up the hills and down into the paddies and across the rivers and up again and down, just humping, one step and then the next and then another, but no volition, no will, because it was (automatic) it was anatomy, and the   35
war was entirely a matter of posture and carriage, the *looks on outside* hump was everything, a kind of inertia, a kind of emptiness, a dullness of desire and intellect and conscience and hope and human sensibility. Their principles were in their feet. Their calculations were   40
biological. They had no sense of strategy or mission. *animal instinct* They searched the villages without knowing what to

? Hmm....

mix of things not normally listed together illness games awards

like a robot- no feelings?!

no purpose

look for, <u>not caring</u>, kicking over jars of rice, frisking
children and old men, blowing tunnels, sometimes
setting fires and sometimes not, then forming up and   45
moving on to the next village, then other villages,
where it would always be the same. They carried their
own lives. <u>The pressures were enormous</u>. In the heat   *the pressure of war*
of early afternoon, they would remove their helmets
and flak jackets, walking bare, which was dangerous   50
but which helped ease the strain. They would often
discard things along the route of march. Purely for
comfort, they would throw away rations, blow their   *always have supplies*
Claymores and grenades, no matter, because by
nightfall the resupply choppers would arrive with   55
more of the same, then a day or two later still more,
fresh **?**<u>watermelons</u> and crates of ammunition and   *odd*
<u>sunglasses</u> and <u>woolen sweaters</u>**?**—the resources were   **? Why send**
stunning—<u>sparklers for the Fourth of July</u>, <u>colored</u>
<u>eggs for Easter</u>. It was the great (American war chest)—   60
the fruits of science, the smokestacks, the canneries,   **Whole U.S. industry**
the arsenals at Hartford, the Minnesota forests, the
machine shops, the vast fields of corn and wheat—they
carried like freight trains; they carried it on their backs
and shoulders—and for all the <u>ambiguities of Vietnam</u>,   65
all the mysteries and unknowns, there was at least the
single abiding certainty that <u>they</u> would never be at a
loss for things to carry.   *carry more than "things"—carry*
                                   emtional baggage

Seems confused by it all.

Planning Your Essay

The essay prompt for Question 2 asks you to determine the attitude of
the narrator toward the war in Vietnam. The prompt tells you that the
passage is about the life of a soldier in Vietnam. As we read the
passage, we notice that the narrator refers to the soldiers as "they";
however, the narrator seems to have intimate knowledge about a
soldier's daily routine and thoughts. The passage is not only about the
objects that each soldier physically carries, but also about the
emotions each soldier carries within. The prompt also tells the reader
that the attitude the narrator has concerning Vietnam is "complex."
The overall purpose of the question is to test your skills in analysis and
interpretation by examining how the details of the passage "echo" the
narrator's view of the war in Vietnam—in particular, the view of an
American soldier in Vietnam. Your task is to determine the narrator's
"complex attitude" toward the war and explain how the use of literary
devices helped create that attitude.

Note that there are no specific literary devices listed in the writing
prompt. This is not to say that prompts for prose analysis don't give
suggested lists; it simply means that *sometimes* they don't. This
prompt simply asks you to identify "literary devices." Be sure to

include those devices that are, in your view, the most important in conveying the author's message.

THE SCORING GUIDELINES

The scoring guidelines, below, follow the concepts and language of the scoring guidelines used by the College Board. To receive a score of 6 or higher, you must successfully respond to the prompt. AP readers score each essay knowing it was composed as a rough draft. Your essay may have mistakes—mistakes are found even in papers scoring a 9. However, an essay with many distracting errors in grammar and mechanics will not be scored higher than a 3.

9–8 Essays in this scoring range illustrate a persuasive, effective, and insightful analysis of how specific literary devices develop the complex attitude of the narrator toward the war in Vietnam. These essays show consistent and effective control of language with writing that is clear, cohesive, and stylistically mature. An essay scoring a 9 is particularly insightful in its interpretation of the passage and uses a sophisticated style appropriate for overall literary analysis.

7–6 Essays in the upper-half range give a reasonable interpretation of the passage and offer an effective analysis of the literary devices used to create the narrator's attitude toward the war. Writers use text evidence to suggest how devices such as point of view, imagery, and punctuation function within the passage. These essays show more consistency in analysis than an essay scored 5 does. Papers scored a 7 exhibit more sophistication in both the effectiveness of their analysis and their overall style.

5 These essays demonstrate an ability to respond to the prompt with an acceptable overall reading of the passage but provide only a superficial analysis. Often these essays show some analysis but then resort to paraphrasing. There is little or no consistency in the development of ideas. These essays may begin to discuss a particular literary device used in the passage but then fail to give an interpretation as to how the device or technique reflects the author's complex attitude toward the war. These essays do show adequate writing skills but are often marred by grammar and punctuation errors. Many times an essay scored a 5 essay will seem formulaic or superficial in its analysis.

4–3 These essays attempt to respond to the prompt but may misinterpret a portion of the passage or fail to develop a cohesive analysis of the passage as a whole. Many essays in this range lack fully developed ideas and resort to paraphrasing the passage rather than analyzing and interpreting it. There is usually a lack of control in some areas of the writing, such as awkward wording and/or problems with punctuation. The essay may be repetitive (saying the same thing over and over). There are few or no textual examples to support any ideas in the essay. An essay score of 3 is given to writing that is particularly simplistic.

2–1 Essays in this range may attempt to answer the prompt but include a serious misreading of the passage or the prompt. They respond to the prompt in a general way, with no specific reference to the passage. These essays may consist of the student's personal views of the Vietnam War, which are separate from the passage. These essays are not well developed in their response to the prompt and lack control in their language. The vocabulary used may be simplistic. These essays fail to show any attempt at analysis and tend to ramble. A score of 1 is given to papers with no development of ideas.

0 An essay that merely repeats the prompt is given a 0.

— This indicates a blank response or the writing was completely off topic.

Sample Student Prose Essays with Comments

A Student Essay Scored 8

One of the most popular authors of the Vietnam War, Tim O'Brien, shows in this passage the myriad of emotions and ideas associated with being a soldier in Vietnam. The narration, in third person and in past tense, uses "they carried" often, suggesting that there is a need to disassociate himself from the action and separate the past and the present. There is a mixture of emotions regarding Vietnam—all represented within various descriptions of what the soldiers carry. There are objects such as "tanning lotion" and "Black Flag insecticide" that are unique to the individual soldier. These individual items characterize the individual personalities, but the focus is on what the soldiers carry in common. What they share with each other. It is a motley list of items that normally do not go together, but in the extreme circumstances of war, they become a part of every soldier. The narrator uses a series of juxtapositions to list the things they carry. There are the wounds of battle carried along with the basketball or the chess set. There are the diseases such as malaria and dysentery mingled with lice and ringworm. The medals of war such as the Purple Heart and the Bronze Star are carried in the same pockets as the dust of Vietnam itself. It is a mixture of courage, stamina, and chance.

The narrator says that the soldiers carry "the whole atmosphere" of Vietnam, which is not seen in a favorable light from the use of imagery provided, "stink of fungus and decay" and the "powdery orange-red dust that covered their boots and fatigues and faces." It seems to be a sort of cursed land to the narrator. Later, the narrator discusses the empty monotony of the soldier's march during the day. The passage is sprinkled with frustration and weariness with "endless march," "without purpose," "nothing won or lost," "dumb," and "unthinking." What is absent is a sense of mission and accomplishment. The narrator does not view the war as an event with a decided purpose. It is a war that is more concerned with appearances than actual realities. He is quick to point out that there is no "sense of strategy or mission" and that the soldiers are functioning more as animals driven by the instinct to survive than by the intellect that man is capable of. The war in all its cruelties has no high purpose, no actual mission to save the world. They are focused on saving themselves. War is an aggressive action that goes against our intellect. He says the "pressures were enormous" that they carried each day. The irony is that the soldiers are given "sparklers for the Fourth of July, colored eggs for Easter," all as part of the American war chest—not gold, medicine, land, glory—all the things we associate with a war chest. The things that are sent to them are not practical, but merely a reminder of the innocence they left behind in a country far away. Despite what each soldier carries, in the end there is no question regarding the fact that the soldier will never have a loss for things to carry. The most important baggage of all is the emotional baggage that each soldier will continue to carry long after the war is over. The end of the passage suggests that as the soldiers go on marching, the war machine of industry keeps on churning out the food and ammunition needed to continue the war. It is the profit of war—a gain of dollars for one and the loss of life for another.

Vietnam becomes a place of "ambiguities" where the narrator points out that at one point they are operating solely on the instinct to survive and the next they are taking off their helmets and jackets, despite the threat of sniper fire, for a reprieve from the heat of the day. The syntax of the passage weaves short statements of fact such as "They moved like mules" with a series of clauses separated by commas. There are no long pauses in the passage that reflect the life of the soldier, for they have no time to rest either. There are scattered thoughts here and there written as dependent clauses, which gives the overall impression of a narrator speaking about his experience in a series of disjointed scenes and thoughts. Everything from the topography of the land to the thinking of the men is described in contrast. Vietnam is not a place only of death, only of frustration, only of a loss of innocence, but a combination of many things including a place of camaraderie. But even the sense of belonging has its price and as the narrator comments "they would never be at a loss for things to carry."

COMMENT
This essay effectively analyzes the passage and discusses the complexity of emotion created by the narrator. The student notes the narrator's point of view, as well as the use of past tense as a means of detachment from a scene that perhaps the author does not want to be a part of. The contrast in objects is noted in the first paragraph of the essay and summed up with "it is a mixture of courage, stamina, and chance." The essay provides examples from the selection and then comments insightfully on their purpose. For example, the student notes the idea that the shipment of "sparklers for the Fourth of July" and "colored eggs for Easter" is especially ironic ; there is no use for

either object in Vietnam, and they only serve to remind the soldiers of the innocent traditions of home. The student also comments on the fact that war is a loss of life for the soldier who fights but a boon for industry in providing the weapons of war. The essay does have some problems with wording, but in general, it shows a mature writing style and, more importantly, insightful analysis.

A Student Essay Scored 6

In the passage from <u>The Things They Carried</u>, the narrator reflects a complex attitude toward the war in Vietnam. First, the soldiers are described as carrying an assortment of objects from "tanning lotion" to "ringworm." Some of the objects they carry are positive or useful—like the tanning lotion—but others are not. The objects that the soldiers carry depict the many aspects of Vietnam and the war. Vietnam is a hot country with plenty of sun so it makes sense to carry tanning lotion, plastic water containers, and insecticide; however, there are other objects that are carried that don't make sense such as Sanders' "starched tiger fatigues." Why would you need to starch anything in the jungle? The Vietnam War is viewed through the things the soldiers carry. The war at times seems rational—something that is necessary like the insecticide and at other times completely senseless like the need to carry starched fatigues. The author uses a lot of juxtaposition in that he draws attention to the contrast between items such as the soldiers "carrying" lice and ringworm at the same time they are carrying Bronze Stars and a PRC-77 scrambler radio.

The narrator describes the soldiers as "simple grunts" perhaps incapable of independent thought. They are described as acting out of instinct rather than obeying a set of rational, well-planned orders. The narrator suggests that perhaps the war in Vietnam was based on gut reaction rather than a well thought-out decision. Regardless of the things they will use along the trail, the soldiers will always have something to carry according to the narrator. The American war chest continues to supply what the soldiers need—for practicality purposes but not for their emotional needs. It is the emotional baggage from the war that the soldiers will carry with them forever.

The narrator is torn between the need to do his duty as an American soldier and to justify the reason for why he was there. The items each soldier's pack carried signified bits and pieces of the puzzle known as Vietnam. The experience itself is complex for the narrator for he remembers the feelings of frustration and exhaustion through each item and as fragmented thoughts throughout the passage much like someone who has suffered trauma. Vietnam is a series of images, mostly negative, that are a part of him forever. However, he says that they "carry their own lives" as though each man is the simply the sum of what he carries on his back.

The passage ends with a surreal scene of soldiers taking off their protective gear (flak jackets) and blowing up their ammunition for fun knowing of course that there is plenty of ammo waiting for them at the end of the day. It's as if for that brief period in the heat of the day, their cares are thrown aside. The baggage is tossed away and the war for a little while gets tossed away as well. However, the ending sentence sums up the narrator's view that "there will always be things to carry" whether they are in the farm fields back home or in the rice fields of Vietnam. The experience of Vietnam will always be baggage, a burden, to carry.

COMMENT

This is a developed essay that does an effective job of analyzing the text and explaining how the literary devices used (juxtaposition, diction) contribute to the narrator's view of the Vietnam War. The sentence structure is varied, and the control of language is apparent; however, the writing is generally unsophisticated in style and diction. The student does understand the connection between the objects carried by the soldiers and their relation to the attitude the narrator has for the war itself.

A Student Essay Scored 4

The soldiers in the passage <u>The Things They Carried</u> reflect the attitude of the narrator. The narrator describes many things that the soldiers are carrying including tanning lotion, empty sandbags, insecticide. They also carry lice, ringworm, and other infectious diseases. The soldiers carry a lot of different things just like the narrator thinks about the Vietnam War. He talks about Vietnam as having monsoons, orange-red dust, stink of fungus and having the people live in villages. Vietnam seems to be a very unpleasant place for the narrator. The narrator also describes the American soldiers as being "unthinking" and "all blood and bone, simple grunts." He doesn't think too highly of the American soldiers because they are only acting on instincts and the war is an example of the "dullness of desire and intellect and conscience and hope and human sensibility." He then goes on to say that the soldiers had enormous pressure on them (line 48). The pressure of course came from the struggle to survive with the threat of sniper fire and mortars. Later in the passage the narrator speaks about the American war chest and how it was full of different things like colored Easter eggs, sparklers, woolen sweaters, sunglasses, and watermelons. The items in the war chest were not practical items except for the ammunition. The reader wonders why such items would be sent to the soldiers in Vietnam which leads you to think about why America sent soldiers to Vietnam. Perhaps both were impractical. In any case, the narrator sees the war in many different ways both dangerous and without purpose.

COMMENT

The essay attempts some analysis of the passage, with the list of items the soldiers carry being related to the narrator's view of the war. Later, the student comments on the fact that the items being shipped in the American war chest were as impractical as the shipment of American soldiers. The student makes assertions but then doesn't fully develop them, such as the comments "Vietnam seems to be a very unpleasant place" and "He doesn't think too highly of the American soldiers." The sentence structure of the essay is simple and rather choppy in places. The vocabulary used is basic, and much of the essay's wording comes directly from quotations and their paraphrasing.

THE OPEN ESSAY QUESTION

The open essay is not an essay you should fear. In fact, this kind of essay allows you to choose the literary work you want to use as the basis of your essay, rather than requiring you to analyze a work chosen by the College Board. The open essay prompt is based on a central question that challenges your ability to think about literature in a broader sense—on the thematic level. As with the exam's first two essays, the essays that score higher on this kind of question are characterized by an ability to write well and in a mature style.

A WORD ABOUT THEME

Let's take a closer look at theme before tackling the open essay question itself. What is a theme? For starters, the word "theme" has several meanings. It can refer to the main idea of an essay; it can also be used to refer to the written essay itself. The word "theme" in relation to the AP exam essay refers to the heart and soul of a piece of literature no matter what its genre may be. It is helpful to identify literary devices and understand the use of rhetorical strategies; however, if you don't understand the heart of the literature, the rest is simply irrelevant. You'll find a discussion of theme in *Perrine's Literature: Structure, Sound, and Sense.*

Considering a theme means looking for a general insight into life or the human condition. The theme of a piece of literature is not the subject itself, but rather some facet of the human condition examined by the work; *a theme is a statement, direct or implied, about the subject.*

Let's look at some differences between subjects and themes. You are probably familiar with the list on the subject side of the table.

SUBJECT (general topic)	THEMES (examples)

The individual in nature
 	
   man versus nature
 	
   man versus animal
	Nature reminds us how vulnerable we really are.
	
	Intellect is no match for the raw forces of nature.

The individual in society
 	
   man versus society
 	
   man versus man
	Strength of character is often measured in how well we can stand by our convictions even when they are considered unpopular or dangerous.
	
	An individual who is committed to change will succeed, even in the most adverse circumstances.

SUBJECT (general topic)	THEMES (examples)
The individual and knowledge man versus technology	*Man's quest for knowledge regardless of his intentions can be disastrous.* *The practice of science without responsibility is immoral.*
Love	*Without love, life has no meaning.* *Love can be a powerful force for change.*
Alienation	*Alienation can lead to self-knowledge.* *Being human requires us to be a part of something greater than just ourselves.*
Initiation and maturation	*Our childhood experiences often shape who we become as adults.* *A person grows only as much as he or she is willing to change.*
Death	*Death is a part of life that can give life itself its ultimate meaning.* *Death is inescapable, despite our efforts to the contrary.*

Here are some general topics from which themes can be created:

abandonment	environment	peace
acceptance	ethical dilemmas	peer pressure
activism	freedom	poverty
anger	friendship	prejudice
belonging	guilt	pride
bullies	hatred	propaganda
challenges	help	racism
choices	honesty	relationships
commitment	hope	resourcefulness
communication	humor	responsibility
community	leadership	safety
convictions	loneliness	self-esteem
courage	loss	social change
customs	love	survival
death and dying	loyalty	teamwork
denial	memories	tragedy
discovery	money	trust
discrimination	mythology	values
diversity	nature	violence
dreams	patriotism	war

Remember that the theme in a story or poem is a statement, usually implied, about the topic—some "insight" into the topic and its relation to the human condition. In general, themes are written without any reference to specific characters, in order to show the "universality" of each theme. In other words, the thematic statement could be applied to a number of different works.

OPEN ESSAY PROMPTS

When responding to the open essay prompt, think about the following before you begin to write:

- What is the prompt really asking you to do?
- Which literary work that you're familiar with relates best to the prompt?
- Is the selection you've chosen of sufficient merit for the exam?

Let's take a look a some kinds of prompts you might encounter.

THEMES

Prompts for Question 3 sometimes deal specifically with theme. For example, you might be asked to address the thematic statement *Intellect is no match against the raw forces of nature*. The question will be accompanied by a list of literary works you might use to explore the theme—for example, *The Tempest, Call of the Wild, The Grapes of Wrath, Their Eyes Were Watching God, The Things They Carried*. Keep in mind that you are not restricted to the suggested works—they are no more than suggestions. You can base your response on a work of your choosing, but be careful that you choose a work of literary merit.

GENRES

Some Question 3 prompts focus on a genre. The College Board might ask you to address one or another aspect of comedy—for example, the goals of comedy, how the literary work you have chosen to write about describes an aspect of society, how a particular character creates humor and furthers the author's purpose, which literary devices the author employs.

For a question of this kind, you'll want to be familiar with the different types of comedy commonly found in literature. In addition, you should be prepared to think about the question thematically. Which plays and novels have you read that have dealt with social problems or pointed out a character's major flaw? What are the comedic devices that created the humor? When you discuss the details of a literary work, avoid simply summarizing the entire plot or even a scene.

If you haven't had an opportunity to become familiar with the more common techniques of creating humor in literature, you will want to acquaint yourself with some of the terms below. Accompanying each term you'll find references to both a work of literary merit and a popular movie or television series. (Remember, however, that *you cannot use TV shows and movies as your examples of a "work of literary merit" in the open essay question*.) Many comedies are a combination of several of the forms of comedy listed below. For example, the television series *M.A.S.H.* included many incidents of low comedy, yet it was, overall, a comedy of ideas.

- FARCE is full of coincidences, mistaken identities, and mistiming. Examples include The Importance of Being Earnest, Seinfeld (TV series), and The Parent Trap (movie).
- COMEDY OF MANNERS usually has a plot centered on class contrasts, particularly involving the upper class. Note the witty language and "put-downs" in this type of comedy. Examples include The Taming of the Shrew, My Fair Lady, and The Fresh Prince of Bel-Air (TV series).
- COMEDY OF IDEAS has a plot that subtly satirizes people and institutions and is filled with witty arguments and clever language. Examples include Gulliver's Travels, M.A.S.H. (TV series and movie), and Forrest Gump (movie).
- LOW COMEDY, as the name implies, centers on exaggerated comedy, often physical. This type of comedy involves dirty jokes, slapstick physical action, and ribald humor. Examples include scenes from Twelfth Night and Romeo and Juliet, Two and a Half Men (TV series), and Young Frankenstein (movie).

CONFLICT

The plot structure in a work of literature often involves a conflict—for example, a parent-child conflict. What have you read that involves conflict? When choosing a novel or play, be sure that you are sufficiently familiar with the work to "analyze the sources of the conflict." Note that the prompt never asks you to summarize the plot. You should choose a novel or play of literary merit, and not a short story or a book that is simplistic, such as a fairy tale. We could write all about Cinderella and her wicked stepmother as a definite example of parental conflict—but should we? What about Hamlet or Frankenstein? These novels are of sufficient complexity and offer universal themes. There would be enough depth in either work to write a solid essay.

Now it's your turn.

A SAMPLE OPEN ESSAY QUESTION

Question 3

"When the world goes mad, one must accept madness as sanity; since sanity is, in the last analysis, nothing but the madness on which the whole world happens to agree."
—George Bernard Shaw (1856–1950)

Select a novel or play in which a character or a situation of "madness" plays an important role. In a well-written essay, explain how the madness is manifested and why it is important to the work as a whole. Then explain how such madness could be viewed as something "on which the whole world happens to agree." You may select a work from the list below or choose another novel or play of literary merit.

1984
A Doll House
A Streetcar Named Desire
A Tale of Two Cities
An Enemy of the People
As I Lay Dying
Beloved
Brave New World
Catch-22
Catcher in the Rye
Crime and Punishment
Death of a Salesman
Fahrenheit 451

Hamlet
Heart of Darkness
Les Misérables
One Flew over the Cuckoo's Nest
Sula
The Awakening
The Color Purple
The Crucible
The Grapes of Wrath
The Things They Carried
Their Eyes Were Watching God
The Red Badge of Courage
Things Fall Apart

PLANNING YOUR ESSAY

This prompt begins with a quote by George Bernard Shaw as a way to jump-start ideas about what the words "madness" and "sanity" mean. When there is a quote at the beginning of your open-essay prompt, read it carefully and try to paraphrase it so that it makes sense to you before attempting to begin your essay. Here Shaw says that when the world goes mad, it is no longer viewed as madness, but becomes sanity, an accepted practice or behavior. What was once considered strange behavior or thought becomes ordinary or acceptable. However, Shaw goes on to say that what society considers sane is really madness that society has come to accept or agree upon.

After you have wrapped your thoughts around the quote, it is time to look at the prompt itself. What is the prompt asking you to do? The prompt calls for an essay based on a work in which "madness" is fundamental, either to the development of a character or to the construction of the plot. Think about novels you have read that deal with madness or insanity. You can write about a work of your choosing, but the list accompanying a Question 3 prompt is worth looking at closely. It may contain a novel or play you are familiar with but had simply forgotten.

Be sure to answer the *entire* prompt—essential for an upper-level score. This prompt has several parts. First, you are asked to describe the madness of a character or situation and how the author uses it. Then you are asked to "explain how such madness could be viewed as something 'on which the whole world happens to agree.'" Did the world or the characters in the novel or play for the most part begin to support the madness or begin to accept the madness as appropriate behavior or sane? Notice that the prompt uses the verb "could be viewed" rather than "was viewed." The characters in the novel or play you choose may not have embraced the madness as sanity, but in what way could the madness be seen as an act of sanity? You will need to discuss how the madness was actually viewed in the literature you selected and then briefly discuss how the madness could have been accepted as a sane act or thought.

THE SCORING GUIDELINES

The scoring guidelines, below, follow the concepts and language of the scoring guidelines used by the College Board. To receive a score of 6 or higher, you must successfully respond to the prompt. AP readers score each essay knowing it was composed as a rough draft. Your essay may have mistakes—mistakes are found even in papers scoring a 9. However, an essay with many distracting errors in grammar and mechanics will not be scored higher than a 3.

9–8 Essays in this scoring range illustrate a persuasive, effective, and insightful analysis of "madness" or the irrational behavior of a character in an appropriate novel or play. They explain the specific "madness" in the literary work, as well as how it's developed. Furthermore, they show how the madness might be judged reasonable by others in the context of the work. These essays show consistent and effective control of language. Writing is clear, cohesive, and mature in style. An essay scoring a 9 is particularly insightful in its interpretation of how the madness is significant to the work as a whole.

7–6 Essays in the upper-half range give a reasonable analysis and interpretation of "madness" or the irrational behavior of a character in an appropriate novel or play. They discuss how others might see the irrational behavior as reasonable in the context of the work and how the behavior relates to the work as a whole. Although there may be insightful analysis, it is less perceptive or specific in detail. Writers of these essays show more consistency in their analysis and overall writing skills than in an essay scored 5. Essays scored 7 exhibit more sophistication in both the effectiveness of their interpretation and their overall style.

5 These essays show that the student is able to respond to the prompt with an acceptable novel or play, but only superficially. Often these essays show some analysis, but only after resorting to plot summary. Sometimes the work selected in response to the topic is not well chosen or the student's assertions are not well supported. There is little or no consistency in the development of ideas. These essays do show adequate writing skills, but often are marred by unsophisticated thinking, immature writing, and usage and mechanical errors. Many times an essay scored a 5 will seem formulaic or lack style.

4–3 These essays attempt to respond to the prompt but may misinterpret a portion of the passage or fail to develop a cohesive analysis of the passage as a whole. Many essays in this range lack fully developed ideas and resort to paraphrasing the passage rather than analyzing and interpreting it. The essay may have usage and punctuation problems and it may be repetitive. Few or no examples are given in support of the ideas in the essay. A score of 3 is given to an essay that is particularly simplistic.

2–1 Essays in this range may attempt to answer the prompt but are only partially successful or they may have an oversimplified understanding of the work discussed. They respond to the prompt in a general way with no specific references or fail to establish how the "madness" is an integral part of the whole work. These essays may consist of the student's own personal views of "madness" apart from the context of the novel or play chosen. These essays are not well developed in their response to the prompt and lack control in their language, with frequent run-ons and/or fragments and wording problems. The vocabulary used may be simplistic. These essays fail to make any attempt at analysis and tend to ramble. A score of 1 is given to papers with no development of ideas.

0 An essay that merely repeats the prompt is given a 0. These essays are weak in their discussion, as well as unacceptably brief. They provide no analysis and are mechanically unsound.

— This indicates a blank response or the writing was completely off topic.

SAMPLE STUDENT OPEN ESSAYS WITH COMMENTS

A STUDENT ESSAY SCORED 8

Beloved is an inspirational novel by Toni Morrison revolving around the main character Sethe, whom the town calls "mad" for murdering her baby daughter. After a closer look, the reader sees that Sethe's intentions are merely to save her baby from the horrible conditions of slavery. The use of flashbacks, the interaction of characters, and imagery all attempt to prove that Sethe's madness is merely a mother's protective love.

In the beginning of the novel, Morrison tells Sethe's story through flashbacks, giving the reader only pieces of information at a time. In this way, the author chooses the order of information so that the reader can first see Sethe's concern for her baby, and then know the details of the murder. Sethe's flashbacks illustrate all the terrible conditions and the overall experience of slavery she endures. From whippings to being viewed as an animal, Sethe's personal trials as a slave form her all-consuming hatred for the institution and her own self-loathing. By presenting the reader with Sethe's background first, Morrison prevents the reader from judging Sethe's actions without understanding her reasoning, unlike the town's mistake of doing so. In this way, the reader can realize Sethe's love for her daughter, and her cruel treatment as a slave brought her to the overwhelming desire to protect her child regardless of the consequences.

Toni Morrison has the characters interact with each other so that it lends justification to Sethe's crime. When the "ghost" of her baby comes in the form of the Beloved, Sethe's attention to Beloved's every desire reveals how much she really cares about her child and the love she has for her even after having murdered her. Sethe stops eating so that Beloved can have more food. This sacrifice shows an attempt on Sethe's part to make up for her "mad" act of murder. Sethe even pushes her lover, Paul, away because her focus is on Beloved now. Paul asserts that Sethe is an animal for having killed her baby and this accusation further drives the couple apart. Sethe begins to question her choice to murder her baby; however, the more she interacts with Beloved and sacrifices for her, the more the murder seems to support the idea that her killing was justified in her love for her daughter.

The deeper meaning in the novel is found in Morrison's imagery of hummingbirds around Sethe's head, signifying the conflict between blacks and whites. Every time Sethe sees a white man she feels like she is in danger of becoming a slave again. She feels a fluttering sensation in her head that is like a madness, allowing her only to react and not think. The hummingbird imagery subtly points out the madness of slavery as a social institution and the emotional toll that is placed on individuals who have had to succumb to the reality of being slaves themselves. The madness is embedded in the practice of slavery and is made manifest through Sethe's hummingbirds. Morrison proves through flashback, imagery, and character interaction that the madness is really found in the horrors of slavery, rather than in the individual who experiences it.

COMMENT

This essay is well written, moving from a specific reference to "madness" in the novel and why the character is seen as being "mad," to the specific motives behind the character's apparent insanity. The essay connects the character's behavior to the more general condition of human slavery and its underlying theme in the novel. The writing is coherent, with few errors.

A STUDENT ESSAY SCORED 6

Darl Bundren was characterized as being somewhat crazy in <u>As I Lay Dying</u>. He was viewed as "different" by the other members of the family because of his personality. Darl played a major role in <u>As I Lay Dying</u> and his individuality, or "madness," was significant in the overall plot; however, he was not seen as crazy by everyone.

Darl's intuitiveness set him apart from most of his family, who failed to view things the way he did. He was aware of what most individuals were not and he knew about Dewey's relationship and how she had become pregnant. It can be inferred that Dewey Dell justifiably considered Darl crazy because he continued to persecute her with his awareness of her thoughts about him, always knowing what she was thinking and reminding her that he knew Darl knew before anyone else that Jewel was unlike the rest of the family. When Darl discovered that Jewel had a different father, he tormented his mother with what he knew. Darl was aware of all his family's secrets and although they were obviously serious and their bearers had wished them private, Darl was always reminding them of their faults. Darl was somewhat of a social outcast because he did not know how to appropriately deal with the information he learned about others. He tormented them rather than seek to help them or simply keep the information to himself. It is because of this that many viewed him as crazy or "not quite right."

The Bundren family may have thought that Darl was insane, but Cora, a family friend, determined that what made Darl different was that he was a genius. She was concerned about him and saw nothing but what she wanted to see. She thought Darl was a good person. Cora believed that Darl's "madness" was not madness at all. Darl could possibly have just been very smart and what he found out may not have been as a result of his "craziness." At least this is what Cora thought. Darl knew too much about his family and their personal lives and given his actions after finding out something about someone, it is no wonder that those he knew secrets about would think him crazy.

Despite Cora's thought that Darl was not insane, he played a major role in <u>As I Lay Dying</u> since it is through him that many of the secrets of the other characters are revealed to the reader. Darl was able to reveal a great deal of thought about his family and provide a different view of the burial of his mother. It took the Bundren family nine days to bury his mother. The nine days leading up to her death were rather funny, suggesting a lack of normalcy in the Bundren Family. Each character is presented during the nine days and the identity of each family member is developed. But it is Darl who gives us insight into the characters through his close observation and knowledge of their secrets. Therefore, it is difficult to determine whether Darl was really mad or just very perceptive.

COMMENT

The essay provides an example of "madness" in a character; however, the essay tends to stray somewhat and doesn't clearly connect the idea of madness to the theme. The student does note that Darl's perceived madness can be justified in saying that "Darl was somewhat of a social outcast because he did not know how to appropriately deal with the information he learned about others." The connection between Darl and the overall novel is made clear in the comment "since it is through him that many of the secrets of the other characters are revealed to the reader." However, more analysis and concrete examples are needed for a higher score.

A STUDENT ESSAY SCORED 4

We often shy away from being labeled "mad." If someone is labeled as being "crazy" people automatically prejudge the person as not fit for general society and not worthy of having true friends. In the novel <u>One Flew over the Cuckoo's Nest</u> one character who is thought of as mad is Randal McMurphy. On closer examination the reader can see that McMurphy madness can be seen as something else. His illness has a great importance to his work. First of all, McMurphy's madness can be seen as the behavior of a sane not insane man. He is seen as unstable mentally because he fights a lot, drinks alchohol, and sleeps with women too much. McMurphy chose the mental ward because it was either that or prison. He was also accused of having sex with an underage minor, but the charges were dropped. These are the actions of any normal person who just likes to have a little fun. A lot of people drink too much and get into fights. As to the statutory rape, well, McMurphy claims that he didn't know how young she really was. For these reasons, McMurphy's sanity is open to interpretation.

Secondly, McMurphy's illness plays a crucial role in the work. McMurphy is very confrontational which is why he gets into so much trouble. When he comes to the mental ward he notices that the nurse, Nurse Ratched, the head nurse has all of the men under her control. The men have no freedom or allowed any individuality and they do not know that anything is wrong. When McMurphy sees all this, he frees the men from her control by making Nurse Ratched lose control herself. The men are able to be individuals by the end of the story and taste freedom along with being able to drink beer and have prostitutes. He is able to turn them in to men again.

In <u>One Flew over the Cuckoo's Nest</u>, McMurphy is said to be crazy. He proves that this is not true, and because of his so called "symptoms" he cures the entire mental ward. McMurphy plays a important role in this novel by helping to take away some of Nurse Ratched's power and give it to the patients.

COMMENT

The essay begins by explaining why McMurphy is seen as "mad" by general society; however, the essay does not analyze the reasons why the main character chooses to act as he does, other than to say it was "either that or prison." The connection between McMurphy's behavior and individuality is loose. The essay tends to summarize the plot of the story more than answer questions of how McMurphy's actions could be justified beyond saying "[a] lot of people drink too much." It also doesn't connect McMurphy's actions to a greater theme in the novel. The essay hints at "freedom" and "individuality" but doesn't connect them clearly to McMurphy's supposed "madness." The language is limited and there are a number of spelling and other grammatical errors.

Part III

Practice Tests

PRACTICE TEST 1

AP ENGLISH LITERATURE AND COMPOSITION EXAMINATION
Section I: Multiple-Choice Questions
Number of questions: 55
Total time: 1 hour

DIRECTIONS: This part consists of selections from literary works and questions on their content, form, and style. After reading each passage, choose the best answer to the accompanying questions.

QUESTIONS 1–11. The following passage is the opening of D. H. Lawrence's short story "The Horse Dealer's Daughter." Read it carefully before choosing your answers.

"Well, Mabel, and what are you going to do with yourself?" asked Joe, with foolish flippancy. He felt quite safe himself. Without listening for an answer, he turned aside, worked a grain of tobacco to the tip of his tongue, and spat it out. He did not care about anything, since he felt safe himself.

The three brothers and the sister sat round the desolate breakfast-table, attempting some sort of desultory consultation. The morning's post had given the final tap to the family fortunes, and all was over. The dreary dining-room itself, with its heavy mahogany furniture, looked as if it were waiting to be done away with.

But the consultation amounted to nothing. There was a strange air of ineffectuality about the three men, as they sprawled at table, smoking and reflecting vaguely on their own condition. The girl was alone, a rather short, sullen-looking young woman of twenty-seven. She did not share the same life as her brothers. She would have been good-looking, save for the impassive fixity of her face, "bull-dog," as her brothers called it.

There was a confused tramping of horses' feet outside. The three men all sprawled round in their chairs to watch. Beyond the dark holly bushes that separated the strip of lawn from the high-road, they could see a cavalcade of shire horses swinging out of their own yard, being taken for exercise. This was the last time. These were the last horses that would go through their hands. The young men watched with critical, callous look. They were all frightened at the collapse of their lives, and the sense of disaster in which they were involved left them no inner freedom.

Yet they were three fine, well-set fellows enough. Joe, the eldest, was a man of thirty-three, broad and handsome in a hot, flushed way. His face was red, he twisted his black moustache over a thick finger, his eyes were shallow and restless. He had a sensual way of uncovering his teeth when he laughed, and his bearing was stupid. Now he watched the horses with a glazed look of helplessness in his eyes, a certain stupor of downfall.

The great draught-horses swung past. They were tied head to tail, four of them, and they heaved along to where a lane branched off from the high-road, planting their great hoofs floutingly in the fine black mud, swinging their great rounded haunches sumptuously, and

5

10

15

20

25

30

35

GO ON TO THE NEXT PAGE

trotting a few sudden steps as they were led into the lane, round the corner. Every movement showed a massive, slumbrous strength, and a stupidity which held them in subjection. The groom at the head looked back, jerking the leading rope. And the cavalcade moved out of sight up the lane, the tail of the last horse, bobbed up tight and stiff, held out taut from the swinging great haunches as they rocked behind the hedges in a motion-like sleep. 40

Joe watched with glazed hopeless eyes. The horses were almost like his own body to him. He felt he was done for now. Luckily he was engaged to a woman as old as himself, and therefore her father, who was steward of a neighboring estate, would provide him with a job. He would marry and go into harness. His life was over, he would be a subject animal now. 45 50

He turned uneasily aside, the retreating steps of the horses echoing in his ears. Then, with foolish restlessness, he reached for the scraps of bacon-rind from the plates, and making a faint whistling sound, flung them to the terrier that lay against the fender. He watched the dog swallow them, and waited till the creature looked into his eyes. Then a faint grin came on his face, and in a high, foolish voice he said: "You won't get much more bacon, shall you, you little b—?" 55

1. All of the following reinforce the tone of the second paragraph EXCEPT
(A) "desultory consultation"
(B) "morning's post"
(C) "desolate breakfast table"
(D) "final tap"
(E) "dreary dining-room"

2. The first indication that the story is being told by an omniscient narrator comes in the phrase
(A) "Without listening for an answer, he turned aside" (lines 2–3)
(B) "'Well, Mabel, and what are you going to do with yourself?'" (line 1)
(C) "with foolish flippancy" (line 2)
(D) "He did not care about anything" (line 4)
(E) "attempting some sort of desultory consultation" (line 7)

3. The phrase that most clearly signals a difference between the men and their horses is
(A) "floutingly in the fine black mud" (lines 36–37)
(B) "planting their great hoofs" (line 36)
(C) "tied head to tail" (line 34)
(D) "they heaved along" (line 35)
(E) "a massive, slumbrous strength" (line 39)

4. The comment that Joe would be a "subject animal now" is best understood to mean that he would
(A) need to care for his sister
(B) become the central character in the story
(C) now be free to marry
(D) be happier working on the "neighbouring estate"
(E) owe obedience to others

5. The characters in the passage are characterized chiefly by their
(A) physical descriptions
(B) clothes and belongings
(C) dialogue and diction
(D) thoughts and feelings
(E) behaviors and actions

6. Which of the following best describes the tone of the passage?
(A) patronizingly apprehensive
(B) resignedly fatalistic
(C) meditatively reflective
(D) brusquely vitriolic
(E) indignantly remorseful

7. The primary effect of the statement that Joe would "go into harness" (line 49) is to
(A) emphasize his eagerness to work
(B) recall his unspoken love for the horses
(C) link him again with the horses
(D) reflect his feelings of security
(E) suggest that he will be forced into hard labor

8. The central opposition in the passage is between
(A) the brothers and their horses
(B) the brothers and their sister
(C) the brothers' past and future
(D) Joe's father and the owner of the neighboring estate
(E) the sister's passions and her responsibilities

9. The passage is best described as an example of
(A) expository characterization
(B) descriptive interlude
(C) rhetorical argument
(D) operational definition
(E) authorial comment

10. The passage establishes an implied metaphor that links
(A) the people and the animals
(B) the men and the land
(C) the sister and her brothers
(D) the past and the future
(E) the landed gentry and the workers

11. Joe's actions are characterized primarily as
(A) menacing and impulsive
(B) irresponsible and reckless
(C) thoughtful and prudent
(D) sorrowful and cerebral
(E) irrational and silly

QUESTIONS 12–22. Carefully read "One day I wrote her name upon the strand" by Edmund Spenser before choosing your answers.

One day I wrote her name upon the strand,
But came the waves and washèd it away:
Again I wrote it with a second hand,
But came the tide, and made my pains his prey.
"Vain man," said she, "that dost in vain assay   5
A mortal thing so to immortalize.
For I myself shall, like to this, decay,
And eek[1] my name be wipèd out likewise."
"Not so," quoth I, "let baser things devise
To die in dust, but you shall live by fame: 10
My verse your virtues rare shall eternize,
And in the heavens write your glorious name,
Where whenas death shall all the world subdue
Our love shall live, and later life renew."

12. The speaker in the poem is
(A) a heavenly spirit
(B) a lifeguard
(C) a poet in love
(D) a religious leader
(E) a passing stranger

[1] Also.

GO ON TO THE NEXT PAGE

13. The phrase "came the tide, and made my pains his prey" (line 4) is best interpreted to mean
    (A) the tide wiped out all my hard work
    (B) the tide caught me and caused me physical pain
    (C) the water temporarily alleviated my emotional pains
    (D) history turned against all my best intentions
    (E) the heavens would not hear my prayer

14. The poet begins line 5 with the word "vain" in order to
    I. set up the pun on the same word later in the line
    II. allow the woman to gently mock the speaker's claim
    III. introduce the main idea of the poem's second quatrain
    (A) I only
    (B) I and II only
    (C) I and III only
    (D) II and III only
    (E) I, II, and III

15. The pronoun "she" in line 5 refers to the same person as
    (A) the strand (line 1)
    (B) "her" (line 1)
    (C) the name (line 1)
    (D) the tide (line 4)
    (E) the prey (line 4)

16. When "she" says "I myself shall, like to this, decay" (line 7), by "this" she means
    (A) the relationship between the speaker and herself
    (B) the verse the speaker has constructed
    (C) the speaker's own death
    (D) her name, which the speaker has written in the sand
    (E) the pains the speaker has taken on her behalf

17. By "my name" (line 8) the woman means
    (A) earthly memory of her
    (B) her good reputation
    (C) her earthly life
    (D) her physical beauty
    (E) her moral character

18. The speaker's attitude toward his "verse" (line 11) is best characterized as
    (A) intensely ashamed
    (B) insecurely hesitant
    (C) coolly distant
    (D) wholly confident
    (E) quietly content

19. All of the following are true of line 14 EXCEPT
    (A) it introduces a striking new idea into the poem
    (B) the rhythm is quickened by the alliterative "L"s
    (C) it is true, since we are still reading the poem today
    (D) it completes the rhyming couplet begun by line 13
    (E) the speaker uses it to close his argument with a promise

20. The two clear shifts in the poem come after lines
    (A) 2 and 10
    (B) 4 and 8
    (C) 4 and 10
    (D) 4 and 12
    (E) 8 and 12

21. The tone of the speaker in the poem is best described as
    (A) wistful and nostalgic
    (B) frustrated and disappointed
    (C) jocund and sardonic
    (D) incredulous and scornful
    (E) reassuring and secure

22. The lines that best state the main idea of the poem are
    (A) 1 and 2
    (B) 1 and 3
    (C) 5 and 6
    (D) 7 and 8
    (E) 11 and 14

QUESTIONS 23–33. Carefully read the poem by Philip Larkin before choosing your answers.

Aubade

I work all day, and get half drunk at night.
Waking at four to soundless dark, I stare.
In time the curtain-edges will grow light.
Till then I see what's really always there:
Unresting death, a whole day nearer now,   5
Making all thought impossible but how
And where and when I shall myself die.
Arid interrogation: yet the dread
Of dying, and being dead,
Flashes afresh to hold and horrify.   10

The mind blanks at the glare. Not in remorse
—The good not done, the love not given, time
Torn off unused—nor wretchedly because
An only life can take so long to climb
Clear of its wrong beginnings, and may never;   15
But at the total emptiness for ever,
The sure extinction that we travel to
And shall be lost in always. Not to be here,
Not to be anywhere,
And soon; nothing more terrible, nothing more true.   20

This is a special way of being afraid
No trick dispels. Religion used to try,
That vast moth-eaten musical brocade
Created to pretend we never die,
And specious stuff that says *No rational being*   25
Can fear a thing it will not feel, not seeing
That this is what we fear—no sight, no sound,
No touch or taste or smell, nothing to think with,
Nothing to love or link with,
The anaesthetic from which none come round.   30

And so it stays just on the edge of vision,
A small unfocused blur, a standing chill
That slows each impulse down to indecision.
Most things may never happen: this one will,
And realization of it rages out   35
In furnace-fear when we are caught without
People or drink. Courage is no good:
It means not scaring others. Being brave
Lets no one off the grave.
Death is no different whined at than withstood.   40

Slowly light strengthens, and the room takes shape.
It stands plain as a wardrobe, what we know,
Have always known, know that we can't escape,
Yet can't accept. One side will have to go.

GO ON TO THE NEXT PAGE

> Meanwhile telephones crouch, getting ready to ring   45
> In locked-up offices, and all the uncaring
> Intricate rented world begins to rouse.
> The sky is white as clay, with no sun.
> Work has to be done.
> Postmen like doctors go from house to house.   50

23. The speaker in this poem is best identified as
    (A) a man who has been taken into police custody for drunkenness
    (B) a man who awakens in his bedroom during the night
    (C) a man who awakens in a frightening, unfamiliar place
    (D) a patient who awakens in a hospital critical care unit
    (E) a doctor who has risen early to make house calls to his dying patients

24. The phrase "arid interrogation" in line 8 is best understood to mean that the speaker
    (A) cannot speak the answers because of "dry mouth" caused by medication
    (B) fears he will not have answers for the questions at the Last Judgment
    (C) is dehydrated from alcohol abuse
    (D) knows he can't find answers to his questions
    (E) has awoken in his bed with "night sweats"

25. Which of the following best identifies the source of the "glare" in line 11?
    (A) "the curtain-edges" that "grow light" (line 3)
    (B) "dying, and being dead" (line 9)
    (C) "the dread of dying" (lines 8–9)
    (D) the "[a]rid interrogation" (line 8)
    (E) the "[m]aking all thought impossible" (line 6)

26. The poet uses the phrases "The good not done, the love not given, time / Torn off unused" (lines 12–13) to
    (A) contradict the idea expressed by "the dread / Of dying" (lines 8–9)
    (B) enumerate some of the causes of the potential "remorse" (line 11)

    (C) contrast with the thought of "[m]aking all thought impossible" (line 6)
    (D) foreshadow the "wrong beginnings" of life (line 15)
    (E) provide examples of actions that "hold and horrify" (line 10)

27. Which of the following is implicit after the phrase "may never" in line 15?
    (A) "die" (line 7)
    (B) "[t]orn off unused" (line 13)
    (C) "take so long" (line 14)
    (D) "climb / Clear of its wrong beginnings" (lines 14–15)
    (E) "travel to" [extinction] (line 17)

28. Which of the following best identifies what the speaker calls "terrible" and "true" in line 20?
    (A) "love not given" (line 12)
    (B) life taking "so long" (line 14)
    (C) "wrong beginnings" (line 15)
    (D) the "good not done" (line 12)
    (E) "Not to be anywhere" (line 19)

29. In the context of the poem, the phrase "moth-eaten musical brocade" (line 23) is intended to suggest all of the following EXCEPT
    (A) rich opulence
    (B) elaborateness
    (C) heaviness
    (D) the natural world
    (E) ineffectiveness

30. Which of the following best paraphrases line 33?
    (A) that makes our bodies incapable of responding to external stimuli
    (B) that draws us, in spite of our efforts, toward our deaths
    (C) that helps us make up our minds to move slowly and surely
    (D) that suppresses our impulses but also increases our momentum
    (E) that robs us of the emotional stamina to perform our duties

31. One purpose of line 40 is to
    (A) reinforce the idea that being brave when faced with death is meaningless
    (B) suggest that resisting and even complaining when death threatens can bring strength
    (C) counter the argument that "Being brave / Lets no one off the grave" (lines 38–39)
    (D) assert again that religion teaches us how to avoid whining when faced with death
    (E) present a metaphor that helps makes sense of death

32. The diction in line 45 suggests that the speaker sees telephones as
    (A) an aggressive presence that stalks humans
    (B) a reassuring metaphor for the link between humans and the divine
    (C) a comforting symbol of the return to calm normalcy after the fears of the night
    (D) a mechanical piece of an indifferent daily life of routine
    (E) a call to action against "all the uncaring" world

33. An aubade is a song or poem greeting the dawn, a morning love song, or a poem about the parting of lovers at dawn, so its use as the title here brings to the poem
    (A) a softening reassurance
    (B) a lyrical intensity
    (C) a climactic culmination
    (D) a mordant irony
    (E) a promise of hope

QUESTIONS 34–44. In this passage from the opening scene of Oscar Wilde's *The Importance of Being Earnest*, Jack is calling on his friend in Algernon's London flat. Read it carefully before choosing your answers.

ALGERNON. How are you, my dear Ernest? What brings you up to town?

JACK. Oh, pleasure, pleasure! What else should bring one anywhere? Eating as usual, I see, Algy!

ALGERNON [stiffly]. I believe it is customary in good society to take some 5 slight refreshment at five o'clock. . . .

JACK. Hallo! Why all these cups? Why cucumber sandwiches? Why such reckless extravagance in one so young? Who is coming to tea?

ALGERNON. Oh! merely Aunt Augusta and Gwendolen.

JACK. How perfectly delightful! 10

ALGERNON. Yes, that is all very well; but I am afraid Aunt Augusta won't quite approve of your being here.

JACK. May I ask why?

ALGERNON. My dear fellow, the way you flirt with Gwendolen is perfectly disgraceful. It is almost as bad as the way Gwendolen 15 flirts with you.

JACK. I am in love with Gwendolen. I have come up to town expressly to propose to her.

ALGERNON. I thought you had come up for pleasure? . . . I call that business. 20

JACK. How utterly unromantic you are!

ALGERNON. I really don't see anything romantic in proposing. It is very romantic to be in love. But there is nothing romantic about a definite proposal. Why, one may be accepted. One usually is, I believe. Then the excitement is all over. The very essence of romance is uncertainty. 25 If ever I get married, I'll certainly try to forget the fact.

GO ON TO THE NEXT PAGE

JACK. I have no doubt about that, dear Algy. The Divorce Court was specially invented for people whose memories are so curiously constituted.

ALGERNON. Oh! there is no use speculating on that subject. Divorces 30 are made in Heaven—*[Jack puts out his hand to take a sandwich. Algernon at once interferes.]* Please don't touch the cucumber sandwiches. They are ordered specially for Aunt Augusta. *[Takes one and eats it.]*

JACK. Well, you have been eating them all the time. 35

ALGERNON. That is quite a different matter. She is my aunt. *[Takes plate from below.]* Have some bread and butter. The bread and butter is for Gwendolen. Gwendolen is devoted to bread and butter.

JACK *[advancing to table and helping himself]*. And very good bread and butter it is too. 40

ALGERNON. Well, my dear fellow, you need not eat as if you were going to eat it all. You behave as if you were married to her already. You are not married to her already, and I don't think you ever will be.

JACK. Why on earth do you say that?

ALGERNON. Well, in the first place, girls never marry the men they flirt 45 with. Girls don't think it right.

JACK. Oh, that is nonsense!

ALGERNON. It isn't. It is a great truth. It accounts for the extraordinary number of bachelors that one sees all over the place. In the second place, I don't give my consent. 50

JACK. Your consent!

ALGERNON. My dear fellow, Gwendolen is my first cousin. And before I allow you to marry her, you will have to clear up the whole question of Cecily. *[Rings bell.]*

JACK. Cecily! What on earth do you mean? What do you mean, Algy, by 55 Cecily! I don't know any one of the name of Cecily.

[Enter Lane.]

ALGERNON. Bring me that cigarette case Mr. Worthing left in the smoking-room the last time he dined here.

LANE. Yes, sir. *[Lane goes out.]* 60

JACK. Do you mean to say you have had my cigarette case all this time? I wish to goodness you had let me know. I have been writing frantic letters to Scotland Yard about it. I was very nearly offering a large reward.

ALGERNON. Well, I wish you would offer one. I happen to be more than 65 usually hard up.

JACK. There is no good offering a large reward now that the thing is found.

[Enter Lane with the cigarette case on a salver.
Algernon takes it at once, Lane goes out.] 70

ALGERNON. I think that is rather mean of you, Ernest, I must say. *[Opens case and examines it.]* However, it makes no matter, for, now that I look at the inscription inside, I find that the thing isn't yours after all.

JACK. Of course it's mine. *[Moving to him.]* You have seen me with it a 75 hundred times, and you have no right whatsoever to read what is written inside. It is a very un-gentlemanly thing to read a private cigarette case.

ALGERNON. Oh! it is absurd to have a hard and fast rule about what one should read and what one shouldn't. More than half of modern 80 culture depends on what one shouldn't read.

JACK. I am quite aware of the fact, and I don't propose to discuss modern culture. It isn't the sort of thing one should talk of in private. I simply want my cigarette case back.

ALGERNON. Yes; but this isn't your cigarette case. This cigarette case is a present from someone of the name of Cecily, and you said you didn't know anyone of that name. 85

JACK. Well, if you want to know, Cecily happens to be my aunt.

ALGERNON. Your aunt!

JACK. Yes. Charming old lady she is, too. Lives at Tunbridge Wells. Just give it back to me, Algy. 90

ALGERNON [*retreating to back of sofa*]. But why does she call herself little Cecily if she is your aunt and lives at Tunbridge Wells? [*Reading.*] "From little Cecily with her fondest love."

JACK. My dear fellow, what on earth is there in that? Some aunts are tall, some aunts are not tall. That is a matter that surely an aunt may be allowed to decide for herself. You seem to think that every aunt should be exactly like your aunt! That is absurd! For Heaven's sake give me back my cigarette case. [*Follows Algernon round the room.*] 95

ALGERNON. Yes. But why does your aunt call you her uncle? "From little Cecily, with her fondest love to her dear Uncle Jack." There is no objection, I admit, to an aunt being a small aunt, but why an aunt, no matter what her size may be, should call her own nephew her uncle, I can't quite make out. Besides, your name isn't Jack at all; it is Ernest. 100

JACK. It isn't Ernest; it's Jack. 105

ALGERNON. You have always told me it was Ernest. I have introduced you to every one as Ernest. You answer to the name of Ernest. You look as if your name was Ernest. You are the most earnest-looking person I ever saw in my life. It is perfectly absurd your saying that your name isn't Ernest. It's on your cards. Here is one of them. [*Taking it from case.*] "Mr. Ernest Worthing, B. 4, The Albany." I'll keep this as a proof that your name is Ernest if ever you attempt to deny it to me, or to Gwendolen, or to any one else. [*Puts the card in his pocket.*] 110 115

JACK. Well, my name is Ernest in town and Jack in the country, and the cigarette case was given to me in the country.

ALGERNON. Yes, but that does not account for the fact that your small Aunt Cecily, who lives at Tunbridge Wells, calls you her dear uncle. Come, old boy, you had much better have the thing out at once. 120

JACK. My dear Algy, you talk exactly as if you were a dentist. It is very vulgar to talk like a dentist when one isn't a dentist. It produces a false impression.

ALGERNON. Well, that is exactly what dentists always do. Now, go on! Tell me the whole thing. I may mention that I have always suspected you of being a confirmed and secret Bunburyist; and I am quite sure of it now. 125

JACK. Bunburyist? What on earth do you mean by a Bunburyist?

ALGERNON. I'll reveal to you the meaning of that incomparable expression as soon as you are kind enough to inform me why you are Ernest in town and Jack in the country. 130

JACK. Well, produce my cigarette case first.

ALGERNON. Here it is. [*Hands cigarette case.*] Now produce your explanation, and pray make it improbable. [*Sits on sofa.*]

GO ON TO THE NEXT PAGE

34. The irony in Algernon's statement in lines 5–6 that "I believe it is customary in good society to take some slight refreshment at five o'clock" results from
(A) Algernon's "I believe" implying that he is not sure
(B) its not being five o'clock
(C) Jack's hunger when he sees the sandwiches
(D) the fact that the characters are not "in society" but alone
(E) the sandwiches having been brought by Lane, not Algernon

35. The humor in Jack's speech in lines 7–8 grows from the incongruity between
(A) "all these cups" and "who is coming"
(B) "cups" and "sandwiches"
(C) "one so young" and "who is coming"
(D) "reckless extravagance" and "cucumber sandwiches"
(E) "sandwiches" and "tea"

36. "The fact" Algernon says in line 26 he will try to forget is best identified as
(A) his being married
(B) the acceptance of a "definite proposal"
(C) the romance of being in love
(D) the romance of proposing
(E) the uncertainty of romance

37. The statement that produces humor by inverting a common adage is
(A) "Divorces are made in Heaven" (lines 30–31)
(B) "Please don't touch the cucumber sandwiches" (lines 32–33)
(C) "The Divorce Court was specially invented for people whose memories are so curiously constituted" (lines 27–29)
(D) "there is no use speculating on that subject" (line 30)
(E) "They are ordered specially for Aunt Augusta" (line 33)

38. Algernon's attitude toward marriage is best described as one of
(A) anxious apprehension
(B) distressed abhorrence
(C) enthusiastic attraction

(D) mischievous cynicism
(E) sneering misanthropy

39. The passage's clearest example of hyperbole is the lines
(A) "the way you flirt with Gwendolen is perfectly disgraceful. It is almost as bad as the way Gwendolen flirts with you" (lines 14–16)
(B) "But there is nothing romantic about a definite proposal. Why, one may be accepted" (lines 23–24)
(C) "The bread and butter is for Gwendolen. Gwendolen is devoted to bread and butter" (lines 37–38)
(D) "girls never marry the men they flirt with. Girls don't think it right" (lines 44–45)
(E) "I have been writing frantic letters to Scotland Yard about it. I was very nearly offering a large reward" (lines 61–63)

40. Jack's comment about his aunt's height in lines 93–95 is absurd because
(A) Jack himself is not very tall
(B) he is embarrassed that his aunt is abnormally short
(C) he knows his aunt is actually quite tall
(D) people can't choose their height
(E) people in Tunbridge Wells are known for their tall stature

41. Algernon includes the word "small" in referring to Cecily in line 116 in order to
(A) cast suspicion on Jack's earnestness
(B) express doubt that Jack has a place in the country
(C) imply that Jack can't really be called Ernest
(D) maintain that Jack's aunt is actually relatively tall
(E) mock Jack's illogical explanation

42. The primary function of the comment "It is very vulgar to talk like a dentist when one isn't a dentist. It produces a false impression" in lines 119–21 is to
(A) couple the puns on "have the thing out" and "false impression"
(B) define what is "vulgar" in polite society

(C) mock dentists as tradesmen who
   must work for a living
(D) suggest that Algernon failed in his
   attempt to become a dentist
(E) tease Algernon about his fear of
   dentists

43. In the context, the word
   "incomparable" in line 127 most nearly
   means
   (A) fancy
   (B) inexpressible

(C) newly coined
(D) ubiquitous
(E) unique

44. Algernon's final comment, "pray make
   it improbable" (in lines 132), reinforces
   his tone of
   (A) annoyed displeasure
   (B) apprehensive skepticism
   (C) mock seriousness
   (D) patient forbearance
   (E) wounded dismay

QUESTIONS 45–55. Carefully read the poem by Linda Pastan before choosing your answers.

Ethics

In ethics class so many years ago
our teacher asked this question every fall:
if there were a fire in a museum
which would you save, a Rembrandt painting
or an old woman who hadn't many   5
years left anyhow? Restless on hard chairs
caring little for pictures or old age
we'd opt one year for life, the next for art
and always half-heartedly. Sometimes
the woman borrowed my grandmother's face   10
leaving her usual kitchen to wander
some drafty, half imagined museum.
One year, feeling clever, I replied
why not let the woman decide herself?
Linda, the teacher would report, eschews   15
the burdens of responsibility.
This fall in a real museum I stand
before a real Rembrandt, old woman,
or nearly so, myself. The colors
within this frame are darker than autumn,   20
darker even than winter—the browns of earth,
though earth's most radiant elements burn
through the canvas. I know now that woman
and painting and season are almost one
and all beyond saving by children.   25

45. The speaker in the poem is best
   identified as
   (A) a school student
   (B) a painter
   (C) an older woman
   (D) a young woman
   (E) a teacher

46. The setting of the poem is
   (A) a child's room
   (B) a classroom, then a museum
   (C) an artist's studio
   (D) a school classroom
   (E) a hospital or rest home

GO ON TO THE NEXT PAGE

47. The speaker changes the phrasing "a Rembrandt painting / or an old woman" in lines 4–5 to "pictures or old age" in line 7 to reflect
    (A) the rapid aging of both the artwork and the people
    (B) the impersonal and generic nature of the students' perceptions
    (C) the cleverness of the students in completing their assignments
    (D) the important role played by museums in the students' lives
    (E) the frustration of the teacher faced with indifferent pupils

48. The speaker's statement that "the woman borrowed my grandmother's face" (line 10) is best understood to mean that
    (A) to identify with the old woman in line 5, the speaker as a child needed to picture her own grandmother in her place
    (B) the speaker is angry that her choice was made difficult by the resemblance of the old woman in line 5 to her grandmother
    (C) the speaker feels fortunate that the painter would use her own grandmother as a model
    (D) the teacher would try to get her students to take the assignment seriously by calling up their memories of their grandparents
    (E) the lighting in the museum made the woman in the painting look like the speaker's own grandmother

49. The diction in the teacher's response to the suggestion of letting "the old woman decide herself" (line 14) carries a tone of
    (A) unforgiving and severe censure
    (B) mocking but mild reproach
    (C) rueful but nostalgic regret
    (D) untroubled but aloof indifference
    (E) vehement but poignant anger

50. The phrase "old woman" in line 18 refers to
    (A) the woman in the painting by Rembrandt
    (B) the teacher
    (C) a museum guard or docent
    (D) an anonymous painter
    (E) the speaker herself

51. The seasons autumn and winter in the context of lines 20–21 are best understood to suggest
    (A) aging and death
    (B) the children and the old woman
    (C) holidays and festivals
    (D) the carelessness of humans toward the environment
    (E) the museum as shelter from rough weather

52. The most significant shift in the poem comes
    (A) in line 9
    (B) between lines 12 and 13
    (C) between lines 16 and 17
    (D) in line 19
    (E) in line 23

53. The tone that prevails throughout the poem is best characterized as
    (A) wistful and nostalgic
    (B) whimsical and mischievous
    (C) pessimistic and suspicious
    (D) mournful and crestfallen
    (E) reflective and realistic

54. The speaker most closely identifies with
    (A) the teacher (line 2)
    (B) the woman in the "Rembrandt painting" (line 4)
    (C) the "old woman who hadn't many / years left anyhow" (lines 5–6)
    (D) the children, "[r]estless on hard chairs" (line 6)
    (E) her grandmother (line 10)

55. The poem as a whole implies that "all [are] beyond saving by children" for all the following reasons EXCEPT

(A) children are more immediately concerned with their own physical comfort than with questions of ethics and values

(B) children are like the girl Linda in lines 15–16, who "eschews / the burdens of responsibility"

(C) children make ethical decisions at random

(D) children are closer to "the browns of earth" (line 21) than the older people and more interested in the seasons than in art

(E) children lack the maturity and the experience to understand the value of the "woman and painting and season" (lines 23–24)

STOP
END OF SECTION I

Section II: Essay Questions
Number of questions: 3
Reading time: 15 minutes
Writing time: 2 hours
Suggested time for each essay: 40 minutes

Section II of this examination requires answers in essay form. Each question counts for one-third of the total essay section score. The two hours are yours to divide among the three essay questions as you think best. To help you use your time well, the proctor may announce the time at which each question should be completed. If you finish any question before time is announced, you may go on to another question. You may go back at any time and work on any essay question you want.

Each essay will be judged on its clarity and effectiveness in dealing with the assigned topic and on the quality of the writing. In response to Question 3, select a work of recognized literary merit appropriate to the question. A good general rule is to use works of the same quality as those you studied in your Advanced Placement literature course(s).

After completing each question, you should check your essay for accuracy of punctuation, spelling, and diction; you are advised, however, not to attempt many longer corrections. Remember that quality is far more important than quantity.

Write your essays clearly and legibly in dark-blue or black ink. Cross out any errors you make.

Question 1

In the fairy tale of Hansel and Gretel, the brother and sister, who have been stranded in a forest by their wicked stepmother, are captured by a witch. As the witch prepares to cook Hansel, Gretel pushes her into the oven instead, and the children are saved and reunited with their father when they learn that their stepmother is also dead. In the following poem, poet Louise Glück considers the characters after their return home. Carefully read the poem. Then write an essay in which you analyze both the attitude of the speaker and the techniques that convey that attitude, taking the title of the poem into consideration. In your essay consider elements such as point of view, imagery, and diction.

Gretel in Darkness

This is the world we wanted.
All who would have seen us dead
are dead. I hear the witch's cry
break in the moonlight through a sheet
of sugar: God rewards.   5
Her tongue shrivels into gas. . . .
        Now, far from women's arms
and memory of women, in our father's hut
we sleep, are never hungry.
Why do I not forget?   10
My father bars the door, bars harm
from this house, and it is years.

No one remembers. Even you, my brother,
summer afternoons you look at me as though   15
you meant to leave,
as though it never happened.
But I killed for you. I see armed firs,
the spires of that gleaming kiln—

Nights I turn to you to hold me
but you are not there.
Am I alone? Spies   20
hiss in the stillness, Hansel
we are there still, and it is real, real,
that black forest, and the fire in earnest.

GO ON TO THE NEXT PAGE

Question 2

The following passage is the opening of "A Family Supper," a 1990 story by English author Kazuo Ishiguro. Read the passage carefully. Then write an organized essay in which you analyze the author's presentation of the three characters and the relationship among them.

Fugu is a fish caught off the Pacific shores of Japan. The fish has held a special significance for me ever since my mother died through eating one. The poison resides in the sexual glands of the fish, inside two fragile bags. When preparing the fish, these bags must 5 be removed with caution, for any clumsiness will result in the poison leaking into the veins. Regrettably, it is not easy to tell whether or not this operation has been carried out successfully. The proof is, as it were, in the eating. 10

Fugu poisoning is hideously painful and almost always fatal. If the fish has been eaten during the evening, the victim is usually overtaken by pain during his sleep. He rolls about in agony for a few hours and is dead by morning. The fish became extremely 15 popular in Japan after the war. Until stricter regulations were imposed, it was all the rage to perform the hazardous gutting operation in one's own kitchen, then to invite neighbours and friends round for the feast. 20

At the time of my mother's death, I was living in California. My relationship with my parents had become somewhat strained around that period, and consequently I did not learn of the circumstances surrounding her death until I returned to Tokyo two 25 years later. Apparently, my mother had always refused to eat fugu, but on this particular occasion she had made an exception, having been invited by an old schoolfriend whom she was anxious not to offend. It was my father who supplied me with the details as we 30 drove from the airport to his house in the Kamakura district. When we finally arrived, it was nearing the end of a sunny autumn day,

"Did you eat on the plane?" my father asked. We were sitting on the tatami floor of his tea-room. 35

"They gave me a light snack."

"You must be hungry. We'll eat as soon as Kikuko arrives."

My father was a formidable-looking man with a large stony jaw and furious black eyebrows. I think 40 now in retrospect that he much resembled Chou En-lai, although he would not have cherished such a comparison, being particularly proud of the pure samurai blood that ran in the family. His general presence was not one which encouraged relaxed 45 conversation; neither were things helped much by his odd way of stating each remark as if it were the concluding one. In fact, as I sat opposite him that

afternoon, a boyhood memory came back to me of the
time he had struck me several times around the head
for "chattering like an old woman." Inevitably, our
conversation since my arrival at the airport had been
punctuated by long pauses.

"I'm sorry to hear about the firm," I said when
neither of us had spoken for some time. He nodded
gravely.

"In fact the story didn't end there," he said. "After
the firm's collapse, Watanabe killed himself. He didn't
wish to live with the disgrace."

"I see."

"We were partners for seventeen years. A man of
principle and honor. I respected him very much."

"Will you go into business again?" I said.

"I am—in retirement. I'm too old to involve myself
in new ventures now. Business these days has become
so different. Dealing with foreigners. Doing things
their way. I don't understand how we've come to this.
Neither did Watanabe." He sighed. "A fine man. A
man of principle."

The tea-room looked out over the garden. From
where I sat I could make out the ancient well which as
a child I had believed haunted. It was just visible now
through the thick foliage. The sun had sunk low and
much of the garden had fallen into shadow.

"I'm glad in any case that you've decided to come
back," my father said. "More than a short visit, I
hope."

"I'm not sure what my plans will be."

"I for one am prepared to forget the past. Your
mother too was always ready to welcome you back—
upset as she was by your behavior."

"I appreciate your sympathy. As I say, I'm not sure
what my plans are."

"I've come to believe now that there were no evil
intentions in your mind," my father continued. "You
were swayed by certain—influences. Like so many
others."

"Perhaps we should forget it, as you suggest."

"As you will. More tea?"

Just then a girl's voice came echoing through the
house.

"At last." My father rose to his feet. "Kikuko has
arrived."

Despite our difference in years, my sister and I had
always been close. Seeing me again seemed to make
her excessively excited and for a while she did nothing
but giggle nervously. But she calmed down somewhat
when my father started to question her about Osaka
and her university. She answered him with short
formal replies. She in turn asked me a few questions,
but she seemed inhibited by the fear that her questions
might lead to awkward topics. After a while, the

GO ON TO THE NEXT PAGE

conversation had become even sparser than prior to Kikuko's arrival. Then my father stood up, saying: "I must attend to the supper. Please excuse me for being burdened down by such matters. Kikuko will look after you." 105

My sister relaxed quite visibly once he had left the room. Within a few minutes, she was chatting freely about her friends in Osaka and about her classes at university. Then quite suddenly she decided we should walk in the garden and went striding out onto the veranda. We put on some straw sandals that had been left along the veranda rail and stepped out into the garden. The daylight had almost gone. 110 115

"I've been dying for a smoke for the last half-hour," she said, lighting a cigarette.

"Then why didn't you smoke?"

She made a furtive gesture back towards the house, then grinned mischievously. 120

"Oh I see," I said.

Question 3

Many works of imaginative literature develop characters who, throughout a work or for some part of it, try to pass themselves off as something they are not, pretending to be a different person, or a different *kind* of person.

From a novel, play, or epic poem you have studied, choose such a character. In a well-written essay, analyze the character's feigning and explain clearly the contribution it makes to the meaning of the work as a whole. You may choose a work from the list below or select another of comparable literary merit. Do not summarize the plot.

A Clockwork Orange
A Streetcar Named Desire
A Tale of Two Cities
Blindness
Brave New World
Death of a Salesman
Elmer Gantry
Hamlet
Henderson the Rain King
Invisible Man
King Lear
Les Misérables

M. Butterfly
One Flew Over the Cuckoo's Nest
Pride and Prejudice
Pygmalion
The Adventures of Huckleberry Finn
The Bourgeois Gentleman
The Catcher in the Rye
The Great Gatsby
The Importance of Being Earnest
The Mayor of Casterbridge
The Scarlet Letter
Twelfth Night

END OF EXAMINATION

ANSWERS AND EXPLANATIONS FOR SECTION I

MULTIPLE-CHOICE ANSWER KEY

Using the table below, determine how many questions you answered correctly, how many incorrectly. Then look over the answer explanations.

1. B	2. D	3. A	4. E	5. E
6. B	7. C	8. C	9. A	10. A
11. E	12. C	13. A	14. E	15. B
16. D	17. A	18. D	19. A	20. B
21. E	22. E	23. B	24. D	25. C
26. B	27. D	28. E	29. D	30. E
31. A	32. A	33. D	34. D	35. D
36. A	37. A	38. D	39. E	40. D
41. E	42. A	43. E	44. C	45. C
46. B	47. B	48. A	49. B	50. E
51. A	52. C	53. E	54. C	55. D

EXPLANATIONS FOR THE MULTIPLE-CHOICE ANSWERS

1. **ANSWER: B.** *A tone question.* The dismally hopeless tone of the paragraph is reinforced by the words "desultory" in A, "desolate" in C, "final" in D, and "dreary" in E, leaving B as the best choice.

2. **ANSWER: D.** *A point of view question.* The question asks about an omniscient narrator—that is, one who knows the thoughts of all of the characters. A carries no sign of omniscience because the narrator simply reports what all can see. B repeats what the character has said for all to hear. C and E characterize Joe's movement, but without any insight into his thoughts. D tells what Joe is thinking and thus establishes the narrator as omniscient.

3. **ANSWER: A.** *A diction question.* A does not fit the men; they have nothing to flout—no reason to feel comfort or superiority—and nothing about them or their surroundings qualifies as sumptuous. All the rest do tie the horses to Joe or his brothers. B links the horses' "motionlike sleep" to the "stupor" in Joe's eyes (line 33). The horses' being "tied head to tail" in C foreshadows Joe's going "into harness"

(line 49). The "stupidity which held them in subjection" in D recalls Joe's "stupid" bearing (line 31), and the horses' "massive, slumbrous strength" in E recalls the brothers' description as "fine, well-set fellows" (line 27) and Joe's as "broad," as well as the sprawling and stupor that Lawrence uses to characterize the men.

4. **ANSWER: E.** *A diction question.* Nothing in the passage suggests that Joe will be looking after his sister; in fact, the opening question suggests strongly that he will not, so A is incorrect. B misconstrues the word "subject," which here is not the noun meaning a central person or thing but the adjective meaning owing obedience to another. C will not work because although the passage establishes that he is engaged, there is no indication that he was ever not free to marry. D is inaccurate because although working for the neighbor may rescue him from the situation, the mood of the entire passage makes it clear that "happy" is an exaggerated description. E matches the meaning of "subject" in the context and is the best choice.

5. **ANSWER: E.** *A characterization question.* The passage provides a direct physical description of the characters. It then reinforces the portrayal with the animal imagery that runs throughout, linking the men with the horses and the sister with the "bull-dog." So A best describes the method of characterization. B and D are inaccurate because we are told almost nothing about what they might be wearing, thinking, or feeling. C is clearly wrong because the passage includes only one sentence spoken by any character, and E because it includes almost no actions at all.

6. **ANSWER: B.** *An interpretation question.* The inactivity of the characters and their quiet show that they are resigned to their unlucky fate, the loss of "the family fortunes," and seem powerless to change that fate, making B the best response. The characters have no one to patronize, so A is wrong. B echoes the word "reflecting" from line 13 of the passage, but that reflection is "vague" and we don't know their thoughts. The description of them "sprawled at table, smoking" reinforces the idea that reference to their reflection as "meditative" would not be supported by the text. D is indefensible because no one is brusque and there is no vitriol in the piece. If there are feelings of remorse, the passage does not reveal them.

7. **ANSWER: C.** *An interpretation question.* Lawrence's choice of the phrase "into harness" links Joe once again to the horses because a harness is most often used on draught horses. A can't be right because although Joe seems willing to work, there's no indication of any eagerness. Nor is there any indication of affection for the horses. They are his workhorses and his livelihood, but not pets for which he feels affection, so B is out. D tries to impose the idea of fear into the context where it does not exist. There are implications that Joe is not looking forward to his new position, but nothing indicates that he fears it. E presents a misreading of the passage, where the imagery suggests strongly that the men have been hard workers all their lives.

8. **ANSWER: C.** *A conflict question.* Choice A misreads the passage, in which Lawrence repeatedly links the men with the horses. B is a weak

choice, supported only by the nickname the brothers give their sister, and which they do not use in the passage. Even if there is opposition there, it cannot qualify as "central." D is wrong because Joe's father is never mentioned. So too is E, because we don't know enough about the sister to know what her passions might be. The passage details the change in the family's life, and the conflict between the security of the way they have lived contrasted with the uncertainty of their futures creates that central opposition, making C the best choice.

9. **ANSWER: A.** *A rhetorical purpose question.* Choice A accurately identifies the passage as expository; it introduces us to the characters and the setting but focuses on the brothers and the girl. An interlude must by definition come between other parts, as this passage does not, eliminating B. C and D are incorrect because there is no argument made and no stated term to be defined. E is unacceptable because the passage includes comment from the narrator but not from the author.

10. **ANSWER: A.** *A figurative language or imagery question.* The strong association of the men with their horses runs throughout the passage. They are built alike and work alike. Even the sister is said to have the tenacity of a bulldog. Although we sense that land matters here, the passage never mentions it, so B is inaccurate. C contradicts the statement that the sister "did not share the same life as her brothers." Although the break with the past is implied, no metaphor separates it from the future, and no "landed gentry" appear in the passage, eliminating D and E.

11. **ANSWER: E.** *A characterization question.* Joe has few actions in the selection. His comment to his sister is probably imprudent, but there's nothing rash about it. B won't stand up because "reckless" would be an exaggeration in describing anything in the piece. We might take the characters' quiet for thoughtfulness, but nothing shows them to be "prudent," eliminating C. There may be sorrow, although the signs are slim, but in a question like this, both claims must stand up, and the imagery contradicts the idea of "cerebral." E is the best choice; the narrator says outright that Joe's opening question is foolish and flippant.

12. **ANSWER: C.** *A speaker question—a common type, especially with poetry.* The speaker is a poet who has written "verse." Choice E has no basis in the poem. A and D may appear linked to the mention of "heavens" in the poem, but they have no such link to the speaker. Choice B might sound connected to the beach setting, but it can be quickly eliminated.

13. **ANSWER: A.** *An interpretation question.* What the tide "preys" on, or destroys, is what the speaker has taken pains to write in the sand. Nothing in the poem supports the idea that he is in any physical or emotional pain, eliminating B and C, and D and E stray even further from the poem.

14. **ANSWER: E.** *A diction question.* Beware of the trap of letting a "Roman numeral question" eat up too much of your time. Their form is complex, but they tend to be somewhat straightforward. Here, I is true since the word means conceited or foolish in the first mention and

useless in the phrase "in vain." II is true because the woman teases the speaker by pointing out that her name in the sand is gone and that she, too, will die. Since the second quatrain presents that idea, that the speaker is foolish to think he can fight nature, III is also correct.

15. ANSWER: **B.** *A grammar question.* The woman whose name the speaker writes is the only woman in the poem, so B is the quick choice. C doesn't make sense because "she" is the speaker (or at least the one being quoted) in lines 5–8, and "the name" would not say "my name be wiped out." E won't work for the same reason because "prey" also refers to the name in the sand. We can eliminate A and D since it makes no sense for either the strand or the tide to speak of its own decay.

16. ANSWER: **D.** *A grammar question.* What has decayed in the poem is the name written in the sand. A and C find no support in the poem, and B fails because the speaker claims that the verse will not decay. E sounds acceptable at first, but it is a less satisfying choice than D because the speaker may have taken the pains on her behalf, but more likely did so on his own.

17. ANSWER: **A.** *An interpretation question.* The woman can only mean her name in the sense of records of her and her life. Nothing in the poem has established that she has a good reputation, beauty, or moral character to have wiped out, so B, D, and E don't work. C is a possible choice, but she has already said she will decay like the name in the sand—that is, completely—so C would be simply a restatement. A adds the idea that not only will she die, but the world will forget her after she does so.

18. ANSWER: **D.** *A question of tone and attitude.* The speaker argues resolutely that his poetry will make the woman immortal—maybe a huge claim, but he makes it. B is wrong because there is no insecurity about him. A and E don't work because there's no shame in his tone and nothing quiet about the way he brags about his verse. C is wrong because he seems intent on breaking down *her* distance, not adding his own.

19. ANSWER: **A.** *A question of structure and interpretation.* Poems, especially sonnets, do not introduce new ideas in a final line. "L" sounds—as "liquid sounds"—do speed up a line, the line does form a couplet with line 13, and the speaker promises that their love will outlast mortal life. Even C is true; he was right.

20. ANSWER: **B.** *A structure question.* Punctuation is the easiest clue here; end stops finish lines 4 and 8 and no others. That first shift marks the move from the speaker's vain attempt and the tide's destruction to the new idea—the woman's belief that people don't last forever either. Line 9 then shifts to the speaker's counter-argument that he can make her last forever through his poetry. The rhyme helps some; it does change after line 4 and after line 8, but also after line 12. The shift in speaker reinforces the choice of B since the man speaks lines 1–4, he quotes the woman in 5–8, and returns to his own voice for 9–14.

21. **ANSWER: E.** *A tone question.* The word "secure" leads to E, and "reassuring" may understate the speaker's intent but it is accurate. The "scornful" in D might be tempting if we take it to mean scornful of the earthly decay he claims to be surmounting (probably not what the question means), but "incredulous" clearly does not fit. A weak argument might be made that he's disappointed, but B is wrong because he is certainly not frustrated. As the bold "Not so" shows, he's well prepared with his counter-argument. The others are not supported by any details from the poem.

22. **ANSWER: E.** *A "main idea" question—a very common type.* Since we're looking for two lines that "state the main idea," we need two lines that come close to saying the same thing. Since line 11 says "My poem will make you immortal" and line 14 says "Our love will be immortal," we have a close match. Another clue is that the "main idea" of a sonnet nearly always comes in the closing quatrain or sestet, not near the start.

23. **ANSWER: B.** *A speaker question.* The speaker is normally identified early in a poem. Here the word "I" alerts us, and in the second line we get the answer. The other choices echo words or ideas found in the poem, but in other contexts.

24. **ANSWER: D.** *An interpretation question.* The speaker cannot find the answers to his questions in the previous line, where and when he will die. Choices A, C, and E all appeal to the literal meaning of "arid," but the meaning here is metaphorical. B is not supported by the poem.

25. **ANSWER: C.** *An interpretation question.* The "glare" here comes from the "flashes," and what flashes is the "dread of dying." Choice A picks up on the idea of light, since light glares, but here it's in a different context. The other choices are not supported by details in the poem.

26. **ANSWER: B.** *An interpretation question.* All three phrases are examples of wasted opportunities that bring feelings of remorse. That remorse adds to, rather than lessens, the "dread of dying," so A is wrong. C won't work because it's the death in line 5 that "makes all thought impossible." D is wrong because of logic: actions done or not done during life can't foreshadow its beginnings. E is the best of the wrong choices, but grammatically it can't work because what "hold and horrify" are the flashes of the dread in line 8.

27. **ANSWER: D.** *A question of grammar and interpretation.* The semicolon at the end of line 25 indicates the end of a grammatical unit, so we have to back up to find what it refers to. The other choices make no grammatical sense

28. **ANSWER: E.** *A question of grammar and interpretation.* Unless there's strong evidence that we should look elsewhere, we stay in the same sentence to find grammatical relationships. So what's "terrible and true" here is the idea of not being at all. The context supports this choice as well, since the speaker has established that what he dreads is dying and disappearing. The other choices are too far away—both grammatically and in meaning.

29. **ANSWER: D.** *An interpretation question.* The natural world is far from the speaker's ideas about religion. All the others fit. Brocade is a heavy, rich silk fabric ornamented in gold, eliminating A, B, and C. "Moth-eaten" eliminates E.

30. **ANSWER: E.** *A reading and paraphrase question.* The line is nearly literal: the fear of death becomes a blur that undoes our impulses and leave us incapable of taking any action. D starts well but then reverses itself. C has a positive tone that the poem does not support, and A mistakes a psychological meaning for a physical one. B makes little sense.

31. **ANSWER: A.** *A paraphrase question.* The line means that our reaction to death has no effect on it. None of the other choices are supported by the poem; C is contradicted by it.

32. **ANSWER: A.** *A diction question.* The words "crouch, getting ready" are normally used to describe predatory animals. Choices B, C, and D contradict that image, and E misreads the poem as calling for action. The poem simply laments what it sees as a demoralizing reality.

33. **ANSWER: D.** *A question of diction and tone.* Since the poem contradicts every element in the definition of aubade, its use in the title here is ironic. Choices A and E represent a serious misreading of this bleak poem, and C does not specify what is being concluded. B is the best of the wrong choices because the poem is certainly intense; the lyricism, however, is not the lyricism implied by the definition of aubade.

34. **ANSWER: D.** *An irony question.* The passage includes plenty of discussion about behavior with others, but here the two men are alone, so the irony comes from Algernon's nonsensical pretending that they are "in good society," and D is the best choice. Even after a short passage we know Algernon well enough to understand that when he says "I believe," he doesn't mean that he isn't sure. Choice A is close, but the comment is simple sarcasm rather than irony. B is not a good choice because the time has not been established, and C won't work because neither Jack nor anyone else has mentioned his hunger. E is based on an irrelevant detail—who actually brought in the sandwiches doesn't matter.

35. **ANSWER: D.** *A humor question.* There is nothing incongruous about A because Jack's seeing a large number of teacups would logically lead him to assume that Algernon was expecting company. Both cups and sandwiches would be set out for guests, eliminating B. The phrases in C are not incongruous but simply unrelated. D is the best choice because "reckless extravagance" calls up objects or events much more dramatic than sandwiches, and especially those as bland as cucumber. E presents two closely related objects, the sandwiches and tea; they are normally served together, so there is nothing incongruous about their being coupled in the line.

36. **ANSWER: A.** *An interpretation question.* Both logic and placement mark the phrase in A as the correct choice. C, D, and E are all circumstances Algernon says he does not want to forget and so do not fit the question. He might want to forget B, the acceptance of a "definite proposal," but certainly not as much as actually being married. This

question is unusual. Questions about reference generally ask you to find an antecedent that lies at some distance from the referent. Here the two are side by side.

37. ANSWER: **A.** *An allusion question.* Like all questions on references and allusions, this one assesses both your understanding of the text and your previous knowledge. The common saying this question expects you to know is "Marriages are made in Heaven." None of the other choices fit any common saying or idiom. (The answer to the question of how you are supposed to know all these sayings is reading. Reading widely will supply the cultural literacy these questions—and an enjoyment of this play and other entertainment—call on.)

38. ANSWER: **D.** *A tone question.* The tone Algernon takes toward marriage (and just about everything else) is one of questioning and doubt, but always with the attitude of a playful rascal, so D is the best choice here. He is not fearful (A) and expresses no hatred or loathing (B). He is certainly not enthusiastic about marriage, eliminating C; nor does he show any kind of the spiteful dislike of people that E implies.

39. ANSWER: **E.** *An interpretation question.* Because hyperbole is an enormous exaggeration not meant to be taken literally, only E qualifies. Jack knows that the Scotland Yard police headquarters would not react well to a series of letters about a lost cigarette case, especially "frantic letters." The offering of a "large reward" is a substantial exaggeration, given the nature of the loss. The only other choice with an exaggeration is the claim in D that "girls never marry the men they flirt with," but Algernon offers the comment only as a reversal of what is known to be true, not as an exaggeration.

40. Answer: **D.** *An interpretation question.* The absurdity of an aunt, or anyone else, being able to "decide for herself" marks D as the best choice. We do not "choose" our height. E presents an irrelevant observation. A, B, and C are eliminated because there is no reference to Jack's height nor to the real height of his aunt, and he shows no embarrassment about anything.

41. ANSWER: **E.** *A humor question.* Algernon is mocking Jack's statement that his aunt is short because he knows the woman called Cecily is not Jack's aunt in the first place. He never says he suspects Jack's aunt is tall, nor that Jack might not have a country home, which eliminates B and D. A and C are directly contradicted by the text in lines 106–08 and so can't be correct.

42. ANSWER: **A.** *A diction question.* Choice A brings together the silly dentistry puns about having a tooth pulled and having an impression made for a filling or crown. None of the other choices have any support in the text because dentists have not been mentioned.

43. ANSWER: **E.** *A diction question.* The question, a common type on most AP exams, is really more of a vocabulary question than anything else. If something is incomparable, it can't be compared to anything else; it is one of a kind. That makes E the best choice because "unique" most commonly means that something has no like or equal. The other choices are all words with unrelated meanings, except for D, which

offers a word almost opposite in meaning—"ubiquitous" means existing everywhere.

44. **ANSWER: C.** *A diction question.* Algernon is pretending to be highly formal and serious when he says "pray" rather than "please." But that he is not at all serious becomes apparent when he reverses what a listener expects. The audience thinks he is going to ask for a believable excuse, but he does the opposite, and we see that he is not serious at all. He does not show any signs of being annoyed or apprehensive, but seems to be looking forward to Jack's explanation, eliminating A and B. D starts well because he seems patient, but forbearance implies that he is restraining himself, something of which he seems incapable. E represents a misreading of the scene because Algernon is never seriously dismayed and seems incapable of being wounded.

45. **ANSWER: C.** *A speaker question.* The speaker identifies herself in lines 18–19, "old woman / or nearly so, myself." Choices B, D, and E name people who are mentioned but who do not speak the lines. Choice A is closer since the student who is the subject of lines 13–16 is the same person as the woman in line 18, but the speaker tells the story of the poem as an older woman, not as the student, who (the poem says) would not see the story as worth telling.

46. **ANSWER: B.** *A setting question.* In a literal sense, the setting is the museum because the speaker "thinks through" the whole piece while standing in that museum, but there is no "museum only" choice. The poem's story that makes up the speaker's thought begins in the classroom with the teacher's question. In line 17 it moves to the "real museum," where the speaker is standing for the rest of the poem. Choice D fails to see that change. The places named in A, C, and E don't exist in the poem.

47. **ANSWER: B.** *A question of diction and interpretation.* The teacher poses the question, identifying a painting by a specific artist—Rembrandt—and an old woman. When the speaker gives us the children's point of view in line 7, the specificity of the Rembrandt painting fades into the generic term "art," and the old woman is stripped of her gender and even her humanity as she becomes "old age." Choice E might at first appear defensible, but the poem doesn't give us the teacher's reaction, so we don't know if he or she in fact feels frustration.

48. **ANSWER: A.** *An interpretation question.* The speaker as a child cannot picture an "old woman," since she thinks only in terms of "old age." In order to get a specific image in her mind, she turns to the only "old" woman she can think of, her grandmother (who probably has much longer to live than the "old woman" the teacher has in mind). The speaker then uses "borrow" as a metaphor for her own moving of the face from one woman to another. Choices B and C specify emotions not present in the poem, E strays from the text because there's no mention of lighting, and D is wrong because the teacher doesn't mention grandparents.

49. **ANSWER: B.** *A diction and tone question.* The teacher chooses the overly formal word "eschews" instead of the more natural "avoids" or more

conversational "is trying to get out of" that the children would understand more easily. The teacher is rebuking Linda, but the scolding is indirect and fairly gentle. Choices A and E far overstate the tone of the teacher's remark. Choice D is correct in identifying the aloof tone, but if the teacher were either untroubled or indifferent, there would have been no rebuke at all. The word "nostalgia" eliminates C.

50. **ANSWER: E.** *A reference question.* The old woman is the speaker, as is made clear by the surrounding pronouns "I" in line 17 and "myself" in line 19. A is wrong because we are not told the subject of the Rembrandt painting, and C and D are incorrect because the people named don't appear in the poem. B can't be right because we don't know the teacher's age or gender.

51. **ANSWER: A.** *A symbol question.* The seasons often symbolize a human life from the youth of spring, maturing of summer, aging of autumn, and death of winter. That's the case here. Nothing about the children would link them to autumn, eliminating A. Choices C, D, and E have nothing in the poem to defend choosing them.

52. **ANSWER: C.** *A structure question.* Every poem will have at least one shift. Here the two parts are each introduced by the announcement of a place and time. Line 1 gives us "[I]n . . . class so many years ago," and line 17, "[t]his fall in a real museum." That change in setting marks the poem's move from a more narrative section to a more reflective one. Choice E could be defended as the place where the poem turns from all past observations to a concluding sentence, but it lacks the structural reinforcement of the abrupt setting change at line 17. Choice D is harder to support because although the poem moves into metaphor there, it moves back in the next sentence. Choices A and B have little to suggest a major shift.

53. **ANSWER: E.** *A tone question.* The reflective nature of the whole poem results in the realistic conclusion that the children cannot yet understand enough to make the decision the teacher has asked for. Choice A is inaccurate because only half the poem is set in the past, and the look back carries no nostalgia. There is no whimsy to justify choice B, and while the speaker may be disappointed that the children cannot understand, there is nothing pessimistic or "mournful" in her realization, so C and D are wrong.

54. **ANSWER: C.** *A speaker question.* The speaker here identifies with the teacher's "old woman," even calling herself "old woman" in line 18. We are not told what is in the Rembrandt, eliminating B. Choice A is wrong because the speaker doesn't identify with the teacher. The speaker understands that the question the teacher poses has little meaning to the children; there is no evidence that the teacher does. Although she sympathizes to some extent with the children on their "hard chairs," she is far from feeling herself one of them, eliminating D. Only choice E offers some temptation, but the speaker puts the grandmother in an "imagined museum" and contrasts it explicitly with the "real museum" she is in.

55. **ANSWER: D.** *A question about the main idea—a most common type.* All the choices have support in the poem except the idea that the children are "closer to 'the browns of earth.'" In fact, the speaker unequivocally includes "season" in the list of things "beyond saving by children." The hard chairs distract children from their task, ruling out A. Linda and, we can safely assume, the other children would rather skip the question than answer it, so B is out. Choice C can't be the exception because the children are inconsistent in their choices, and E is wrong, because it nearly paraphrases the poem's conclusion.

SCORING GUIDELINES FOR SECTION II

The score reported for each essay reflects the reader's judgment of the quality of the essay as a whole. Readers are instructed to reward the writers for what they do well. The score for an exceptionally well-written essay may be raised by one point. A poorly written essay can be scored no higher than a 3.

SCORING GUIDELINES FOR QUESTION 1

9–8 These detailed, well-written essays provide insightful analysis of Glück's poem. They marshal apt and specific details from the poem to lead compellingly to well-founded conclusions. They acknowledge that "happily ever after" does not operate here, and they give some sort of expression to the idea that this Gretel can be seen to represent more people than the girl in the fairy tale. They elaborate effectively on the "darkness" in the title and relate it to the darkness in the poem. They select significant techniques and illustrate their impact on a meaning of the poem, one the essay states or implies clearly. These essays may propose a range of readings and explain a variety of techniques. They may not be flawless, but they sustain their control over the elements of effective writing and manage some measure of style.

7–6 These competent essays offer a consistent understanding of the poem, including both its darkness for Gretel and its divergence from the standard fairy tale ending. They deal specifically with the title, although possibly less thoroughly than the top essays. Their interpretations may weaken in some particulars or exaggerate or exploit an idea beyond its worth, or they may be less detailed or precise. They link their discussion to an expressed meaning of the poem but may do so less convincingly. While they may not demonstrate the same control or sophistication as the 9–8 essays, they do provide evidence of an ability to express logical ideas with clarity and some control.

5 These essays demonstrate some understanding of Gretel's attitude, but they may tend to be more superficial and less compelling than the upper-half essays. They recognize the darkness but may relate it only in part or to a meaning of the poem as a whole. Their argument may slight part of the prompt or rest on insufficient support from concrete detail in the text. They may present minor misreading but show an understanding of the poem's central ideas. There may be some paraphrase, but there are attempts to use it in analysis. The writing shows some control, although maybe not a comfortable command. Mechanical errors are not so distracting as to force rereading, and the diction is not so bland or vague as to obscure meaning. They may not be as well planned or developed as those scoring higher, but they are adequate.

4–3 These lower-half essays reveal an incomplete understanding of the poem, the task, or both. They may suffer more serious misreading or slight their discussion of the poem in favor of the fairy tale. They may fail to recognize the poetic techniques at work in the poem, or they may simply name them without attempting to link them to their intended effect on a reader. They may present interpretations that are not supported by the detail in the poem or that misrepresent or seriously exaggerate what should be minor concerns. The writing may ramble or veer away from the task, or it may fall into extended paraphrase without links to meaning. These essays show an ability to express basic ideas but demonstrate uncertain control over writing beyond the sentence level. Essays that include significant misreading or unskilled writing should be scored 3.

2–1 These essays compound the weaknesses of the 4–3 essays. They may be unacceptably brief or may badly misread the poem. Although they make some attempt to respond to the task, they do so without clarity, organization, or supporting example. They may be poorly written on several counts and include distracting errors in grammar and mechanics that frequently force rereading. Essays with little coherent discussion of the poem should be scored 1.

0 These essays may make no more than a reference to the task.

— These essays are either left blank or are completely off topic.

Scoring Guidelines for Question 2

9–8 These top essays present a persuasive analysis of all three characters and of their relationship. They will not omit Kikuko, although the passage focuses on the father and son. They examine such techniques as diction and tone. The strongest will attend to what is not said and to pauses in conversations. They will reflect perceptive reading and recognize the complexities of the characterizations. Their references to the text will alternate with smooth effectiveness with analysis and will be specific and appropriate. These essays are drafts and may not be free of error, but they show sustained control over the standard language of literary analysis.

7–6 These essays present a reasonable analysis of the characters and of their relationships. They will discuss specific techniques and recognize the complexities of the characterizations, but may do so with less precision and insight than essays scoring higher. They may lack the thorough development of the best essays, but their references are clear and appropriately chosen and alternate appropriately with analysis. They will not be error free, but these essays demonstrate an ability to analyze and to present that analysis with control and clarity.

5 These essays tend to handle the assigned analysis with a plausible interpretation. They are often superficial and predictable in their understanding of the characters and of the techniques used to establish them. They may slight the relationships and focus exclusively on the three characters. They will often present readings more literal than the better essays, missing the subtleties, including the importance of what the characters omit from conversation. The evidence they present may be less aptly chosen, and the balance between detail from the passage and the analysis may be less effective. Surface errors of mechanics and usage may mar the writing, and the diction will show less sophistication, but the essays demonstrate an acceptable command of standard written discourse.

4–3 These lower-half essays present an inadequate interpretation of the characters. They show a partial misunderstanding of the passage or the assigned task, or both. Although they explicitly attempt analysis, they may surrender to summary and paraphrase. They may show misreadings of the text, especially in those scored 3, where the lack of understanding renders the analysis insufficient. The writing may fall short of acceptable control over written expression appropriate to the task. Errors may accumulate or be more troublesome. The essays may force rereading to untangle or clarify ideas.

2–1 These essays fail to mount an explanation of the characters and their relationships, often relying on brief summary or repetitive paraphrase. They may demonstrate a lack of understanding of the text, even on a literal level. Writing difficulties obstruct understanding. The essays may be too brief to communicate any understanding of the passage and the task. Essays void of any attempt at analysis will be scored a 1.

0 These essays refer to the passage or to the prompt but do little more.

— These essays are blank or do not refer to the passage or the prompt.

SCORING GUIDELINES FOR QUESTION 3

9–8 These persuasive essays identify a character in an appropriate novel, play, or epic who takes on another identity or nature. They explain with precision and rich concrete detail from the text the differences between the character's true nature and the feigned identity. They articulate clearly a meaning of the work as a whole and show compellingly how the role they have defined relates to the character's adopted identity. While the change in identity may not be central to the literary work, it is to these essays. They are not without flaw, but they are focused and organized, and alternate with skill between the details of the text and the writer's comment on that detail. They show that the student reads with perception and has a practiced and sophisticated control over the techniques of expressing that perception.

7–6 These essays present a rational and credible explanation of the impact on a clearly stated meaning of the work by the character's pretending. The account of that relationship may be more mechanical or less smoothly articulated, and the essays less thorough or specific than the top papers, but they demonstrate both an accurate reading of the work and sufficient control over the elements of writing about literature. Essays scored 7 will have stronger textual support for their claims and, generally, more expertise of expression than those scored 6.

5 These acceptable essays may be superficial in their expression of the relationship of the changed identity to a meaning of the work. They may confuse pretending with delusion, in which the character may not have chosen the new role. They may overexplain the obvious or belabor predictable ideas rather than offer insight. Plot summary may play too large a role, but plot summary is still linked to an attempt at analysis. While the writing may be inexact in diction and lack grace in syntax, it is still adequate to the expression of the writer's ideas.

4–3 These lower-half essays are incomplete in their understanding of either the prompt or the works they purport to analyze, or both. They may choose a character's pretense that they cannot successfully relate to a meaning of the work or they may be unable to articulate such a meaning clearly. They may fail to go beyond restating what is evident in a plot line or be carried away by plot summary. The writing may fail to show organization and control over the content and the form. This is the highest score for an essay that avoids identifying a meaning of the work as a whole or whose organizational or mechanical weakness forces continuous rereading and backtracking.

2–1 These essays compound the weaknesses of the 3–4 papers. They may completely misconstrue the actual purpose of an author's changing a character's identity or nature or may pay little heed to the instructions. Typically they are unacceptable in form, in content, or both. While they address the prompt, they do so in a cursory, fleeting, or ineffective way. Essays scored 2 include some analysis, however rudimentary. Essays scored 1 include no worthwhile comment on the work.

0 These essays may refer to the prompt but make no attempt to respond to it.

— These essays are blank or write completely off the task.

CALCULATING YOUR AP EXAM GRADE FOR PRACTICE TEST 1

Please keep in mind that these numbers are approximate. Two variables affect the computation every year: the number of multiple-choice questions and the difficulty levels of the essays. There is a slight adjustment every year in terms of the numbers. However, remember that earning 15 points on the three essays combined and getting 55 percent right on the multiple-choice questions will generally produce a score of 3.

SCORING THE MULTIPLE-CHOICE SECTION

$$\underline{\hspace{5cm}} = \underline{\hspace{5cm}}$$
number correct   multiple-choice score

SCORING THE FREE-RESPONSE SECTION

$$\underline{\hspace{3cm}} + \underline{\hspace{3cm}} + \underline{\hspace{3cm}} = \underline{\hspace{3cm}}$$

Question 1   Question 2   Question 3   total essay score
(0–9 score)   (0–9 score)   (0–9 score)

CALCULATING THE COMPOSITE SCORE

$$1.23 \times \underline{\hspace{4cm}} = \underline{\hspace{4cm}}$$
multiple-choice score   weighted section I score

$$3.05 \times \underline{\hspace{4cm}} = \underline{\hspace{4cm}}$$
free-response score   weighted section II score

$$\underline{\hspace{4cm}} + \underline{\hspace{4cm}} = \underline{\hspace{4cm}}$$
weighted section I   weighted section II   composite score

DETERMINING YOUR AP EXAM GRADE

You now have a number between 0 and about 150. The composite scores are divided into five ranges, one for each AP grade. Each year that scale is adjusted. Generally, it goes like this:

Composite Score Range	AP Grade
112–150	5
95–111	4
76–94	3
50–75	2
0–49	1

PRACTICE TEST 2

AP ENGLISH LITERATURE AND COMPOSITION EXAMINATION
Section I: Multiple-Choice Questions
Number of questions: 55
Total time: 1 hour

DIRECTIONS: This part consists of selections from literary works and questions on their content, form, and style. After reading each passage, choose the best answer to the accompanying questions.

QUESTIONS 1–11. Carefully read the poem by John Donne before choosing your answers.

Song: Go and catch a falling star

Go and catch a falling star,
    Get with child a mandrake root,
Tell me where all past years are,
    Or who cleft the devil's foot,
Teach me to hear mermaids singing,   5
    Or to keep off envy's stinging,
        And find
        What wind
Serves to advance an honest mind.

If thou be'st born to strange sights,
    Things invisible to see,   10
Ride ten thousand days and nights,
    Till age snow white hairs on thee;
Thou, when thou return'st, wilt tell me
    All strange wonders that befell thee,
        And swear   15
        No where
Lives a woman true and fair.

If thou find'st one, let me know;
    Such a pilgrimage were sweet.
Yet do not; I would not go,   20
    Though at next door we might meet.
Though she were true when you met her,
    And last till you write your letter,
        Yet she
        Will be   25
False, ere I come, to two or three.

GO ON TO THE NEXT PAGE

1. The instructions in the first stanza have in common that they all
   (A) have a religious connotation
   (B) list tasks the speaker considers impossible
   (C) relate directly to love and marriage
   (D) are references to the Bible or mythology
   (E) foreshadow line 20

2. The chief effect of the two-syllable rhymes, in lines 5–6, 14–15, and 23–24, is to
   (A) accentuate the most critical words in the lines
   (B) contrast them with each other
   (C) continue the rhyme of the preceding four lines
   (D) help establish the tone by adding humor to the lines
   (E) keep the poem's rhythm steady

3. The details the speaker lists in the first stanza represent all of the following EXCEPT
   (A) the natural world
   (B) religious symbolism
   (C) mythological reference
   (D) human psychology
   (E) health and medicine

4. Which of the following best paraphrases line 10?
   (A) if your parents were uncommon people
   (B) if you were born far off in a place of mysterious sights
   (C) if you were an unusual-looking child
   (D) if you have a lifetime of experience seeing peculiar things
   (E) if you have been carried away to exotic places

5. The word "snow" (line 13) is best read as
   (A) an adverb modifying the adjective "white"
   (B) a verb whose subject is "age"
   (C) an adjective modifying the noun "hairs"
   (D) a verb whose object is "white hairs"
   (E) the object of the preposition "on"

6. In the context of the poem, lines 17–18 are best interpreted to imply that
   (A) the qualities of honesty and justice make a woman true to herself
   (B) women who tell the truth are being just to men
   (C) women are less likely than men to be accurate and precise
   (D) no woman exists who is both beautiful and faithful
   (E) women who appear to treat others fairly can be untruthful

7. The antecedent of the pronoun "one" in line 19 is
   (A) "thee" (line 13)
   (B) "thou" (line 14)
   (C) "wonders" (line 15)
   (D) "woman" (line 18)
   (E) "pilgrimage" (line 20)

8. Which of the following pairs of words refers to different entities?
   (A) me (line 3) and who (line 4)
   (B) me (line 5) and I (line 27)
   (C) woman (line 18) and one (line 19)
   (D) thou (line 14) and thee (line 15)
   (E) her (line 23) and she (line 25)

9. The idea in lines 21–27 is best understood as the speaker's
   (A) resolve to wait for word from his messenger
   (B) encouragement to redouble the effort in the search
   (C) desire to carry out the search by letters rather than visits
   (D) abandonment of what he says would be a futile chore
   (E) gratification by the success of his search

10. The best example of hyperbole appears in
    (A) line 10
    (B) line 12
    (C) line 13
    (D) line 15
    (E) line 23

11.   The poem as a whole is best
      characterized as
      (A) an anguished appeal to God for
          help in finding any good in human
          nature
      (B) an acknowledgment of the
          exhilaration brought by love,
          though with overtones of
          misgiving
      (C) an appreciation of youth and love,
          but one apprehensive of the
          approach of old age and death
      (D) an overstated, and thereby
          somewhat tongue-in-cheek,
          bemoaning of the faithlessness of
          woman
      (E) an appreciative comparison of the
          wonders of life—natural, divine,
          and human

QUESTIONS 12–22. Carefully read the following passage, the opening of the short story "Battle Royal" by Ralph Ellison, before choosing your answers.

It goes a long way back, some twenty years. All my life I had been looking for something, and everywhere I turned someone tried to tell me what it was. I accepted their answers too, though they were often in contradiction and even self-contradictory. I was naïve. I was looking for myself and asking everyone except myself questions which I, and   5
only I, could answer. It took me a long time and much painful boomeranging of my expectations to achieve a realization everyone else appears to have been born with: That I am nobody but myself. But first I had to discover that I am an invisible man!

And yet I am no freak of nature, nor of history. I was in the cards,   10
other things having been equal (or unequal) eighty-five years ago. I am not ashamed of my grandparents for having been slaves. I am only ashamed of myself for having at one time been ashamed. About eighty-five years ago they were told that they were free, united with others of our country in everything pertaining to the common good, and, in   15
everything social, separate like the fingers of the hand. And they believed it. They exulted in it. They stayed in their place, worked hard, and brought up my father to do the same. But my grandfather is the one. He was an odd old guy, my grandfather, and I am told I take after him. It was he who caused the trouble. On his deathbed he called my   20
father to him and said, "Son, after I'm gone I want you to keep up the good fight. I never told you, but our life is a war and I have been a traitor all my born days, a spy in the enemy's country ever since I give up my gun back in the Reconstruction. Live with your head in the lion's mouth. I want you to overcome 'em with yeses, undermine 'em with   25
grins, agree 'em to death and destruction, let 'em swoller you till they vomit or bust wide open." They thought the old man had gone out of his mind. He had been the meekest of men. The younger children were rushed from the room, the shades drawn and the flame of the lamp turned so low that it sputtered on the wick like the old man's breathing.   30
"Learn it to the younguns," he whispered fiercely; then he died.

GO ON TO THE NEXT PAGE

But my folks were more alarmed over his last words than over his dying. It was as though he had not died at all, his words caused so much anxiety. I was warned emphatically to forget what he had said and, indeed, this is the first time it has been mentioned outside the family circle. It had a tremendous effect upon me, however. I could never be sure of what he meant. Grandfather had been a quiet old man who never made any trouble, yet on his deathbed he had called himself a traitor and a spy, and he had spoken of his meekness as a dangerous activity. It became a constant puzzle which lay unanswered in the back of my mind. And whenever things went well for me I remembered my grandfather and felt guilty and uncomfortable. It was as though I was carrying out his advice in spite of myself. And to make it worse, everyone loved me for it. I was praised by the most lily-white men of the town. I was considered an example of desirable conduct—just as my grandfather had been. And what puzzled me was that the old man had defined it as *treachery*. When I was praised for my conduct I felt a guilt that in some way I was doing something that was really against the wishes of the white folks, that if they had understood they would have desired me to act just the opposite, that I should have been sulky and mean, and that that really would have been what they wanted, even though they were fooled and thought they wanted me to act as I did. It made me afraid that some day they would look upon me as a traitor and I would be lost. Still I was more afraid to act any other way because they didn't like that at all. The old man's words were like a curse. On my graduation day I delivered an oration in which I showed that humility was the secret, indeed, the very essence of progress. (Not that I believed this—how could I, remembering my grandfather?—I only believed that it worked.) It was a great success. Everyone praised me and I was invited to give the speech at a gathering of the town's leading white citizens. It was a triumph for our whole community.

35
40
45
50
55
60

12. The speaker says that he was "naïve" (line 4) in that he
(A) found the answers of others contradictory
(B) recognized that he had to discover his own invisibility
(C) expected that others would be able to tell him who he really was
(D) was embarrassed at having been ashamed to be descended from slaves
(E) was "looking for myself" (lines 4–5)

13. In the context of the passage, the speaker asserts that he is "invisible" (line 8) especially to
(A) "our whole community" (line 61)
(B) his grandfather
(C) the "lily-white men of the town" (lines 44–45)
(D) his parents
(E) the audience at the graduation speech

14. The phrase "no freak of nature, nor of history" (line 10) is best understood to imply that the speaker sees himself as
    (A) free of any legacy from his ancestors
    (B) a natural consequence of the historical forces of the mid-19th century
    (C) destined to be an unusual departure from what would be normal for the era
    (D) different from most other young people in his search for his own identity
    (E) having been confused in his youth by the lack of consistent advice he received

15. When the speaker says he was "in the cards" (line 10), he means
    (A) his freedom was in question
    (B) his makeup and his very being had been decided
    (C) his grandfather had predicted his birth
    (D) he was involved in gambling
    (E) he was reading about history

16. The simile of "the fingers of the hand" (line 16) refers most directly to the phrase
    (A) the "boomeranging of my expectations" (line 7)
    (B) "nobody but myself" (line 8)
    (C) "no freak of nature" (line 10)
    (D) "in the cards" (line 10)
    (E) "(or unequal)" (line 11)

17. All of the following reflect some result of the grandfather's advice to "Live with your head in the lion's mouth" (lines 24–25) EXCEPT
    (A) "I could never be sure of what he meant" (lines 36–37)
    (B) "It had a tremendous effect upon me" (line 36)
    (C) "I was carrying out his advice in spite of myself" (lines 42–43)
    (D) "Grandfather had been a quiet old man" (line 36)
    (E) "The old man's words were like a curse" (lines 55–56)

18. The passage employs all of the following contrasts EXCEPT one between
    (A) the speaker and his grandfather
    (B) the different answers the speaker gets from those trying to help
    (C) the speaker's trying both to fulfill the expectations of others and to be himself
    (D) the grandfather's life and his dying words
    (E) what the "white folks" wanted and what they thought they wanted

19. The grandfather uses the pronoun "'em" (lines 25–26) to refer to
    (A) the powerful whites and their allies
    (B) the principles of living honorably
    (C) the principles of living dishonorably
    (D) the "fingers of the hand"
    (E) the speaker's parents, including the grandfather's own son

20. The passage is developed chiefly through
    (A) definition with an extended example
    (B) comparison but with minor contrast
    (C) classification and division
    (D) delineating the steps in a process
    (E) exposition and narrative

21. When the speaker says, "[E]veryone loved me for it," (line 44) "it" refers to
    (A) feeling guilty and uncomfortable (line 42)
    (B) the "constant puzzle" in the back of his mind (line 40)
    (C) forgetting what his grandfather had said (line 34)
    (D) carrying out his grandfather's advice (line 43)
    (E) "learn[ing] it to the younguns" (line 31)

GO ON TO THE NEXT PAGE

22. The main purpose of the passage is to
    (A) differentiate the speaker from his grandfather
    (B) build a justification for the graduation oration
    (C) substantiate the validity of the grandfather's advice to the speaker
    (D) disapprove of the "lily-white men of the town" (lines 44–45)
    (E) introduce the speaker's attempt to define who he is

QUESTIONS 23–33. Carefully read the poem by Dylan Thomas before choosing your answers.

Fern Hill

Now as I was young and easy under the apple boughs
About the lilting house and happy as the grass was green,
    The night above the dingle starry,
        Time let me hail and climb
    Golden in the heydays of his eyes,   5
And honored among wagons I was prince of the apple towns
And once below a time I lordly had the trees and leaves
        Trail with daisies and barley
    Down the rivers of the windfall light.

And as I was green and carefree, famous among the barns   10
About the happy yard and singing as the farm was home,
    In the sun that is young once only,
        Time let me play and be
    Golden in the mercy of his means,
And green and golden I was huntsman and herdsman, the calves 15
Sang to my horn, the foxes on the hills barked clear and cold,
        And the sabbath rang slowly
    In the pebbles of the holy streams.

All the sun long it was running, it was lovely, the hay
Fields high as the house, the tunes from the chimneys, it was air 20
    And playing, lovely and watery
        And fire green as grass.
    And nightly under the simple stars
As I rode to sleep the owls were bearing the farm away,
All the moon long I heard, blessed among stables, the nightjars 25
    Flying with the ricks, and the horses
        Flashing into the dark.

And then to awake, and the farm, like a wanderer white
With the dew, come back, the cock on his shoulder: it was all
    Shining, it was Adam and maiden,   30
        The sky gathered again
    And the sun grew round that very day.
So it must have been after the birth of the simple light
In the first, spinning place, the spellbound horses walking warm

Out of the whinnying green stable   35
        On to the fields of praise.

And honored among foxes and pheasants by the gay house
Under the new made clouds and happy as the heart was long,
        In the sun born over and over,
                I ran my heedless ways,   40
        My wishes raced through the house high hay
And nothing I cared, at my sky blue trades, that time allows
In all his tuneful turning so few and such morning songs
        Before the children green and golden
                Follow him out of grace,   45

Nothing I cared, in the lamb white days, that time would take me
Up to the swallow thronged loft by the shadow of my hand,
        In the moon that is always rising,
                Nor that riding to sleep
        I should hear him fly with the high fields   50
And wake to the farm forever fled from the childless land.
Oh as I was young and easy in the mercy of his means,
        Time held me green and dying
        Though I sang in my chains like the sea.

23. Which of the following lines is closest in meaning to lines 1 and 6?
(A) line 10
(B) line 19
(C) Line 29
(D) Line 33
(E) Line 54

24. The phrasing in line 7 most clearly echoes
(A) medieval tales of knights and castles, but exaggerated
(B) mythological stories of Greece and Rome, but contrasted with each other
(C) the role of plants from Greek mythology, but personified
(D) fairy tales, but in a playfully inverted form
(E) the reference to the house in line 2

25. The clause "the owls were bearing the farm away" (line 24) is best understood to suggest that
(A) the child enjoyed playing in the grass and hay but feared that the owls might attack
(B) the owls are carrying small plants and animals away from the farm as the child sleeps
(C) the child was afraid to go to sleep because of fears of nightmares about birds
(D) the child's dreams of riding horses were interrupted by nightmares about owls
(E) the child hears owls outside as dreams come on and move the child's perceptions away from the farm

GO ON TO THE NEXT PAGE

26. The choice of the word "maiden"
    (line 30) most clearly suggests that the
    speaker
    (A) is aware that the child would not
        know the biblical story
    (B) wants to accentuate the absolute
        parallel between the farm and the
        Garden of Eden
    (C) is intentionally avoiding the
        connotations of a mention of Eve's
        name
    (D) is trying to emphasize the
        dominance of the man over the
        woman
    (E) wants to establish the contrast
        with the animals named in the
        poem

27. The phrase "out of grace" (line 45) is
    best understood to mean
    (A) as a result of their prayers
    (B) because of their gratitude
    (C) in a way that shows refinement
        and elegance
    (D) away from their childhood
        innocence
    (E) away from the natural country way
        of life

28. The abstraction most clearly
    personified in the poem as a whole is
    (A) time
    (B) death
    (C) childhood
    (D) innocence
    (E) nature

29. The child's relation to nature in the
    poem is best characterized as a blend
    of
    (A) distance and indifference
    (B) competition and rivalry
    (C) control, harmony, and awe
    (D) respect, fear, and suspicion
    (E) power, domination, and friction

30. The musical rhythm of the poem is
    amplified by all the following EXCEPT
    (A) the occasional rhyme
    (B) the length of the lines
    (C) the rhythmic patterns
    (D) the animal references
    (E) the parallel lines

31. The colors that dominate in the poem
    are best interpreted to represent all of
    the following EXCEPT
    (A) youth and life
    (B) immaturity and innocence
    (C) plants and growth
    (D) wealth and comfort
    (E) richness and ripeness

32. The poem is marked most heavily by
    (A) intricate patterns of rhyme
    (B) realistic and detailed description
    (C) imagery of light and color
    (D) repeated parallel similes
    (E) unusual and random punctuation

33. The poem as a whole is best
    characterized as
    (A) a spiteful indictment of the loss
        suffered by a child who has to
        grow up in the city
    (B) a lament that even childhood
        happiness leads finally only to
        death
    (C) an exuberant affirmation of the
        joys of childhood, even in the face
        of human mortality
    (D) a derisive mocking of the youthful
        foolishness of childhood
    (E) a warning of some of the dangers
        that can come with childhood
        naïveté

QUESTIONS 34-44. The following excerpt is the opening of "Araby," a story by James Joyce published in 1914. Read the passage carefully before answering the questions that follow it.

> North Richmond Street, being blind, was a quiet street except at the
> hour when the Christian Brothers' School set the boys free. An
> uninhabited house of two storeys stood at the blind end, detached
> from its neighbours in a square ground. The other houses of the
> street, conscious of decent lives within them, gazed at one another   5
> with brown imperturbable faces.

The former tenant of our house, a priest, had died in the back drawing-room. Air, musty from having been long enclosed, hung in all the rooms, and the waste room behind the kitchen was littered with old useless papers. Among these I found a few paper-covered books, the pages of which were curled and damp: *The Abbot,* by Walter Scott, *The Devout Communicant,* and *The Memoirs of Vidocq.* I liked the last best because its leaves were yellow. The wild garden behind the house contained a central apple-tree and a few straggling bushes under one of which I found the late tenant's rusty bicycle-pump. He had been a very charitable priest; in his will he had left all his money to institutions and the furniture of his house to his sister.

When the short days of winter came dusk fell before we had well eaten our dinners. When we met in the street the houses had grown sombre. The space of sky above us was the color of ever-changing violet and towards it the lamps of the street lifted their feeble lanterns. The cold air stung us and we played till our bodies glowed. Our shouts echoed in the silent street. The career of our play brought us through the dark muddy lanes behind the houses where we ran the gauntlet of the rough tribes from the cottages, to the back doors of the dark dripping gardens where odors arose from the ashpits, to the dark odorous stables where a coachman smoothed and combed the horse or shook music from the buckled harness. When we returned to the street, light from the kitchen windows had filled the areas. If my uncle was seen turning the corner we hid in the shadow until we had seen him safely housed. Or if Mangan's sister came out on the doorstep to call her brother in to his tea, we watched her from our shadow peer up and down the street. We waited to see whether she would remain or go in and, if she remained, we left our shadow and walked up to Mangan's steps resignedly. She was waiting for us, her figure defined by the light from the half-opened door. Her brother always teased her before he obeyed and I stood by the railings looking at her. Her dress swung as she moved her body and the soft rope of her hair tossed from side to side.

Every morning I lay on the floor in the front parlor watching her door. The blind was pulled down to within an inch of the sash so that I could not be seen. When she came out on the doorstep my heart leaped. I ran to the hall, seized my books and followed her. I kept her brown figure always in my eye and, when we came near the point at which our ways diverged, I quickened my pace and passed her. This happened morning after morning. I had never spoken to her, except for a few casual words, and yet her name was like a summons to all my foolish blood.

Her image accompanied me even in places the most hostile to romance. On Saturday evenings when my aunt went marketing I had to go to carry some of the parcels. We walked through the flaring streets, jostled by drunken men and bargaining women, amid the curses of laborers, the shrill litanies of shop-boys who stood on guard by the barrels of pigs' cheeks, the nasal chanting of street-singers, who sang a *come-all-you* about O'Donovan Rossa, or a ballad about the troubles in our native land. These noises converged in a single sensation of life for me: I imagined that I bore my chalice safely through a throng of foes. Her name sprang to my lips at

GO ON TO THE NEXT PAGE

moments in strange prayers and praises which I myself did not understand. My eyes were often full of tears (I could not tell why) and at times a flood from my heart seemed to pour itself out into my bosom. I thought little of the future. I did not know whether I would ever speak to her or not or, if I spoke to her, how I could tell her of   65
my confused adoration. But my body was like a harp and her words and gestures were like fingers running upon the wires.

One evening I went into the back drawing-room in which the priest had died. It was a dark rainy evening and there was no sound in the house. Through one of the broken panes I heard the rain   70
impinge upon the earth, the fine incessant needles of water playing in the sodden beds. Some distant lamp or lighted window gleamed below me. I was thankful that I could see so little. All my senses seemed to desire to veil themselves and, feeling that I was about to slip from them, I pressed the palms of my hands together until they   75
trembled, murmuring: *'O love! O love!'* many times.

34. The allusion in "The wild garden behind the house contained a central apple-tree and a few straggling bushes" (lines 13–15) links the boy most strongly to
   (A) the brutal ending of the Trojan War
   (B) the innocence of Eden
   (C) the transformation of Moses on Mount Horeb
   (D) the discord sown by the Greek goddess Eris
   (E) the loneliness of Wandering Aengus

35. The strongest irony in the statement that "her name was like a summons to all my foolish blood" (lines 49–50) is that
   (A) the boy hides to watch for her
   (B) she is actually the sister of the boy's friend
   (C) the boy has not spoken to her
   (D) the boy passes her every morning
   (E) the narrator has not given her name

36. The narrator's comment that "her name was like a summons to all my foolish blood" (lines 49–50) can best be understood to imply that the narrator looks at his younger self with
   (A) scorn for his immaturity
   (B) ridicule at his feelings
   (C) remorse over his silliness
   (D) sympathy for his situation
   (E) empathy for his sharp anger

37. The purpose of the description of the city streets (lines 53–59) is to present the boy's
   (A) care to protect his aunt's parcels from damage or theft
   (B) efforts to link his love to the excitement and color of the city
   (C) love for his city and its people
   (D) struggle to lift his love above the mundanity of everyday life
   (E) love for the girl as secondary to his love for his native land in spite of its "troubles"

38. The chief source of the imagery in lines 59–67 is
   (A) Celtic art
   (B) Greek mythology
   (C) Irish history
   (D) Christian religion
   (E) medieval romance

39. The boy's comments about Mangan's sister combine to suggest his outlook is
   (A) confident but casual
   (B) upbeat and optimistic
   (C) idealistic and romantic
   (D) calculating and manipulative
   (E) despairing but melancholy

40. The point of view of the excerpt is best described as
   (A) the story's main character speaking at the time of the story
   (B) an omniscient speaker outside the story
   (C) a grown narrator looking back on his early youth

(D) free indirect discourse
(E) a third-person involved narrator

41. At her first actual appearance
(lines 33–41) the girl stands in contrast
to the rest of the paragraph because of
(A) her calling her brother for tea
(B) her hair being braided like rope
(C) her brother's teasing her before
   going in
(D) the light that defines her
(E) the boys' standing in the shadow

42. Which of the following best describes
the tone of the passage?
(A) wistfully nostalgic
(B) whimsically euphoric
(C) apprehensively dispassionate
(D) ominously timorous
(E) disdainfully disapproving

43. The clearest example of
personification occurs in line(s)
(A) 22–23
(B) 39
(C) 19
(D) 59–60
(E) 8

44. The sentence using the figure of the
harp (lines 66–67) is best interpreted to
mean that
(A) the memory of the music of the
   harness (lines 29–30) has made the
   boy unresponsive to the girl
(B) the girl wants to manipulate the
   boy, playing on his feelings
(C) the boy is captive to his feelings
   and is played on by them
(D) the music the girl plays on the harp
   makes her attractive to the boy
(E) the music of the harp reminds the
   boy of the dead priest

QUESTIONS 45–55. Carefully read the poem by Richard Wilbur before choosing your answers.

The Writer

In her room at the prow of the house
Where light breaks, and the windows are tossed with linden,
My daughter is writing a story.

I pause in the stairwell, hearing
From her shut door a commotion of typewriter-keys   5
Like a chain hauled over a gunwale.

Young as she is, the stuff
Of her life is a great cargo, and some of it heavy:
I wish her a lucky passage.

But now it is she who pauses,   10
As if to reject my thought and its easy figure.
A stillness greatens, in which

The whole house seems to be thinking,
And then she is at it again with a bunched clamor
Of strokes, and again is silent.   15

I remember the dazed starling
Which was trapped in that very room, two years ago;
How we stole in, lifted a sash

And retreated, not to affright it;
And how for a helpless hour, through the crack of the door,   20
We watched the sleek, wild, dark

GO ON TO THE NEXT PAGE

And iridescent creature
Batter against the brilliance, drop like a glove
To the hard floor, or the desk-top,

And wait then, humped and bloody,   25
For the wits to try it again; and how our spirits
Rose when, suddenly sure,

It lifted off from a chair-back,
Beating a smooth course for the right window
And clearing the sill of the world.   30

It is always a matter, my darling,
Of life or death, as I had forgotten. I wish
What I wished you before, but harder.

45. The phrase "windows are tossed with linden" (line 2) is best understood to stress the similarity between
   (A) the trees and the structure of the house
   (B) the daughter and the trees
   (C) the trees and waves on the ocean
   (D) the speaker and the daughter's room
   (E) the linden and the starling

46. The phrase "and some of it heavy" (line 8) is best read to refer to
   (A) the difficulties of learning to write
   (B) the "commotion" of the typewriter keys
   (C) the speaker's inability to help
   (D) the dissatisfaction with "its easy figure" (line 11)
   (E) the "heavy" parts of the daughter's life

47. The "easy figure" (line 11) that dominates lines 1–15 is made up of
   (A) auditory imagery
   (B) nautical images
   (C) the parts of the house
   (D) the speaker's wishes (line 9)
   (E) silences

48. The speaker most likely calls the figure "easy" because it
   (A) offends the daughter
   (B) is ordinary and overused
   (C) is the speaker's creation and not the daughter's
   (D) can be understood by many

   (E) lacks the obscurity the context requires

49. The phrase "[a] stillness greatens" (line 12)
   I. plays inventively with grammar
   II. presents a paradox
   III. suggests the intensity of the daughter's thinking
   (A) I only
   (B) I and II
   (C) I and III
   (D) II and III
   (E) I, II, and III

50. The shift at line 15 is made evident by a change in all the following EXCEPT the
   (A) alliterative pattern
   (B) punctuation
   (C) chronology
   (D) main character
   (E) controlling image

51. The speaker means all the following words and phrases to relate to the bird *and* the daughter EXCEPT
   (A) "sleek, wild, dark" (line 21)
   (B) "trapped in that very room" (line 17)
   (C) "batter against the brilliance" (line 23)
   (D) "wait . . . / For the wits to try it again" (lines 25–26)
   (E) "suddenly sure" (line 27)

52. The speaker's closing wish for his daughter also includes a reminder to himself of
    (A) the dangers of adolescence
    (B) the unintentional ingratitude of children
    (C) his own inevitable death
    (D) the awe-inspiring significance of writing
    (E) his sadness at her rejection of his "figure" (line 11)

53. Lines 31–33 have all of the following functions EXCEPT to
    (A) allow the speaker to address the daughter directly for the first time
    (B) differentiate lines 1–15 from lines 16–30
    (C) offer reassurance to the daughter about her writing
    (D) repeat and intensify the wish in line 9
    (E) end the poem on a simple, prayerlike wish

54. In the phrases "easy figure" (line 11) and "I had forgotten" (line 32),
    (A) the speaker finishes with an ironic contradiction of the meaning of lines 1–15
    (B) the speaker implies that previous poems he had written using the same extended metaphor left him dissatisfied
    (C) the speaker fears his daughter is taking her writing too seriously
    (D) the speaker implies that he sees his own poem as weak because he has not sustained the original metaphor throughout
    (E) it is clear that the poem is about both the speaker's daughter's writing and his own attempts to write about his daughter's writing

55. The tone throughout the poem is best characterized as
    (A) playfully serious
    (B) affectionately pensive
    (C) ironically grim
    (D) solemnly melancholic
    (E) irrevocably despondent

STOP
END OF SECTION I

Section II: Essay Questions
Number of questions: 3
Reading time: 15 minutes
Writing time: 2 hours
Suggested time for each essay: 40 minutes

Section II of this examination requires answers in essay form. Each question counts for one-third of the total essay section score. The two hours are yours to divide among the three essay questions as you think best. To help you use your time well, the proctor may announce the time at which each question should be completed. If you finish any question before time is announced, you may go on to another question. You may go back at any time and work on any essay question you want.

Each essay will be judged on its clarity and effectiveness in dealing with the assigned topic and on the quality of the writing. In response to Question 3, select a work of recognized literary merit appropriate to the question. A good general rule is to use works of the same quality as those you studied in your Advanced Placement literature course(s).

After completing each question, you should check your essay for accuracy of punctuation, spelling, and diction; you are advised, however, not to attempt many longer corrections. Remember that quality is far more important than quantity.

Write your essays clearly and legibly in dark-blue or black ink. Cross out any errors you make.

Question 1

Carefully read the poem by Henry Reed, taking into account the different voices. Then write a well-organized essay in which you analyze how the poet achieves his purpose. In your discussion you may wish to consider such literary techniques as contrast, repetition, rhythm, and detail.

Naming of Parts

Today we have naming of parts. Yesterday,
We had daily cleaning. And tomorrow morning,
We shall have what to do after firing. But today,
Today we have naming of parts. Japonica
Glistens like coral in all of the neighboring gardens,   5
    And today we have naming of parts.

This is the lower sling swivel. And this
Is the upper sling swivel, whose use you will see,
When you are given your slings. And this is the piling swivel,[1]
Which in your case you have not got. The branches   10
Hold in the gardens their silent, eloquent gestures,
    Which in our case we have not got.

This is the safety-catch, which is always released
With an easy flick of the thumb. And please do not let me
See anyone using his finger. You can do it quite easy   15
If you have any strength in your thumb. The blossoms
Are fragile and motionless, never letting anyone see
    Any of them using their finger.

And this you can see is the bolt. The purpose of this
Is to open the breech, as you see. We can slide it   20
Rapidly backwards and forwards: we call this
Easing the spring. And rapidly backwards and forwards
The early bees are assaulting and fumbling the flowers:
    They call it easing the Spring.

They call it easing the Spring: it is perfectly easy   25
If you have any strength in your thumb: like the bolt,
And the breech, and the cocking-piece, and the point of balance,
Which in our case we have not got; and the almond-blossom
Silent in all of the gardens and the bees going backwards and forwards,
    For today we have the naming of parts.   30

---

[1] A piece that allows rifles to be stacked.

GO ON TO THE NEXT PAGE

Question 2

Carefully read the short story by Lan Samantha Chang, printed here in its entirety. Then write an essay in which you show how the writer reveals the meaning of the story through the interplay of the contemporary setting and action with the ancient legend. In your essay you might want to consider such elements as title, detail, and symbol.

Water Names

Summertime at dusk we'd gather on the back porch, tired and sticky from another day of fierce encoded quarrels, nursing our mosquito bites and frail dignities, sisters in name only. At first we'd pinch and slap each other, fighting for the best—least ragged—folding chair. Then we'd argue over who would sit next to our   5 grandmother. We were so close together on the tiny porch that we often pulled our own hair by mistake. Forbidden to bite, we planted silent toothmarks on each other's wrists. We ignored the bulk of house behind us, the yard, the fields, the darkening sky. We even forgot about our grandmother. Then suddenly we'd hear her old,   10 dry voice, very close, almost on the backs of our necks.

"*Xiushila!*" Shame on you. Fighting like a bunch of chickens."

And Ingrid, the oldest, would freeze with her thumb and forefinger right on the back of Lily's arm. I would slide my hand away from the end of Ingrid's braid. Ashamed, we would shuffle   15 our feet while Waipuo calmly found her chair.

On some nights she sat with us in silence, the tip of her cigarette glowing red like a distant stoplight. But on some nights she told us stories, "just to keep up your Chinese," she said, and the red dot flickered and danced, making ghostly shapes as she moved her   20 hands like a magician in the dark.

"In these prairie crickets I often hear the sound of rippling waters, of the Yangtze River," she said. "Granddaughters, you are descended on both sides from people of the water country, near the mouth of the great Chang Jiang, as it is called, where the river is so   25 grand and broad that even on clear days you can scarcely see the other side.

"The Chang Jiang runs four thousand miles, originating in the Himalaya mountains where it crashes, flecked with gold dust, down steep cliffs so perilous and remote that few humans have ever seen   30 them. In central China, the river squeezes through deep gorges, then widens in its last thousand miles to the sea. Our ancestors have lived near the mouth of this river, the ever-changing delta, near a city called Nanjing, for more than a thousand years."

"A thousand years," murmured Lily, who was only ten. When   35 she was younger she had sometimes burst into nervous crying at the thought of so many years. Her small insistent fingers grabbed my fingers in the dark.

"Through your mother and I you are descended from a line of great men and women. We have survived countless floods and   40 seasons of ill-fortune because we have the spirit of the river in us. Unlike mountains, we cannot be powdered down or broken apart. Instead, we run together, like raindrops. Our strength and spirit wear down mountains into sand. But even our people must respect the water."   45

She paused, and a bit of ash glowed briefly as it drifted to the floor.

"When I was young, my own grandmother once told me the story of Wen Zhiqing's daughter. Twelve hundred years ago the civilized part of China still lay to the north, and the Yangtze valley lay unspoiled. In those days lived an ancestor named Wen Zhiqing, a resourceful man, and proud. He had been fishing for many years with trained cormorants, which you girls of course have never seen. Cormorants are sleek, black birds with long, bending necks which the fishermen fitted with metal rings so the fish they caught could not be swallowed. The birds would perch on the side of the old wooden boat and dive into the river." We had only known blue swimming pools, but we tried to imagine the sudden shock of cold and the plunge, deep into water.

"Now, Wen Zhiqing had a favorite daughter who was very beautiful and loved the river. She would beg to go out on the boat with him. This daughter was a restless one, never contented with their catch, and often she insisted they stay out until it was almost dark. Even then, she was not satisfied. She had been spoiled by her father, kept protected from the river, so she could not see its danger. To this young woman, the river was as familiar as the sky. It was a bright, broad road stretching out to curious lands. She did not fully understand the river's depths.

"One clear spring evening, as she watched the last bird dive off into the blackening waters, she said, 'If only this catch would bring back something more than another fish!'

"She leaned over the side of the boat and looked at the water. The stars and moon reflected back at her. And it is said that the spirits living underneath the water looked up at her as well. And the spirit of a young man who had drowned in the river many years before saw her lovely face."

We had heard about the ghosts of the drowned, who wait forever in the water for a living person to pull down instead. A faint breeze moved through the mosquito screens and we shivered.

"The cormorant was gone for a very long time," Waipuo said, "so long that the fishermen grew puzzled. Then, suddenly, the bird emerged from the waters, almost invisible in the night. Wen Zhiqing grasped his catch, a very large fish, and guided the boat back to shore. And when Wen reached home, he gutted the fish and discovered, in its stomach, a valuable pearl ring."

"From the man?" said Lily.

"Sshh, she'll tell you."

Waipuo ignored us. "His daughter was delighted that her wish had been fulfilled. What most excited her was the idea of an entire world like this, a world where such a beautiful ring would be only a bauble. For part of her had always longed to see faraway things and places. The river had put a spell on her heart. In the evenings she began to sit on the bank, looking at her own reflection in the water. Sometimes she said she saw a handsome young man looking back at her. And her yearning for him filled her heart with sorrow and fear, for she knew that she would soon leave her beloved family.

"'It's just the moon,' said Wen Zhiqing, but his daughter shook her head. 'There's a kingdom under the water,' she said. 'The prince

GO ON TO THE NEXT PAGE

is asking me to marry him. He sent the ring as an offering to you.' 100
'Nonsense,' said her father, and he forbade her to sit by the water again.

"For a year things went as usual, but the next spring there came a terrible flood that swept away almost everything. In the middle of a torrential rain, the family noticed that the daughter was missing. 105 She had taken advantage of the confusion to hurry to the river and visit her beloved. The family searched for days but they never found her."

Her smoky, rattling voice came to a stop.
"What happened to her?" Lily said. 110
"It's okay, stupid," I told her. "She was so beautiful that she went to join the kingdom of her beloved. Right?"
"Who knows?" Waipuo said. "They say she was seduced by a water ghost. Or perhaps she lost her mind to desiring."
"What do you mean?" asked Ingrid. 115
"I'm going inside," Waipuo said, and got out of her chair with a creak. A moment later the light went on in her bedroom window. We knew she stood before the mirror, combing out her long, wavy silver-gray hair, and we imagined that in her youth she too had been beautiful. 120

We sat together without talking, breathing our dreams in the lingering smoke. We had gotten used to Waipuo's abruptness, her habit of creating a question and leaving without answering it, as if she were disappointed in the question itself. We tried to imagine Wen Zhiqing's daughter. What did she look like? How old was she? 125 Why hadn't anyone remembered her name?

While we weren't watching, the stars had emerged. Their brilliant pinpoints mapped the heavens. They glittered over us, over Waipuo in her room, the house, and the small city we lived in, the great waves of grass that ran for miles around us, the ground 130 beneath as dry and hard as bone.

Question 3

In many works of imaginative literature, money plays a significant role. Characters see or want money for its own sake, just for survival, or as a symbol of success, power, status, or other abstractions. Some look at money in terms of what they can accomplish with it.

Select such a novel, play, or epic poem you have studied. Then, in a well-written essay, characterize specifically and account for the role money—or its equivalent—plays for one or a group of characters. Explain the contribution it makes to the meaning of the work as a whole. You may choose either a work from the list below or another of comparable literary merit. Do not summarize the plot.

A Doll House
A Raisin in the Sun
A Streetcar Named Desire
A Thousand Acres
All My Sons
All the King's Men
An Enemy of the People
Beowulf
Crime and Punishment
Cry, the Beloved Country
Death of a Salesman
Great Expectations
Major Barbara
Middlemarch
Moll Flanders

Oliver Twist
Pride and Prejudice
Rabbit Is Rich
Tartuffe
The Apprenticeship of Duddy Kravitz
The Brothers Karamazov
The Glass Menagerie
The Grapes of Wrath
The Great Gatsby
The Importance of Being Earnest
The Little Foxes
The Merchant of Venice
The Moor's Last Sigh
The Octopus
The Taming of the Shrew

END OF EXAMINATION

ANSWERS AND EXPLANATIONS FOR SECTION I

MULTIPLE-CHOICE ANSWER KEY

Using the table below, determine how many questions you answered correctly, how many incorrectly. Then look over the answer explanations.

1. B	2. D	3. E	4. D	5. B
6. D	7. D	8. A	9. D	10. B
11. D	12. C	13. C	14. B	15. B
16. E	17. D	18. A	19. A	20. E
21. D	22. E	23. A	24. D	25. E
26. C	27. D	28. A	29. C	30. D
31. D	32. C	33. C	34. B	35. E
36. D	37. D	38. D	39. C	40. C
41. D	42. A	43. A	44. C	45. C
46. E	47. B	48. B	49. E	50. A
51. A	52. D	53. B	54.E	55. B

EXPLANATIONS FOR THE MULTIPLE-CHOICE ANSWERS

1. **ANSWER: B.** *An interpretation question.* The tasks are all either physically impossible or hopeless because they depend on myth and legend, like the shape of the Devil's foot or the singing mermaids. Only the reference to the Devil has a religious connotation, eliminating A and D. The "envy" might relate to love (C), but the others could do so only metaphorically. Because they're all impossible, none would relate to line 20.

2. **ANSWER: D.** *A rhyme question.* Multi-syllable rhymes are nearly always intended to bring a smile. The "singing / stinging" rhyme of lines 5–6 begins to suggest humor; the humor in the rhyme of "tell me / befell thee" in lines 14–15 is even stronger, and the almost silly "met her/letter" (lines 23–24) makes the humorous intent inescapable. A careful reading reveals that the words involved have no special importance, eliminating A. B doesn't work because the three sets are not related in any way. The lines don't continue the *abab* rhyme that precedes them, but break it, eliminating C, and E has to be a distractor because the rhythm is neither steady nor broken by the rhyme.

3. **ANSWER: E.** *An interpretation question.* The star, the root, and the wind are from the natural world, the Devil is a religious figure; mermaids come to us from mythology; and envy is a psychological emotion. None on the list, though, relate directly to health.

4. **ANSWER: D.** *An interpretation/vocabulary question.* The meaning of the line depends on the word "born," used here in the sense of "destined from birth." A, B, and C all build on a different definition of being born, and E offers a choice based on another word entirely, the verb "to bear," meaning "to carry or support."

5. **ANSWER: B.** *A grammar question.* The verb "to snow" is normally intransitive. Here, it's used in its transitive sense of "to cause to fall like snow." The image is of the white hair descending to cover the head as the person ages.

6. **ANSWER: D.** *A vocabulary and implication question.* The lines say that a woman both "true" (faithful) and "fair" (beautiful) lives "no where." The distractors all play on a misreading of the two adjectives describing the woman.

7. **ANSWER: D.** *A grammar question.* In these questions the pronoun rarely refers to the most recent noun. Here, though, it does. The second stanza establishes that the search is for "a woman true, and fair." The speaker here asks to be told if "one," meaning such a woman, is found.

8. **ANSWER: A.** *A grammar question.* "Me" refers to the speaker; the "who" in the next line refers to whatever power gave the Devil feet like a goat, presumably God, but certainly not the speaker. Both the choices in B refer to the speaker, those in D refer to the person addressed, and those in C and E refer to the theoretical woman.

9. **ANSWER: D.** *An interpretation question.* The opening words of line 21 make it clear that the speaker is giving up the hunt even before it begins. The rest of the stanza only adds "even though" phrases to reinforce his abandoning the search. All the others imply or state that the speaker wants to keep looking.

10. **ANSWER: B.** *A figurative language question.* Riding for ten thousand days works out to over 27 years on the horse; that qualifies easily as hyperbole, or extravagant exaggeration.

11. **ANSWER: D.** *A thematic question.* The idea that the speaker could not in a lifetime find one woman to fit the search is so exaggerated that we know he's not entirely serious. He sounds unhappy, and we can make some guesses about why. That unhappiness eliminates B, C, and E, and because God doesn't figure in the poem, A is wrong.

12. **ANSWER: C.** *An interpretation question.* Immediately after calling himself naïve, the speaker speaks of the questions "which I, and only I, could answer." He will come to understand that others cannot tell him who he is.

13. **ANSWER: C.** *An interpretation question.* It is the white community that doesn't see the narrator as an individual. A, D, and E can be eliminated because of the declaration that the graduation oration was "a triumph for our whole community," and that would include his parents and the audience. The grandfather singles him out for his deathbed advice, eliminating B.

14. **ANSWER: B.** *An interpretation question.* The narrator maintains that he is a distinct individual but that his grandparents' being enslaved and then freed but still unequal is the history that makes him who he is. A, C, and D have to be wrong because they contradict the text. He is, as he says, what history has made him, regardless of any advice he may have received.

15. **ANSWER: B.** *An interpretation question.* The phrase means inevitable, so he means his future had been decided. D and E misunderstand the word "cards." A contradicts the text, and, contrary to predicting anything for him, his grandfather gives him advice.

16. **ANSWER: E.** *A question of reference.* The reference is to unequal civil rights. The image of the hand with separate fingers that work together hints at the concept that races in America could be given "separate but equal" facilities and rights. So the fingers here are a symbol of inequalities of opportunity. The other choices refer to the text, but inappropriately.

17. **ANSWER: D.** *A question of chronology and interpretation.* Since D refers to the grandfather's behavior before he made the statement, it cannot "result" from it. All the others list the changing stages of the narrator's realization of different meanings of the advice.

18. **ANSWER: A.** *A contrast question.* We see no major difference between the grandfather and the narrator, who, in fact, says he carried out the old man's advice. The differences between the two elements in each of the other choices are explicitly named in the text. He says the answers of others were "often in contradiction" (lines 3–4), eliminating B. He says he was "asking everyone," but realized they were questions "only I could answer" (lines 5–6), and that he "accepted their answers" (line 3) but that "I am nobody but myself" (line 8), eliminating C. The grandfather had been "the meekest of men" (line 28), in contrast to his deathbed words, eliminating D. Finally, E can't be the answer because the narrator says that "the white folks, . . . if they had understood they would have desired me to act just the opposite" (lines 49–50).

19. **ANSWER: A.** *A grammar question.* The grandfather identifies "'em" in line 23 as "the enemy." Since he has had no conflict with the family, E can be ruled out. The grandfather never speaks of undermining principles of any kind, eliminating B and C. D won't work because the image of the hand is the narrator's, not the grandfather's.

20. **ANSWER: E.** *A structure question.* Although it is principally expository, the passage narrates the grandfather's advice and mentions other events, such as the graduation oration. The other choices name rhetorical patterns that the narrator does not use here.

21. **ANSWER: D.** *A grammar question.* The narrator admits to feeling guilty about carrying out his grandfather's advice, even more because others approved of his behavior. The "constant puzzle" is private to the narrator and, as such, could not bring approval, eliminating B. C contradicts the text because the narrator says he carries the advice constantly. The text doesn't support E because we see no interaction between the narrator and the "younguns."

22. **ANSWER: E.** *A question of purpose.* The narrator states his task clearly in the opening paragraph and then goes on to develop it. Although he questions his grandfather's advice, he follows it, eliminating A. The oration needs no justification since everyone praises it, eliminating B. How valid the grandfather's advice is we don't learn in the passage; we know only that the narrator questions it throughout, eliminating C. The expressed disapproval of the white men is brief and too general to serve as a main purpose.

23. **ANSWER: A.** *A question of similarities.* The two lines establish the child's idyllic relationship with the farm, with the wagons honoring him. In line 10 the relationship is reinforced, and the child is now "famous among the barns." B, C, and D fail to work because none of them mention the child at all. E does but the child is now in chains, so the meaning has shifted.

24. **ANSWER: D.** *An allusion question.* The line turns the conventional fairytale opening of "once upon a time" to the playful "once below a time." The word "lord" might appear at first to suggest medieval or mythological stories, but nothing further supports the idea, eliminating A and B. C has no basis in either the poem or Greek myth, and there is no link to the house in line 2, so E is wrong.

25. **ANSWER: E.** *An interpretation question.* As the child lies in that halfway place between waking and sleep, he hears owls outside and associates the sound with slipping into dreams. Nothing in the poem suggests any harmful or frightful aspects of owls, eliminating the other choices.

26. **ANSWER: C.** *An allusion question.* A mention of the "story of Adam and Eve" suggests the serpent and the coming of sin. The speaker here wants the Garden of Eden image, but while it is still "shining" and pure. To keep that purity, the speaker substitutes "maiden" for Eve's name. The child's ignorance of the story is irrelevant to the poem, eliminating A. B is contrary to the speaker's intention, and D and E have no support in the text.

27. **ANSWER: D.** *An allusion question.* The allusion is to the child's state of grace, or innocence, a state that lines 44–45 suggest time will one day end. A, B, and C build on other meanings of the word "grace," meanings not intended here. E has no basis in the text; the "natural country way of life" would probably not be consistent with the innocence intended here.

28. **ANSWER: A.** *A figurative language question.* The speaker personifies time beginning in lines 4, 13, 42, 46, and 53. None of the others are named explicitly in the poem.

29. ANSWER: **C.** *An interpretation question.* The child has control as a "famous," "honored," and "lordly" "prince." The child repeatedly shows respect and awe to, among others, the "holy streams" and "blessed" "nightjars." That awe eliminates A, with its mention of indifference, B because of the idea of rivalry, and D because there is no fear. The lack of friction eliminates E.

30. ANSWER: **D.** *A structural question.* The animal references enrich the poem but have no effect on the musical rhythm. The others all do. The rhyme, strongest in the first and sixth lines of each stanza but the last, eliminates A. The alternating line lengths work here as they do in many songs, so B is out. C is wrong because the poem is highly musical; both the lilting rhythm and the heavy alliteration accentuate its lyric quality. The repetition of lines parallel in structure and content (lines 1 and 10, 2 and 11, 3 and 12, and the like) eliminates E.

31. ANSWER: **D.** *A question of symbol and image.* Green and gold pervade the poem from line 2 to line 52. The green symbolizes youth and growth in both plant life and the child. Gold has been a symbol of innocence since ancient Greece, a time before the corruption of humanity—the "golden time" of Shakespeare and the "gold" that "can't stay" of Frost. Money, though, is out of place in the world of this poem.

32. ANSWER: **C.** *A poetic technique question.* The colors pervade the poem from line 2 ("grass was green") to the closing couplet ("green and dying"). The light does the same, including stars (line 3), the "windfall light" (line 9), the sun (line 19), the moon (line 25), AND the "shining" (line 30). The rhyme helps the poem, but fewer than a quarter of the lines rhyme, eliminating A. The description is detailed but not at all realistic, so B won't work. The poem is crowded with metaphor but has only four similes, eliminating D. E isn't right because the punctuation is conventional and predictable, not random.

33. ANSWER: **C.** *A thematic question.* The A, B, D, and E answers all include negative influences (spite, lament, mocking, danger) that are not present in the poem. The piece does have the affirmation in choice C.

34. ANSWER: **B.** *An allusion question.* References to gardens often imply at least a suggestion of the Garden of Eden, especially in passages involving young people—in particular, young people starting to grow up. Here the reference is redoubled with the mention of a fruit tree, another common allusion to the story in Genesis. So B is the best response. C might be seen as an allusion to the biblical story of Moses and the burning bush, but the reference is too thin, especially compared with the more complex garden image. There's neither brutality nor war involved, eliminating A. D does have an apple link—Eris throws out the "golden apple of discord," sparking chaos at a dinner for the Greek gods—but again the connection is weak; nothing else in the story of Eris lines up with this excerpt. The reference in E is to the Irish god Aengus, who in one story searches for a year for a girl he had seen only in dreams. The echoes of that tale do run through Joyce's story, but nothing in the question's quotation provides any links to it.

35. **ANSWER: E.** *An irony question.* Irony often provides the opposite of what we would expect. Here the mention of a name that does not appear in the passage (or in the whole story, in fact) is unlikely to move a reader—certainly not in the way the boy is moved. So E is the best choice. D runs a distant second and would work as a response if there were any indication that seeing the girl had become nothing special to the boy, but that is not the case. Neither A nor B involves any irony, and C misreads the passage since the boy *has* spoken to her (line 49).

36. **ANSWER: D.** *A tone question.* The word *foolish* implies that the narrator looks back on his reaction as something irrational, but the formal diction of "summons" and the suggestion that it was the young blood of youth responding contradict any interpretation of scorn (A), ridicule (B) or remorse (C). Inasmuch as there is no "sharp anger" in the comment, E is eliminated. D is the proper response because the narrator looks back on the foolishness with understanding and sympathy.

37. **ANSWER: D.** *An interpretation question.* In this scene, the boy notices little positive about the city streets. He and his aunt are jostled; the men are drunk; the women, bargaining. The laborers curse, the singing is nasal, even the songs about Ireland are about not the beauty or the history but the troubles. So B, C, and E are contradicted by the text. There is no sign of his concern for the parcels. In fact, he imagines them transformed into something else. So A is inaccurate. That something else is his "chalice," the cup that holds his love and that he works to keep away from the corrupting effects of the life of real people in the real city.

38. **ANSWER: D.** *An imagery question.* The major images in those lines come from Christian religion: the use of the chalice as a sacred object, the mention of the boy's "prayers and praises," the idea of adoration, and the harp, frequently associated in art with angels. Of the other choices, A, B, and C have no relation to the text. E could be justifiable because the same images are common in medieval romance, but the more specific identification of religion makes D the stronger choice. Remember that many questions may have more than one answer that is "correct." You are looking for the one that is best.

39. **ANSWER: C.** *An interpretation question.* Characteristics of romance and idealism (C) run throughout the passage. Like the heroes of medieval romance, the boy loves from afar, loves with a fiery love, and sees his love shining with the light of ideal and perfection. A and B are inaccurate because if he were confident or upbeat, his behavior would be entirely different, and nothing about him could be called casual. Although the boy does calculate (D) his timing in his efforts to see her, the passage shows no example of his trying to manipulate her. E is incorrect because he doesn't despair anywhere in the excerpt.

40. **ANSWER: C.** *A point of view question.* The narrator looks back on his youth (C) with understanding and compassion for the boy as he was going through a difficult—though certainly not unpleasant—time. This point of view provides an opportunity for the quiet humor of

retrospection that comes from the distance between the narrator and the boy he once was. (Dylan Thomas achieves the same effect in "A Child's Christmas in Wales." So, too, does Jean Shepherd in his novel *In God We Trust, Others Pay Cash,* part of which became the now-classic movie *A Christmas Story.*) The narrator here is looking back, eliminating A, and is not omniscient (B), because he sees only the thoughts of the boy, not those of the girl or any other characters. Much of the narration shares characteristics of free indirect discourse (D), but the story is told in the first, not third, person, which also eliminates E.

41. ANSWER: D. *An imagery question.* The imagery of the passage before the girl's appearance concentrates on a lack of light. The word *dark* appears three times; *blind,* twice. The colors are brown and violet. Yellow is used, but to describe a book's pages that were once white but have darkened. The "somber" "dusk" is broken only by the light from the kitchen windows. When the girl appears in the doorway with the light coming from behind her she takes on a nimbus, or aura, the glow surrounding gods or holy people often seen in paintings. Nothing in her calling to her brother (A) or having hair braided like rope (B) contrasts in any way with the context of her appearance. The boys' being in shadows (E) only serves to accentuate the light on the girl. Nothing about A or C contrasts with anything else in the passage, and B offers no contrast because hers is the only hair mentioned.

42. ANSWER: A. *A tone question.* Other questions may have helped with this one; that is not unusual on the AP exam. Like most tone questions, this one is also a vocabulary question. A is the best choice here because the narrator looks with thoughtful reminiscence on a scene he now sees with different eyes. Although the boy may feel a certain euphoria (B), the narrator does not, and neither is whimsical. The passage shows no real apprehension or fear, eliminating C and D. Choice E represents a misreading of the passage—it comes closest to directly contradicting the actual tone.

43. ANSWER: A. *A figure of speech question.* The image of the lamps (A) gives them the human ability to lift and lower objects. All the rest of the options include verbs commonly used to describe actions by objects as well as humans.

44. ANSWER: C. *A figure of speech question.* The feelings the girl creates in the boy overwhelm him, making C the best choice. The idea in A that he is unresponsive is the opposite of what the text says. The girl does not manipulate the boy (B); in fact, the passage gives no indication that she is aware he exists. Choice D implies the existence of an actual musical instrument when there is none, and the dead priest (E) is far from the boy's mind at this point.

45. ANSWER: C. *A metaphor question.* The speaker introduces in the opening line the metaphor of the house as a ship with a "prow." Here he begins to extend the metaphor by implying a comparison of the leafy linden trees outside the windows with the waves outside a ship. The other choices present comparisons the poem neither states nor implies.

46. **ANSWER: E.** *An interpretation question.* The "it" in line 8 refers to "the stuff of her life." Choice A might be a part of that "stuff" but is too specific about the "stuff." In this context, the word includes more of her life than only the writing. The "heavy" stuff implies some of the difficulties of life she may be writing about, but they are difficulties that would be problems even if she weren't writing about them. The "commotion" in choice B comes from the daughter's writing about the "stuff" rather than being part of it. The heaviness of not being able to help in choice C and the inadequate "figure" in choice D are both part of the narrator's cargo, so to speak—not the daughter's.

47. **ANSWER: B.** *A figurative language question.* Only B accounts for all the details in the figure—"the prow," "tossed," "gunwale," "cargo," and "passage." Choices A, C, and D are incomplete because they focus on only one aspect of the figure: A on the typing sounds, C on "the prow," D on the "passage." The silences come only in lines 12 and 15, after the narrator has abandoned the ship image as "easy," eliminating E.

48. **ANSWER: B.** *An interpretation/vocabulary question.* The "we are all like ships on the sea" image is so common as to have become trite. Choice A is wrong because we don't get reactions from the daughter to anything. C misreads the speaker's role here; we suspect the narrator writes, too, and the suspicion is confirmed in lines 31–32, so while the speaker may judge his own images more harshly than he would his daughter's, he would not—could not—reject one simply because it is his. Both D and E make the serious error of assuming that writers include "hidden meanings" that they don't want readers to find. Writers write to be understood. The job of a poet is to bring meaning out, not to obscure it.

49. **ANSWER: E.** *A diction question.* The remarkable phrase toys with grammar by converting the adjective "great" into a verb. Stillness is quiet, and if it becomes greater, or quieter still, there is less noise, not more. Here, though, the stillness becomes greater, and we understand the paradox. The stillness comes from the pause in the loud noises of the typewriter, leading us to see the daughter thinking about what she will type next. The two words accomplish all three purposes.

50. **ANSWER: A.** *A structure question.* The poem has little alliteration—maybe the H and W sounds in lines 21 and 32–33, almost certainly the Bs in line 23. That is not enough to establish a "pattern." The punctuation shifts; four of the five stanzas in the first part ends with a full stop, but the next five stanzas make up only one sentence. The time changes from the present to "two years ago." The first section focuses on the daughter, the second on the starling, and the image shifts from the ship to the bird.

51. **ANSWER: A.** *A figurative language question.* Since the speaker doesn't show us the daughter, we can't see if anything about her suggests that she is in any way "sleek" or "dark." Her typing may sound "wild," but one out of three isn't enough. We do know, however, that at times she is "suddenly sure," because of her typing that suddenly resumes. She is in the same room as the starling, although trapped in a different way. Both C and D mark points in her writing as she tries to avoid

superficial flashiness ("batter against the brilliance") and stops, waiting for words and ideas ("the wits to try it again").

52. **ANSWER: D.** *An interpretation question.* The narrator has learned what the daughter is learning—the writing, while the writer is doing it, becomes a matter "of life and death," one of awe-inspiring significance. A and B try to impose meanings that the poem doesn't address. There are dangers in adolescence, but the speaker doesn't address them, and we don't know that the daughter is an adolescent. Choice C misreads the word "death" as referring to the speaker's own literal death when the word is used here figuratively. E can be eliminated because the daughter doesn't even know about the image; the speaker only imagines her rejecting it ("as if to reject . . .").

53. **ANSWER: B.** *An interpretation question.* The last stanza doesn't differentiate the two parts of the poem, it unites them by bringing together the daughter's attempts—noisy and thoughtful—to write her story with the "life or death" attempts of the starling to "clear . . . the sill of the world." The last three lines accomplish all the others.

54. **ANSWER: E.** *An implication question.* Like looking in a mirror that reflects a mirror facing it, we come to see that the speaker is struggling to write about his daughter's struggling to write. A is wrong because the last stanza reinforces the meaning of the first 15 lines, in which the speaker wishes the daughter "a lucky passage." We know nothing about previous poems, eliminating B. C fails to understand that lines 31–32 say she has no choice—and that there's nothing more serious than "life and death." D is wrong because the speaker has intentionally rejected the original metaphor of the ship.

55. **ANSWER: B.** *A tone question.* The speaker meditates on both his daughter's writing and the starling's predicament. He shows affection for both by wishing—twice—for his daughter and by taking care "not to affright" the bird and having his spirit "soar" when it flies free. C, D, and E all infer negative connotations that the poem does not imply. A comes closer but oversimplifies the complexity of the poem. There is little that is "playful" about it except the play with language, and "serious" connotes a solemnity that isn't there.

SCORING GUIDELINES FOR SECTION II

The score reported for each essay reflects the reader's judgment of the quality of the essay as a whole. Readers are instructed to reward the writers for what they do well. The score for an exceptionally well-written essay may be raised by one point. A poorly written essay can be scored no higher than a 3.

SCORING GUIDELINES FOR QUESTION 1

9–8 These detailed, well-written essays provide an insightful analysis of Reed's poem. They marshal from the poem apt and specific details that lead compellingly to well-founded conclusions. They identify the two voices, although some will read them as two or more separate people, others as two voices from one individual whose attention shifts from the classroom or drill setting to the gardens. They elaborate effectively on contrasts in the poem and on techniques the poet uses to both link and differentiate the two settings and voices. They select significant techniques and illustrate their impact on a "purpose" the poet achieves, one the essay states or implies clearly. These essays may propose a range of readings and explain a variety of techniques. Although they may not be flawless, these papers sustain their control over the elements of effective writing and manage some measure of style.

7–6 These competent essays offer a consistent understanding of the poem, including the two settings and the shifting of the voice. They deal specifically with techniques the poet uses both to differentiate the two settings and voices, although possibly less thoroughly than the top essays. Their interpretations may weaken in some particulars or exaggerate or exploit an idea beyond its worth, or they may be less detailed or precise. They link their discussion to an expressed meaning of the poem but may settle for a less complex "purpose" than the best papers and may do so less convincingly. While they may not demonstrate the same control or sophistication as the 9–8 essays, they do provide evidence of an ability to express logical ideas with clarity and some control.

5 These essays demonstrate some understanding of the two voices but may tend to be more superficial and less compelling than the upper-half essays in exploiting their relationships. Their argument may slight one of the voices or rely on insufficient support from concrete detail in the text. They may present minor misreading but show an understanding of the poem's central purpose. There may be some paraphrase, but there are attempts to use it in analysis. The writing shows some control, although maybe not a comfortable command. Mechanical errors are not so distracting as to force rereading, and the diction is not so bland or vague as to obscure meaning. These essays may not be as well planned or developed as those scoring higher, but they are adequate.

4–3 These lower-half essays reveal an incomplete understanding of the poem, the task, or both. They may show more serious misreading, confusing or conflating the two voices, or may show the student didn't understand the task being performed through the activity of "naming the parts," or may show a misreading that suggests the assembled parts produce a rifle. They may fail to link the poet's purpose to war and peace. They sometimes fail to recognize the poetic techniques at work in the poem, or they may simply name them without attempting to link them to their intended purpose. They may present interpretations that are unsupported by the detail in the poem or that misrepresent or seriously exaggerate what should be minor concerns. The writing may ramble or veer away from the task, or it may fall into extended paraphrase without links to meaning. These essays show an ability to express basic ideas but demonstrate uncertain control over writing beyond the sentence level. Essays that include significant misreading or unskilled writing should be scored 3.

2–1 These essays compound the weaknesses of the 4–3 essays. They may be unacceptably brief or may badly misread the poem. Although they make some attempt to respond to the task, they do so without clarity, organization, or supporting example. They may be poorly written on several counts and include distracting errors in grammar and mechanics that frequently force rereading. Essays with little coherent discussion of the poem should be scored 1.

0 These essays may do no more than make reference to the task.

— These essays are either left blank or are completely off topic.

SCORING GUIDELINES FOR QUESTION 2

9–8 These well-constructed essays demonstrate a grasp of the complexity of the relationship between the modern setting of the story and the ancient tale the grandmother tells. They identify, usually explicitly, more than one meaning and link the meanings to the story's title. They may comment perceptively on the differences in the behaviors of the girls in the first three paragraphs and in the last three. They will draw on a range of symbolic interpretations but keep them well grounded in the text. Building on apt references to Chang's text, these essays offer a compelling explanation of the literary techniques (such as detail, symbol, or diction) that create and convey meaning. While they may not be without flaws, these papers attest to an ability to sustain control over the elements of effective writing and manage some measure of style and confidence.

7–6 These competent essays offer a consistent understanding of the story and of ways in which its two parts are related. They will link the story's title to meaning, although possibly with less insight than the best essays. They may not be as responsive to the complexities of the story as the top papers, but they provide apt and specific references to the text. Their analysis may be less persuasive or may exaggerate or exploit a simple idea beyond its worth, and their evidence may be thinner than the 9–8 essays. Although they may lack the fullness and the rich specificity of the top essays, may explain fewer elements, and may have less detail than the top essays, they do provide evidence of an ability to read with some insight and to express logical ideas with clarity and some control.

5 These essays offer a reasonable although often reductive reading of Chang's story. Their attempts to link the two parts of the story and their discussion of meaning may be more superficial and predictable and may be expressed in more pedestrian language. They may slight the title with a simple mention and may fall into plot summary, although with attempts to link that summary to analysis. The organization may be unsuccessful or incomplete. There may be slight misinterpretations or exaggerations. The control of the tools of effective communication will be sufficient. Mechanical errors, though often present, are not serious or prevalent enough to force rereading. These essays are not as well organized or developed as those scoring higher, but they are adequate.

4–3 These lower-half essays reveal an incomplete understanding of the story, the task, or both. Typically they are unable to go beyond the simple surface of the story and fail to see any links between the two parts. They may fail to recognize the literary elements at work in the story, or they may simply name them without attempting to link them to their intended effect on meaning. They may present interpretations that are unsupported by the text or that misrepresent or seriously exaggerate what should be minor concerns. The writing may ramble or veer away from the task, or it may fall into extended plot summary without links to meaning. These essays show an ability to express basic ideas but demonstrate uncertain control over writing beyond the sentence level. Essays that include significant misreading or unskilled writing should be scored 3.

2–1 These essays compound the weaknesses of the 4–3 essays. They may be unacceptably brief or may badly misinterpret the story. Although they attempt to respond to the task, they do so without clarity, organization, or supporting example. They may be poorly written on several counts and include distracting errors in grammar and mechanics that force rereading. Essays with little coherent discussion of the story should be scored 1.

0 These essays may make no more than a reference to the task.

— These essays are either left blank or are completely off topic.

SCORING GUIDELINES FOR QUESTION 3

9–8 These persuasive essays identify an appropriate novel, play, or epic in which money plays a significant role. They articulate clearly a meaning of the work as a whole and show compellingly the role money plays in it. These essays may be the most successful at exploiting the phrase "or its equivalent" and choose to examine the role played by land or possessions, always seeing them in a role money could play. They explain with precision and apt concrete details from the text how the writer uses money to establish, develop, or explain character or to manipulate plot. They are not without flaw, but they are focused and organized, weaving details from the text into their analysis with skill. They show that the writer reads with perception and has practiced and sophisticated control over the techniques of expressing that perception.

7–6 These essays present a lucid and credible explanation of the impact of money on a clearly stated meaning of the work. The account of that relationship may be more mechanical or less smoothly articulated and the essays less thorough or specific than the top papers, but they demonstrate both an accurate reading of the work and sufficient control over the elements of writing about literature. Essays scored 7 will have stronger textual support for their analysis and, generally, more expertise of expression than those scored 6.

5 These acceptable essays may be superficial in their expression of the relationship of money to a meaning of the work. They may misinterpret the prompt's phrase "or its equivalent" to include material possessions too different from money to play an equivalent role. They may choose a work in which the role of money is less pivotal or is exploited to less consequence. They may work with less specificity and show less perception. They may belabor superficial or predictable ideas rather than offer insight. Plot summary may play too large a role, but plot summary will still be linked to an attempt at analysis. While the writing may be inexact in diction and lack grace in syntax, it will still be adequate to the expression of the writer's ideas.

4–3 These lower-half essays are incomplete in their understanding either of the prompt or of the works they purport to analyze, or both. They may identify money that they cannot successfully relate to a meaning of the work or they may be unable to articulate such a meaning clearly. They may fail to go beyond restating what is evident in a plot line or be carried away by plot summary. The writing may fail to show organization and control over the content and the form. This is the highest score for an essay that avoids identifying a meaning of the work as a whole or whose organizational or mechanical weaknesses force continuous rereading and backtracking.

2–1 These essays compound the weaknesses of the 3–4 papers. They may completely misconstrue the actual purpose of an author's use of money or may pay little heed to the instructions. Typically, they are unacceptable in form, in content, or both. While they address the prompt, they do so in a cursory, fleeting, or ineffective way. Essays scored 2 will include some analysis, however rudimentary. Essays scored 1 offer no worthwhile comment on the work.

0 These essays may refer to the prompt but make no attempt to respond to it.

— These essays are blank or write completely off the task.

CALCULATING YOUR AP EXAM GRADE FOR PRACTICE TEST 2

Please keep in mind that these numbers are approximate. Two variables affect the computation every year: the number of multiple-choice questions and the difficulty levels of the essays. There is a slight adjustment every year in terms of the numbers. However, remember that earning 15 points on the three essays combined and getting 55 percent right on the multiple-choice questions will generally produce a score of 3.

SCORING THE MULTIPLE-CHOICE SECTION

$$\frac{\hspace{3cm}}{\text{number correct}} = \frac{\hspace{3cm}}{\text{multiple-choice score}}$$

SCORING THE FREE-RESPONSE SECTION

$$\frac{\hspace{2cm}}{\substack{\text{Question 1}\\(0\text{–}9\text{ score})}} + \frac{\hspace{2cm}}{\substack{\text{Question 2}\\(0\text{–}9\text{ score})}} + \frac{\hspace{2cm}}{\substack{\text{Question 3}\\(0\text{–}9\text{ score})}} = \frac{\hspace{2cm}}{\text{total essay score}}$$

CALCULATING THE COMPOSITE SCORE

$$1.23 \times \frac{\hspace{3cm}}{\text{multiple-choice score}} = \frac{\hspace{3cm}}{\text{weighted section I score}}$$

$$3.05 \times \frac{\hspace{3cm}}{\text{free-response score}} = \frac{\hspace{3cm}}{\text{weighted section II score}}$$

$$\frac{\hspace{2cm}}{\text{weighted section I}} + \frac{\hspace{2cm}}{\text{weighted section II}} = \frac{\hspace{2cm}}{\text{composite score}}$$

DETERMINING YOUR AP EXAM GRADE

You now have a number between 0 and about 150. The composite scores are divided into five ranges, one for each AP grade. Each year that scale is adjusted. Generally, it goes like this:

Composite Score Range	AP Grade
112–150	5
95–111	4
76–94	3
50–75	2
0–49	1

CREDITS: P. 12, Frank O'Connor, "The Drunkard" from *Collected Stories*. The Jennifer Lyons Literary Agency LLC. P. 14, "Mirror" from CROSSING THE WATER by Sylvia Plath. Copyright © 1971 by Ted Hughes. Reprinted by permission of HarperCollins Publishers and Faber & Faber Limited. P. 16, William Shakespeare, Othello, the Moor of Venice from Shakespeare: THE COMPLETE WORKS, edited by G B Harrison. © 1952 by Harcourt Brace & Company, renewed © 1980 by G. B. Harrison. P. 18, James Baldwin, "Sonny's Blues" © James Baldwin Estate. P. 23, Countee Cullen, "Yet Do I Marvel" from Color. Copyright 1925 by Harper & Brothers, renewed 1953 by Ida M. Cullen. Copyrights held by the Amistad Research Center, Tulane University, administered by Thompson and Thompson, Brooklyn, NY. P. 24, Reprinted by permission of Don Congdon Associates, Inc. Copyright © 1950 by the Crowell Collier Publishing Company, renewed 1977 by Ray Bradbury. P. 76, "The Story of an Hour" by Kate Chopin. First published in 1894. P. 89, Reprinted by permission of the publishers and the Trustees of Amherst College from THE POEMS OF EMILY DICKINSON, Thomas H. Johnson, ed., Cambridge, Mass.: The Belknap Press of Harvard University Press. Copyright © 1951, 1955, 1979, 1983 by the President and Fellows of Harvard College. P. 103, "The Most Dangerous Game" by Richard Connell. Copyright © 1924 by Richard Connell. Copyright renewed © 1952 by Louise Fox Connell. Reprinted by permission of Brandt & Hochman Literary Agents, Inc. P. 106, Tim O'Brien, "The Things They Carried" from *The Things They Carried*. Houghton Mifflin Company. P. 131, "The Horse-Dealer's Daughter" by D. H. Lawrence, from COMPLETE SHORT STORIES OF D. H. LAWRENCE by D.H. Lawrence, copyright 1922 by Thomas Seltzer, Inc. Copyright renewed © 1950 by Frieda Lawrence. Used by permission of Viking Penguin, a division of Penguin Group (USA) LLC. P. 135, "Aubade" by Philip Larkin. From COLLECTED POEMS, edited by Anthony Thwaite. The Marvell Press, England and Australia, 1988. © 1988 by The Estate of Philip Larkin. Reprinted with the permission of Farrar, Straus & Giroux, LLC and Faber & Faber, Ltd. P. 137, Oscar Wilde, The Importance of Being Earnest. P. 141, "Ethics," from WAITING FOR MY LIFE by Linda Pastan. Copyright © 1981 by Linda Pastan. Used by permission of W. W. Norton & Company, Inc. P. 145, "Gretel in Darkness" from THE FIRST FOUR BOOKS OF POEMS by LOUISE GLÜCK. Copyright © 1968, 1971, 1972, 1973, 1974, 1975, 1976, 1977, 1978, 1979, 1980, 1985, 1995 by Louise Glück. Reprinted by permission of HarperCollins Publishers. P. 146, Copyright © Kazuo Ishiguro 1982. Reproduced by permission of the author c/o Rogers, Coleridge & White, Ltd., 20 Powis Mews, London W11 1JN. P. 167, "Battle Royal," copyright © 1948 and renewed 1976 by Ralph Ellison; from INVISIBLE MAN by Ralph Ellison. Used by permission of Random House, an imprint and division of Random House LLC. All rights reserved. P. 170, Dylan Thomas, "Fern Hill" from The Poems of Dylan Thomas. Copyright 1952 by Dylan Thomas. Reprinted with the permission of New Directions Publishing Corporation. P. 172, "Araby" by James Joyce. First published in 1914. P. 175, "The Writer" from THE MIND-READER, copyright © 1971 and renewed 1999 by Richard Wilbur, reprinted by permission of Houghton Mifflin Harcourt Publishing Company. All rights reserved. P. 179, *Collected Poems* by Reed (1991) 30 lines from "Naming of Parts." By permission of Oxford University Press, Ltd. P. 180, "Water Names" from HUNGER by Lan Samantha Chang. Copyright © 1998 by Lan Samantha Chang. Used by permission of W. W. Norton & Company, Inc.